The Book of Ascension to the Essential Truths of Sufism

Miʿrāj al-tashawwuf ilā ḥaqāʾiq al-taṣawwuf

The Book of Ascension

to the Essential Truths of Sufism

Miʿrāj al-tashawwuf ilā ḥaqāʾiq al-taṣawwuf

A Lexicon of Sufic Terminology

Aḥmad ibn ʿAjība

(1160–1224/1747–1809)

Arabic text prepared, translated, and annotated
Mohamed Fouad Aresmouk and
Michael Abdurrahman Fitzgerald

FONS VITAE

First published in 2011 by
Fons Vitae
49 Mockingbird Valley Drive
Louisville, KY 40207
http://www.fonsvitae.com
Email: fonsvitaeky@aol.com

Library of Congress Control Number: 2011945059
ISBN 9 7818 9178 5849

Printed in South Korea
Typeset in Minion Pro 11/13

This book is dedicated to our beloved teacher,
Mulay Hāchim al-Belghītī al-Maknāsī.

Contents

Acknowledgments

There are many people who have helped make this work possible. First, our gratitude goes to Jean-Louis Michon whose masterful translation and study of *al-Miʿrāj al-tashawwuf* in French, first published by Vrin nearly forty years ago, opened a window for western scholars onto the then nearly unknown Moroccan Sufi, Aḥmad ibn ʿAjība. A translation of Michon's work into English was originally planned to be published by Fons Vitae in the late 1990s, but for various reasons this project never came to fruition. While the present work has been translated from the original Arabic, Michon's work has been an invaluable resource.

Secondly, we would like to thank Virginia Gray Henry, director of Fons Vitae, for her unflagging support of this project from its very inception and for the many efforts she has made and continues to make toward putting beautiful editions of traditional wisdom into the hands of today's researchers and seekers. We thank our colleagues at the Center for Language and Culture, Marrakesh, Brahim Zoubairi and Hamza Weinman, for their suggestions and help with the translation, ʿAbd al-ʿAzīz Abaya of Rabat for helping us procure a copy of the 1305/1887 manuscript from the General Library of Rabat, Khalid Zahri of the Royal Library of Rabat and Dr. Kenneth Honerkamp of the University of Georgia for helping provide a copy of a previously unknown manuscript of the earliest version of *al-Miʿrāj*, and Jamaleddine Benatia of Marrakesh for the calligraphy which appears on the cover of this work and which reproduces the script used in the earliest manuscript. Additional thanks are due to Professor Honerkamp for taking time out of a very busy schedule to read and comment on this translation. Last, but in no wise least, we would like to thank our families for their patience and support over the two years this project has taken to complete.

Mohammed Fouad Aresmouk
Michael Abdurrahman Fitzgerald
Marrakesh, Morocco
19 Rajab 1432 (21 June 2011)

In the Name of God,
the All-Merciful and Compassionate

Introduction

Miʿrāj al-tashawwuf ilā ḥaqāʾiq al-taṣawwuf (*The Book of Ascension to the Essential Truths of Sufism*) is a lexicon of Sufic terminology written by the thirteenth/eighteenth-century Moroccan scholar, mystic, and spiritual mentor, Aḥmad Ibn ʿAjība al-Ḥasanī. In all likelihood, he produced the first version of this lexicon shortly after he entered the Darqāwī Sufic order in 1208/1793–94 as an easily accessible collection of the terms in al-Qushayrī's *Risāla*, and then wrote an entirely revised version of it in 1221/1806, adding forty additional terms along with the insights and nuances of meaning that he had gathered from more than thirteen years as a traveler in the way.

The Life of Ibn ʿAjība[1]

Sīdī Binʿajība, as he is affectionately known to this day in Morocco, was born in the year 1160 or 1161 (1747 or 48) in the small mountain village of al-Khamīs, about 25 kilometers northwest of Tetouan, into a family known for its piety and virtue. From his earliest years he showed a natural inclination toward learning and by the age of thirteen had memorized the entire Qurʾān. He was then sent to Tetouan where he spent the next five years studying the elementary texts (*al-mutun*) of religious knowledge. From there, he traveled to Qaṣr al-Kebīr, and finally to Fes before returning to Tetouan, still in his early twenties, as a qualified teacher of religious knowledge.

For the next ten years, he led the life of a traditional Moroccan scholar, a life of books, study, and teaching, respectable and respected by all, but never losing his thirst for higher knowledge and whatever would bring him closer to God. As he writes in his autobiography, *al-Fahrasa*, "When I acquired the share of exoteric

1. This biographical information is adapted from our previous translation, *The Immense Ocean* (*al-Baḥr al-Madīd*) (Louisville, Kentucky: Fons Vitae, 2009).

knowledge (*al-ʿulūm al-ẓāhira*) that God had destined for me, I prepared myself to receive esoteric knowledge."[2] This phase, which he describes as moving "from knowledge to practice" (*min al-ʿilm ila l-ʿamal*) began for him in earnest when he was given two books that changed his life: the *Ḥikam* of Ibn ʿAṭāʾ Allāh (d. 709/1309) and its greatest commentary, *al-Muwāhib al-ghaythiyya fī sharḥ al-ḥikam al-ʿaṭāʾiyya* by Ibn ʿAbbād al-Rundī (d. 792/1390). In Ibn ʿAjība's own words:

> After this reading, I abandoned exoteric knowledge and dedicated myself to devotional practice, to the remembrance of God, and to the invocation of blessings upon God's Messenger. Then I felt a desire to practice retreat and I began to detest the world and its denizens: when someone approached me, I fled . . .[3]

So powerful was this state that he finally resolved to sell all his books and retire to nearby Jabal ʿAlam to spend the rest of his life in reclusion and worship near the shrine of Ibn Mashīsh.[4] However, a vision at the tomb of Sīdī Ṭalḥa, a Tetouani saint, convinced him to persevere a little longer in his studies. Nonetheless, as he writes in *al-Fahrasa*,

> My mind was already oriented in its Master's direction, and my entire heart was with God. I took my place in the circle of students out of consideration for the Shaykh who had ordered me to study, but I did not know what the teacher was speaking about, so occupied was I with the invocation of God.[5]

It would be another ten years before Ibn ʿAjība, by this time a married man with children and one of the most respected scholars of Tetouan, was to meet the master who would open the door for him to formally enter the Sufic path. According to his own account, this meeting took place in 1208/1793–94 on a trip back from Fes, when he paid a visit to the well-known *zāwiya* of Mūlay al-ʿArabī

---

2. Aḥmad Ibn ʿAjība (*Fahrasa*) *The Autobiography of a Moroccan Soufi*, translated into French by Jean-Louis Michon and into English by David Streight (Louisville, Kentucky: Fons Vitae, 1999), p. 69.
3. Ibn ʿAjība, *Fahrasa*, pp. 69–70.
4. Jabal ʿAlam (altitude 6000 feet) is a mountain located in the Rif Mountains, roughly halfway between Fes and Tetouan.
5. Ibn ʿAjība, *Fahrasa*, p. 73.

l-Darqāwī in Benī Zarwāl. There he met not only the Shaykh himself, undoubtedly the most famous Moroccan spiritual master of the day, but also one of his foremost disciples and representatives (*muqaddimīn*), Sīdī Muḥammad al-Būzīdī. This latter, at the behest of Mūlay al-ʿArabī, was the person who would initiate Ibn ʿAjība into the *ṭarīqa* and act as his guide through the rigorous course of training (*tarbiyya*) that characterized the Darqāwī path at the time. The first phase of this training was a series of ever more demeaning tasks aimed at "slaying the *nafs*," or breaking the strong sense of ego and pride that might characterize someone of Ibn ʿAjība's status. As his daily litany (*wird*), the respected and honored scholar was told to don a patched cloak (*khirqa*) and sweep the marketplace. When he had done this for some time, he was told to sit at the entrance of the mosque on Fridays and beg. In a matter of weeks, his former colleagues among the *ʿulamāʾ* of Tetouan could scarcely look at him when they passed him in the street or while leaving the mosque on Friday.

The next phase of Ibn ʿAjība's education in the way involved his becoming part of a group of traveling *fuqarāʾ*[6] who would walk, often barefoot, with large-beaded Darqāwī rosaries (*subḥāt*) around their necks, from village to village along the rugged mountain paths of the Anjara region, chanting the *shahāda* or other formulas of praise, and calling the locals to renew their faith through the invocation of God and the company of the pious. In many instances, they would be met with scorn and even volleys of stones, but at other times a whole village would welcome them and join the *ṭarīqa*.

After a brief confrontation with the local authorities which resulted in Ibn ʿAjība and the *fuqarāʾ* being jailed for a short time, Shaykh al-Būzīdī bade them to journey out of the area completely to the towns of Sale and Rabat, about two hundred and fifty kilometers south along the Mediterranean coast of Morocco.

According to *al-Fahrasa*, this period of spiritual travel (*siyāḥa*) lasted about five years, during which time Ibn ʿAjība's life consisted

6. *Fuqarāʾ*, the plural of *faqīr*: someone who is poor, in need. This is the principle term by which the Sufis refer to themselves, based on the Qurʾānic verse (35:15), *O humankind! You are the ones in need* (fuqarāʾ) *and God is independent and praised.* The *faqīr* or *faqīra*, then, is the one who fully realizes his or her essential need for God. We have used this term untranslated throughout the present work.

of nights of communal *dhikr* and spiritual instruction and days of composing a number of short esoteric commentaries on certain writings by Ibn ʿArabī, Ibn al-Fāriḍ, al-Shushtārī, and others. Around 1214/1799, he returned to the north of Morocco and built a house and *zāwiya* near the village of Djimmīj. It was here that he spent the last ten years of his life in devotion and writing.

A physical description of Sīdī Binʿajība during this period left by Muḥammad Būziyyān, another disciple of Shaykh al-Darqāwī and author of *Ṭabaqāt Darqāwiyya*, gives us some inkling of the man who made the journey:

> He was thin and his skin was stretched tightly over his bones as a result of the intense spiritual discipline, asceticism, and scruples that were characteristic of him. He wore a patchwork jellaba and burnoose, as was the custom of the Darqāwa, and when he wrote or participated in *dhikr* circles, he wore a wide belt of palm fibers around his waist. We were unable to maintain his rhythm in the sacred dance, since at that time he became transformed, his eyes staring off, and he invoked God's name with force, intensity, and extraordinary rapture.[7]

By the time of his death in 1224/1809 at the age of around sixty-two, as one of the thousands who succumbed to the plague of 1807,[8] Ibn ʿAjība was recognized as a spiritual master in his own right, testified to by the letters of instruction he wrote to various groups of *fuqarāʾ* in the region.[9] Besides a prolific body of writings numbering over forty works, Sīdī Binʿajība's legacy includes the branch of the Shādhiliyya-Darqāwiyya Sufic line which to this day bears his name, *al-Ṭarīqat al-Darqāwiyya al-ʿAjībiyya*. His tomb, a simple domed structure near the ruins of his house and *zāwiya* in Djimmīj, continues to be the site of a huge yearly spiritual gathering (*mawsim*) in which invocations and praise are carried on through the night.

---

7. Ibn ʿAjība, *Fahrasa*, pp. 12–13.
8. The great plague of West Barbary (1799–1800) is estimated to have claimed from one-third to one-half of the population of the land. In spring of 1806 a deadly strain of influenza also appeared in the north of Morocco. Either of these might have been the cause of Ibn ʿAjība's death.
9. Ibn ʿAjība, *Fahrasa*, p. 172ff.

Writings

Starting from the time he returned to Tetouan as a teacher around 1200/1785 until his death, Ibn ʿAjība never ceased to write. Following Michon, these works can be divided into those he completed before his initiation into the Darqāwī order, numbering about fifteen, and those completed after, numbering about thirty-five. Although Ibn ʿAjība wrote on Sufic subjects before entering the order, including lengthy commentaries on the *Burda*, the *Hamziyya*, the *Waẓifa* of Aḥmad Zarrūq, and the *Ḥizb al-kabīr* of Imām Shādhilī, the writings after 1208 are more clearly suffused with spiritual insight, instruction to his fellow travelers in the way, and the conviction that Sufism is the key to reviving faith. These works included the books he is best known for to this day, both in Morocco and elsewhere in the Arabic-speaking Muslim-majority countries: his marvelous commentary on the book that so changed his life, *Īqāẓ al-himam fī sharḥ al-Ḥikam* (The awakening of aspirations in the commentary on the *Ḥikam*), his commentary on *Mabāḥith al-aṣliyya* by Tujībī entitled *al-Futūḥāt al-ilāhiyya* (Divine illuminations), his *tafsīr* of the entire Qurʾān entitled *al-Baḥr al-madīd* (*The Immense Ocean*), and the present work, *Miʿrāj al-tashawwuf ilā ḥaqāʾiq al-taṣawwuf* (*The Book of Ascension to the Essential Truths of Sufism*). The fact that each of these works has seen numerous new Arabic editions in recent years is a testimony to the relevance of Ibn ʿAjība's writings for present-day seekers of the spiritual heart of Islam.

Miʿrāj al-tashawwuf

DATE OF COMPOSITION

In the opening pages of *Īqāẓ al-himam fī sharḥ al-Ḥikam*, which was completed in 1211/1796, and is considered one of the first major works he wrote after his initiation into the Darqāwī path in 1208/1793–4, he writes:

> In its formal aspect, [Sufism] entails knowing the terminology and language which the Sufis use—terms such as *ikhlāṣ, ṣidq, tawakkul, zuhd, waraʿ, riḍā, taslīm, maḥabba, fanāʾ, baqāʾ, dhāt, ṣifāt, qudra, ḥikma, rūḥāniyya,* and *bashariyya*. It also includes knowing what constitutes a "state" or "inspiration" or "station" and so forth. Al-Qushayrī, at the beginning of his

> treatise, mentions a good number of these terms and I myself have compiled a book called *Miʿrāj al-tashawwuf ilā ḥaqāʾiq al-taṣawwuf* containing one hundred of the essential truths of Sufism. Let anyone who needs help in understanding these terms look there.[10]

On the last page of the manuscript upon which all subsequent editions of the *Miʿrāj* have been based, however, we find this inscription:

> This [copy] was completed on Wednesday, the 4th of Jumādā al-ākhira, in the year 1221, at the hand of its compiler, Aḥmad Ibn ʿAjība al-Ḥasanī, may God deal kindly with him in the two abodes. *And their final supplication is 'Praise be to God, lord of the worlds.'*

This gives a span of ten years between the earliest reference to the book and the date of the completed work, a chronology that is also supported by the author's own list of writings in *al-Fahrasa* which places *Īqāẓ al-himam* sixteenth (but "the first work I completed after meeting the Shaykh"[11]) and the *Miʿrāj* thirty-third.

In his 1970 work on Ibn ʿAjība, Michon referred to this difference in dates saying that "(the *Miʿrāj*) appears to be a long-term work that he enriched little by little from his readings and mediations." Shortly after having completed the present translation, however, we were given a digitalized image of an undated manuscript of the *Miʿrāj* from the Royal Library of Rabat.[12] Upon examination we found that this manuscript contained precisely one hundred terms and appeared in every respect to be a copy of Ibn ʿAjība's first version of *al-Miʿrāj*. Comparing this to the version of the work which has been reprinted in Arabic many times and is translated in the pages to follow, we would say that the *Miʿrāj* is a work that was written twice. The first version was probably completed sometime between 1208 and 1211

10. Ibn ʿAjība, *Īqāẓ al-himam* (Beirut: Dār al-Kutub al-ʿIlmiyya, 1996), p. 27.
11. Ibn ʿAjība, *Fahrasa*, p. 66.
12. Manuscript number 12433, Royal Library, Rabat. We are deeply indebted to Mr. Khalid Zahri, research fellow at the Royal Library of Rabat and Dr. Kenneth Honerkamp for helping to procure this beautiful and previously unstudied manuscript, the first page of which has been included on page xxix below.

(1793 and 1796) as a short collection of Sufic terms, largely gathered from al-Qushayrī's *Risāla*, for the use Ibn ʿAjība's fellow travelers in the Darqāwī path. This early work was then probably set aside and revisited ten to thirteen years later, at which time Ibn ʿAjība, then settled in a home in Djimmīj, was able to re-write the book, clarify some of its entries, add insights that he had gathered, and also expand the collection from one hundred to one hundred and forty-three terms. Some of the differences between the first and second versions of the *Miʿrāj* are dealt with below.

THE TITLE

The name Ibn ʿAjība chose for this work, *Miʿrāj al-tashawwuf ilā ḥaqāʾiq al-taṣawwuf* [*The Book of*] *Ascension to the Essential Truths of Sufism*, gives some indication of how he regarded it. The first association a Muslim reader has with the word *miʿrāj* (ascension) is the night journey and ascension (*al-isrāʾ wa-l-miʿrāj*) of the Prophet Muḥammad, referred to in the Qurʾān (17:1)—*Glory be to the One who carried His servant by night from the sacred mosque to the distant mosque which We have blessed, that We might show him Our signs! Lo! He, only He, is the Hearer, the Seer*—and in (53:13–18): *And he* (the Prophet) *saw Him yet another time. At the lote tree of the furthest boundary, near the garden of the abode, when there enshrouded the lote tree that which enshrouds, and the eye did not turn aside nor exaggerate. Verily he saw one of the greatest signs of his Lord.*

Ḥadīth sources describe this event as having taken place roughly one year before the migration (*hijra*) from Mecca to Medina (1/622). Although there is variation in the details mentioned, most versions agree on the basic elements.

One night as the Prophet was sleeping in the courtyard of the Kaʿaba in Mecca, the archangel Gabriel came to him with a fantastic winged creature, referred to in the narratives as *al-Burāq* (*barq* being the Arabic word for "lightning"). Riding on this creature, the Prophet was transported from Mecca to the "distant mosque" (literally "the furthest place of prostration," *al-masjid al-aqṣā*, which is today the site of the mosque in Jerusalem that stands next to the iconic Dome of the Rock). This phase of the journey is called *al-isrāʾ*, from the Arabic root *saraʾa*, "to travel by night." In the distant mosque, the Prophet met earlier prophets, including Abraham, Moses, and Jesus, whom he led in the ritual prayer (*ṣalāt*), after which he ascended

(*ʿaraja*) with Gabriel through seven heavens,[13] meeting again at each of them one of the earlier prophets, and finally coming to "the lote tree of the furthest boundary" (*sidrat al-muntahā*), beyond which Gabriel could not pass. The Prophet then entered into the divine presence where he held intimate discourse (*munājāt*) with God, at the end of which God enjoined upon the Prophet's community the ritual prayer fifty times a day.[14] He then descended to a lower heaven and there met Moses, who advised him to beg from His Lord to reduce the number. This he did several times until eventually the number was reduced from fifty times of prayer to five, each of which would carry a ten-fold blessing.[15]

For the Sufis, the elements of the Prophet's *miʿrāj* became the quintessential model of the seeker's journey to God, each heaven symbolizing a station (*maqām*) along the way. In the earliest known book describing the Sufic journey, *Kitāb al-ṣidq* (The book of truthfulness), by Abū Saʿīd al-Kharrāz (d. c. 287/900), these stations, in fact, number seven—fear, hope, trust, love, shame, longing, and intimacy—all of which are presented as dimensions of truthfulness (*ṣidq*). In *Manāzil al-ʿubbād min al-ʿibāda* (The devotees' stations of worship), by Ḥakīm al-Tirmidhī (d. 320/932), the seven stations are repentance, renunciation, opposing the ego, love, overcoming desires, reverent fear, and nearness, while in *Kitāb al-lumaʿ* (The book of flashes) by Abū Naṣr al-Sarrāj (d. 378/988), they are repentance, abstinence, renunciation, poverty, patience, trust, and contentment with God, to which al-Sarrāj adds eight states (*aḥwāl*): nearness, love, fear, hope, longing, intimacy, contemplation, and certainty. In his short treatise *Miʿrāj al-sālikīn* (The ascension of the wayfarers), Imām al-Ghazālī (d. 505/1111) divides those who pronounce the testimony of faith (*lā ilāha illā Allāh*) into seven groups and describes seven journeys of ascent (*maʿārij*). One hundred and twenty years later, we find the

13. According to later sources, it was from the huge stone over which was later erected the Dome of the Rock that the ascension began. This rock, according to the Jewish tradition, is believed to be the place where Abraham was going to sacrifice his son.

14. The form of the prayer had already been revealed to the Prophet, but the number and times of prayer had not yet been fixed.

15. For the history and canonic place of the Prophet's *miʿrāj* in Islam, see Frederick Colby, *Narrating Muḥammad's Night Journey* (Albany: State University of New York Press, 2008).

image of the *miʿrāj* reappear in a little-known work by Ibn ʿArabī (d. 628/1240), *Isrāʾ ilā maqām al-asrā* (Night journey to the highest station) also known as *Kitāb al-miʿrāj* (The book of the ascension) in which he describes "the journey of the heart" by means of an allusion-laden discourse between the "traveler," whom we may assume is Ibn ʿArabī, and a youth "of spiritual essence and lordly attributes," who leads him to an ascent through seven heavens, each associated with an esoteric principle and a prophet.[16]

For Ibn ʿAjība, the stations number eighteen, beginning with repentance and ending with gnosis, roughly corresponding to the seven stations and eight states found in al-Sarrāj. He then goes on to define approximately one hundred and ten other Sufic terms, and ends the treatise with an ascending arrangement of fourteen terms used to describe devotees in the way, beginning with *murīd*, or aspirant, and ending with *quṭb*, the spiritual pole or axis of a given time, the highest spiritual state a human being may be granted.

THE FIRST *MIʿRĀJ*, THE SECOND *MIʿRĀJ*, AND THE *RISĀLA*

At the end of the recently discovered manuscript of the first version of the *Miʿrāj* (referred to above), Ibn ʿAjība writes: "This concludes what I have gathered of the essential truths of Sufism, depending largely on al-Qushayrī, Shaykh Zarrūq, and his student al-Kharrūbī." Shaykh Aḥmad Zarrūq (d. 899/1493) is, in fact, cited by name twice in the body of the work[17] but al-Kharrūbī is not mentioned at all. The *Risāla* (Epistle) of al-Qushayrī (d. 465/1072), by contrast, is quoted numerous times in both cited and uncited quotations and in the earlier and later versions of the *Miʿrāj*. In fact, the very terms which Ibn ʿAjība chose to include in his compilation are largely taken from the *Risāla*. In the earlier version of the *Miʿrāj*, out of one hundred terms, all but the last sixteen terms can be found in the *Risāla*[18] and all of these were retained when he rewrote the book ten to thirteen

16. Appendix 1 compares the ways the five earliest works on the stations of the way describe the station of repentance.
17. Neither of these quotations, taken from Zarrūq's *al-Qawāʾid al-taṣawwuf*, appear in the final version of the *Miʿrāj*.
18. These terms are help (*taʾyīd*), support (*naṣr*), and divine protection (*ʿiṣma*), (listed as item 46 in the translation below), wisdom (*ḥikma*), (item 47 below) and then the fourteen terms used to refer to travelers in the way—starting with *ʿubbād* (devotees) and ending with *al-quṭb*

years later. It is very likely, therefore, that Ibn ʿAjība's initial intention in writing the *Miʿrāj* was to make an easy to use, simplified, and abridged version of the lexical part of the *Risāla*.

His reasons for wanting to do this are not hard to imagine. First, the *Risāla* itself must have been extremely rare in Morocco of the early twelfth/eighteenth century. The earliest printed version of this work appeared in Cairo in 1867, over half a century after Ibn ʿAjība's death. This means that any copies that did exist in Morocco in Ibn ʿAjība's time were handwritten. Given the fact that the best-known manuscripts of the *Risāla* are between 150 to 326 pages long, it is likely that the book would have been very hard to come by, and this would have been especially true in the more rural areas of northern Morocco where the Darqāwiyya *ṭarīqa* was spreading. Ibn ʿAjība's first version of the *Miʿrāj*, which occupies a scant fifteen pages in manuscript form, would have been relatively easy to copy and distribute.

Second, the *Risāla* is a book written by a scholar for the scholarly. Nearly every lexical entry is a short treatise unto itself in which so many differing definitions of a term are given that it is often difficult to get a sense of what is most essential. Ibn ʿAjība's treatment of the same terms, however, is generally short and very much to the point.

As a way to further describe the stylistic features of the *Miʿraj* we can compare it to the *Risāla* in respect to a number of elements, as below.

1. LENGTH

As we have said, the most obvious difference is length. Manuscript versions of the *Risāla* (considering only the part of the book devoted to terminology) occupy 75 to 150 pages to define about 100 terms, while the *Miʿrāj* is about fifteen small pages in its earlier manuscript version and about twenty-two in its later version. As a printed work, the entry on repentance (*tawba*), for example, occupies one page in the *Miʿrāj* (as translated below) and nine in the *Risāla*.

2. GENERAL STRUCTURE OF AN ENTRY

In al-Qushayrī—as in Abū Ṭālib al-Makkī's *Qūt al-qulūb* before

(the pole), which conclude both the earlier and later versions of the *Miʿrāj*.

him and al-Ghazālī's *Iḥyāʾ ʿulūm al-dīn* after him—most entries begin with Qurʾānic verses followed by *ḥadīth* that establish the term's scriptural source. These are then followed by al-Qushayrī's explanation of the term and extensive quotations from earlier Sufis.

By contrast, an entry in the *Miʿrāj* usually begins directly with the definition, sometimes quoting al-Qushayrī, but most often in Ibn ʿAjība's own wording, which is short, terse, and usually written in easy to memorize rhyming prose (*sajʿ*).[19] Citations from the Qurʾān appear in only six places and *ḥadīth* in only twenty.

3. OTHER REFERENCES CITED

As mentioned above, the entries in the *Risāla*, apart from citing Qurʾān and *ḥadīth* sources, are often extensive compilations of what earlier Sufis said about the term in question. The *Miʿrāj* contains surprisingly few such quotations—about fifty from Sufis mentioned by name (fifteen of which mention either al-Qushayrī or his shaykh and father-in-law Abū ʿAlī l-Daqqāq), and fewer than twenty quotations of poetry, which begin either by citing the poet by name or simply, "As a poet has said . . ."

4. LEVELS OF MEANING

Most of Ibn ʿAjība's entries in the final version of the *Miʿrāj* contain the threefold definition that he refers in his introduction: "For each of these essential truths, I will mention what pertains to it in the beginning, middle, and end of the way," or what the term means for "the generality of the faithful, the elect, and the elect of the elect."[20]

---

19. For example, the definition of fear (*khawf*, item 4), reads in Arabic: "*Inziʿāj al-qalb min luḥūqi-l-makrūh aw fawāti-l-marghūb*"; of love (*maḥabba*, item 14): "*Maylun dāʾim bi qalbin hāʾim*"; of sanctity (*wilāya*, item 27): "*Ḥuṣūlu-l-uns baʿd al-mukābada, wa iʿtināqu-l-rūḥ baʿd al-mujāhada,*" etc.

20. In translation, terms such "the generality of believers" (*al-ʿāmm*), "the elect" (*al-khāṣṣ*), and "the elect of the elect" (*khāṣṣata-l-khāṣṣ*) might not sound consistent with the virtue of humility, which the Sufis deem as an absolute condition to the path. These terms might also be rendered "the majority," "a particular few," and "a particular few among those," with no implication of superiority. Rather, such designations simply distinguish people of basic faith, who may have every virtue and every chance for salvation, from those whose destiny has impelled

These levels of meaning are almost totally absent from the *Risāla*.[21]

5. TERMS AND MATERIAL NOT FOUND IN AL-QUSHAYRĪ'S *RISĀLA*

About forty terms defined in the *Miʿrāj* are not found in the *Risāla*. A number of these relate to metaphysical or cosmological notions—*aḥadiyya, īhād, fardāniyya, infirād, ḥaqīqat al-dhāt al-ʿaliyya, qudra, ḥikma, ʿamā, ḥiss, maʿnā, mulk, malakūt, jabarūt, anwār, asrār, ḍamāʾir, sarāʾir*—along with the last sixteen terms in the *Miʿrāj* that describe the levels of sanctity. It is possible that Ibn ʿAjība took some of these terms from *al-Futūḥāt al-Makkiyya* by Ibn ʿArabī or from *al-Iṣṭilāḥāt al-ṣūfiyya* by al-Kāshānī (d. 730/1330), which is a compilation based on Ibn ʿArabī's work; it is worth noting that the way in which Ibn ʿAjība defines them is markedly different.

It goes without saying that the final version of *Miʿrāj* also includes quotations which postdate al-Qushayrī: one from Ibn ʿAṭāʾ Allāh's *al-Tanwīr fī isqāṭ al-tadbīr*, one from his *Laṭāʾif al-minan*, and five from his *Kitāb al-ḥikam*. There is one mention each of Ibn ʿAjība's own shaykhs, Muḥammad al-Būzīdī and Mūlay al-ʿArabī l-Darqāwī, and one of Sīdī ʿAlī l-Jamal, whom he refers to as "the Shaykh of our Shaykh."

6. PURPOSE

Beyond these formal considerations, the most important difference between the two works lies in the intention behind each. For al-Qushayrī, who wrote his *Risāla* in 437/1045, the "true Sufis" were nearly extinct and he feared that Sufism as a whole had become misunderstood both by its followers and the Muslim community in general. As he writes in the introduction:

> Since our age keeps bringing only more and more difficulties and the majority of our compatriots continue to adhere stubbornly to their ways. . . . I have begun to fear that the hearts of men might think that this whole affair [Sufism] from the very beginning rested upon all those [faulty] foundations and its early adherents followed the same corrupt habits. So I have

---

them toward the Sufic path. In any case, Ibn ʿAjība's initial mention of "the beginning, middle, and end of the way" should be kept in mind.

21. They are also rarely mentioned in the earlier version of the *Miʿrāj*.

> composed this epistle for you . . . that [it] might strengthen the followers.[22]

A long portion of the introduction is then devoted to enumerating these "corrupt habits." Thus, al-Qushayrī's work, like al-Ghazālī's after him,[23] was undertaken—at least in part—out of a perceived need to correct error and reaffirm the place of Sufism within the framework of Islam as a whole.

This kind of polemic is entirely absent from the *Miʿrāj*. Ibn ʿAjība writes for those who are already on the Sufic path or have resolved to follow it. For him, it enough to know that in the famous *ḥadīth Jibrīl*, the Prophet defined three essential elements of the religion—*islām*, *īmān*, and *iḥsān*—to understand where Sufism fits into the whole picture. If *islām* in this context means devotional practices such as prayer and fasting, *īmān* means beliefs, and *iḥsān* is "to worship God as if you saw Him," then each of these is the source of a religious science, which, in turn, is its elaboration or exposition (*tafsīr*). *Fiqh* explains how to accomplish devotional practices, *ʿaqīda* explains what must be believed concerning the nature of God, the prophets, and the afterlife, and *taṣawwuf* explains how to reach proximity and intimate knowledge of God.

Our Work on this Translation

Our overall goal in translating this work is, we believe, similar to that of its author when he undertook its writing over two hundred years ago: to make these key notions of Sufism accessible to a wide range of people, in this case, those whose first language is not Arabic. To help achieve this goal, we have worked toward a translation that favors the syntax of modern English and have opted for gender neutral pronouns whenever possible. The use of the third person masculine form remains only a convention of the Arabic language, and there is no doubt that many women entered the *ṭarīqa* during Ibn ʿAjība's life and were therefore exposed to its teachings. In addition:

---

22. Abū l-Qasim al-Qushayrī, *Epistle on Sufism*, trans. Alexander D. Knysh (Reading: Garnet, 2007), p. 3.
23. In the introduction to the *Iḥyāʾ ʿulūm al-dīn*, al-Ghazālī devotes a dozen lines of text to addressing a certain censurer or critic (*ʿādhil*) whose errors he hopes this book will correct.

A. We have numbered the terms—originally unnumbered—according to their groupings in the manuscript versions of the *Miʿrāj*, so that those which were originally listed as pairs, triads, or groups are treated as single items. Thus, "Expansion and contraction" is one item (number forty-three) and the total of one hundred and forty-three terms come out to seventy-nine separate items in the present work.

B. For the sake of those readers with an interest in the Arabic language, we have included footnotes for nearly every term defined in the *Miʿrāj*, giving more information about the oldest meanings of the term, its verbal root, and its occurrences in the Qurʾān.

C. Arabic terms are transliterated according to the Brill system.

D. Following the translation, we have included three appendices. Appendix I is a comparison of how the five earliest Sufic lexicons treat a single term. Appendix II is a collection of twenty passages from other works by Ibn ʿAjība which expand upon the meanings of some of the key terms found in the *Miʿrāj*. Appendix III is a biographical index of persons mentioned either in the main text or the appendices, referenced to the item numbers in which they appear.

E. When we considered it useful to cross reference a term mentioned in the *Miʿrāj*, we have followed Michon's practice of adding the transliterated term and its item number in parentheses.

F. All Qurʾānic quotations are italicized and referenced to *sūra* and verse. These are either preceded by the letter Q. or put in parentheses. An index of Qurʾānic verses is also included at the end of this work.

G. We have tried to trace all *ḥadīth* mentioned in the main text and appendices. For references to the six canonic collections (*al-kutub al-sitta*), we have used either Ibn al-Athīr's *Jāmiʿ al-uṣūl fī aḥādith al-Rasūl* and have included Arnāʾūṭ's reference to the original source, or we have referred directly to the source itself. An index of *ḥadīth* is included at the end of this work.

H. With students of language in mind, the entire Arabic text of *Miʿrāj*, largely voweled, is included at the end of the book.

بسم الله الرحمن الرحيم وصلى الله على سيدنا محمد وآله وصحبه

قال الشيخ العلامة

الصوفي الرئيس أبو العباس

سيدي أحمد بن عجيبة رحمه الله

الحمد لله الذي حقق الحقائق وبين الطرائق والصلاة
والسلام على من هدى به الخلائق سيدنا ومولانا محمد المخصوص
بتواتر المعجزات وظهور الخوارق وبعد فإن علم التصوف من أجل
العلوم وأفضلها لأنه من مقام الإحسان الذي فسره جبريل للنبي صلى الله عليه
وسلم كما أن الفقه من مقام الإسلام وأن الأصول من مقام الإيمان وقد اشتمل
حديث سؤال جبريل على الجميع وإذا تقرر أنه أفضل العلوم تبين أن
الاشتغال به أفضل ما يتقرب به إلى الله تعالى لكونه سببا لحصول المعرفة
الخاصة وقد اشتمل على عبارات دقيقة وألفاظ غريبة اصطلح أهل الفن
على استعمالها فينبغي معرفة معانيها قبل الخوض فيه وقد
قيدت في هذا المختصر نبذة صالحة من حقائق هذا العلم واصطلاح
كلامهم لعل الله ينفع بها من يريد الوقوف على كلامهم

وسميته

The first page of the manuscript of the earliest version of *Miʿrāj al-tashawwuf* courtesy of the Royal Library, Rabat, Morocco

The Translation

Miʿrāj al-tashawwuf ilā ḥaqāʾiq al-taṣawwuf

The Book of Ascension
to the Essential Truths of Sufism

بسم الله الرحمن الرحيم

In the Name of God,
the All-Merciful and Compassionate

PRAISE BE TO GOD who has affirmed the essential truths (*al-ḥaqāʾiq*) and made clear the paths (*al-ṭarāʾiq*). May blessings and salutations be upon our master Muḥammad, the first of creation, chosen to receive the extraordinary and miraculous, and may God be well-pleased with his Companions by whom His religion was manifested in the furthest east and the furthest west.

The science of Sufism is the foremost of the [religious] sciences and both the goal and heart of the revealed law. And how could it be otherwise when it is the exposition (*tafsīr*) of the station of excellence (*maqām al-iḥsān*), the station of direct perception and vision, in the same way that theology (*ʿilm al-kalām*) is the exposition of the station of faith (*īmān*), and jurisprudence (*fiqh*) is the exposition of the station of surrender (*islām*), all of which are contained in the *ḥadīth* of Gabriel.[1]

---

1. The well-known *ḥadīth,* reported in Bukhārī, *al-Jāmiʿ al-ṣaḥīḥ* (Jeddah: Dār al-Minhāj, 1422/2001), vol. 1, p. 19; and Muslim, *al-Musnad al-ṣaḥīḥ al-mukhtaṣar min al-sunan* (Riyadh: Dār al-Ṭayba, 1427/2006), vol. 1, p. 24, describes how the angel Gabriel came to the Prophet Muḥammad in the form of a traveler and questioned him about the meaning of surrender (*islām*), faith (*īmān*), and excellence or impeccability (*iḥsān*).

If Sufism is thus, then to immerse oneself in this science is the most excellent way of drawing near to God most high. Indeed, it is a means of realizing gnosis (*maʿrifa*), the knowledge which comes from vision. As such, Sufism involves rare and strange truths and subtle expressions which the Sufis use when speaking of them, and anyone who wants to understand this science needs to understand these expressions.

Therefore I wished—through the power and strength of God—to assemble a useful summary of these essential truths and the terms used to express them in hopes that God might benefit thereby those who want to understand this science, and I have called it (*The Book of*) *Ascension to the Essential Truths of Sufism*. All success is in God and He is the One who guides to the right path.

For each of these essential truths, I will mention what pertains to it in the beginning, middle, and end of the way.

1. Sufism (*taṣawwuf*)

Sufism (*taṣawwuf*) is the science of how to journey into the presence of the King of kings. It is to inwardly purify ourselves from vice and beautify ourselves with virtue, to pass away from creation through consciousness of the Creator and then to return. Its beginning is knowledge, its middle practice, and its end a gift [from God].

The word *taṣawwuf* is said to be derived either from "purity" (*ṣafāʾ*) because it is centered on purification, or from "attribute" (*ṣifa*) because it leads to the attributes of virtue, or from "porch" (*ṣuffa*), that is, the porch outside the Prophet's mosque, inasmuch as the Sufis, in their orientation toward God and their devotion, resemble the People of the Porch, or from "wool" (*ṣūf*), because the Sufis are wont to wear this material in their renunciation of the world, choosing it because it is the material from which were made the garments of God's prophets ﵇.

Linguistically, this last derivation is the most suitable and also most closely fits the literal meaning of the word. [Referring to] a garment of wool is an external description based on appearance, and thus simplest and most direct, while the others are inner interpretations. Just as we say *taqammaṣa* to mean "he put on a shirt (*qamīṣ*)," we say *taṣawwafa* to mean "he put on a garment of wool," and the person so garbed is called *ṣūfī*.

Sahl [al-Tustarī] said, "The Sufi is one who is pure (*ṣafiya*) of turbidity and full of reflection, one who has turned away from humankind in order to turn toward God. For the Sufis, gold and pebbles are of equal worth, for they desire nothing but the guardian Lord."

And al-Junayd said, "The Sufi is like the earth: they cast upon it what is vile and there blossoms forth from it what is beautiful, and upon it both the virtuous and the sinners tread. The Sufi is like the sky which shades all, and like the rain from which all are given to drink."[2]

2. Repentance (*tawba*)

Repentance (*tawba*) is the return from every deed that is ugly to one that is beautiful, from every trait that is base to one that is noble, or from a mind engrossed in the world to one immersed in consciousness of the divine.

Its conditions are that we regret [our sin], rid ourselves of it, and refuse to persist in it. Also, if our sin is one that has wronged another human being, we must try to correct that wrong, but our repentance may be accepted without having done so, just as repentance for one sin may be accepted even while another remains.

For the generality of believers, repentance is from sins, for the elect, it is from faults, and for the elect of the elect, it is from everything that distracts the soul from the divine presence.

Every station of the way necessitates repentance. In the station of repentance itself, another repentance is needed if the first one lacks sincerity. It is needed in the station of fear (*khawf*) if we begin to have an illusory sense of security; in the station of hope (*rajāʾ*) if we experience feelings of despair; in the station of patience (*ṣabr*) if we grow restless and worried; in the station of detachment (*zuhd*) if we are beset by cravings and desires; in the station of scrupulousness (*waraʿ*) if we start looking for too much license in the revealed law or are beset by covetousness; in the station of dependence on God (*tawakkul*) if we start worrying about the future, about our choices, or about the means by which our worldly provision will come to us; in the station of contentment and submission (*riḍā wa taslīm*) when we become bitter and contrary in confronting our destiny; in the station of vigilance (*muraqaba*) for ill behavior (*sūʾ*

2. See also appendix II:1.

al-adab) outwardly and ill thoughts inwardly; in the station of self-examination (*muḥāsaba*) for wasting our time with things that do not bring us closer to God; in the station of love (*maḥabba*) when our hearts incline toward other than the Beloved; in the station of contemplative vision (*mushāhada*) if our innermost consciousness turns toward someone or something other than the One perceived, or we become fixed on something in the sensory world, or cease our ascent along the pathways of souls.

Thus would the Prophet ﷺ ask forgiveness from God seventy or a hundred times in a single assembly.[3]

As for "sincere repentance" (*tawbatan naṣūḥan*),[4] it is comprised of four things: to ask forgiveness for sin with our voices, to abstain from it with our bodies, to rid our hearts from any desire to persist in it, and to stay away from bad companions. Sufyān al-Thawrī said, "The signs of sincere repentance are four: meagerness, weakness, humility, and solitude."[5]

3. Conversion (*ināba*)

Conversion (*ināba*) is more particular than repentance. It means to return to God [with our pride] broken and with a renewed aspiration for the spiritual journey. There are three levels of conversion: turning from sin to repentance, turning from heedlessness to vigilance, and turning from separative consciousness (*farq*) to unitive consciousness in God (*jamʿ ʿalā Allāh*).

4. Fear (*khawf*)

Fear (*khawf*) is the heart's distress at confronting what it abhors or losing what it desires. Its fruits should be a renewed effort to live

3. The *ḥadīth*, with the wording "By God, I ask God for forgiveness and turn in repentance to Him more than seventy times a day and night," appears in Bukhārī, vol. 8, p. 67.
4. This refers to Q. 66:8, *O you who believe, turn to God with a sincere repentance.*
5. This term, from the root t-w-b, "to turn in repentence," occurs in the Qurʾān in verbal and nominative forms approximately 90 times, where it is used both with human beings in the sense of repenting, and God, in the sense of turning in forgiveness. One of the ninety-nine divine names is *al-Tawwāb al-Raḥīm*, the Forgiving and Compassionate One. See also appendix I:1–5 and appendix II:2.

in obedience to God and avoid transgressions. Lacking this, it is only pretension.

The generality fear punishment or losing some reward [in the next world]; the elect fear divine reproach or that they will cease to draw nearer to God; and the elect of the elect fear being veiled from God by their poor comportment.[6]

5. Hope (*rajāʾ*)

Hope (*rajāʾ*) is the tranquility of a heart awaiting the object of its love, along with effort made to accomplish the means which lead to that object. Hope without effort is but vanity and self-deception.

For the generality of the faithful, hope is to reach the best of destinations as reward; for the elect, it is to attain God's pleasure (*riḍwān*) and draw near; and for the elect of the elect, it is to attain stability in the consciousness of God and progress ever higher in knowledge of the mysteries of the worshiped Sovereign.

Fear and hope in the heart are like the two wings of a bird: it cannot fly except with both. However, it may be that hope is more prevalent with the gnostics (*al-ʿārifūn*) and fear with the virtuous (*al-ṣāliḥūn*).[7]

6. Patience (*ṣabr*)

Patience (*ṣabr*) is to keep the heart steady before the order of the Lord. For the generality, this means keeping it steady when it is hard to accomplish acts of obedience or avoid transgressions. For the elect, it means to keep the individual self steady in its devotions and spiritual efforts, and to bear the dangers of the way with a heart vigilant in its concentration on God and its search for the veils to be raised. For the elect of the elect, it means keeping the spirit and soul concentrated in the contemplative and essential vision: ongoing reflection and sustained concentration.[8]

---

6. Forms of the verbal root kh-w-f, "to be afraid," occur in the Qurʾān approximately 120 times.
7. The root r-j-w expresses the idea of hoping for something or expecting something. In various forms it occurs in the Qurʾān about 30 times.
8. Variations of the root ṣ-b-r are found just over 100 times in the Qurʾān and include the divine name *al-Ṣabūr*, the Infinitely Patient. See also appendix II:3.

7. Gratitude (*shukr*)

Gratitude (*shukr*) is the heart's joy at receiving some benefaction, using the limbs of the body to obey the Benefactor, and humbly acknowledging that the Benefactor is God.

Gratitude thus has three expressions: by the tongue, in its humble acknowledgment of God's gifts, by the body in its readiness to serve, and by the heart in its witnessing the Benefactor in the benefaction, all of which is summed up in the words of al-Junayd, "[Gratitude] is that you do not use the gifts God has given you to sin against Him."

For the generality of the faithful, gratitude is verbal praise; for the elect, it is service (*khidma*) through the pillars of the religion; and for the elect of the elect, it is to be immersed in consciousness of the Giver (*al-Mannān*).[9]

8. Scrupulousness (*wara*ʿ)

Scrupulousness (*wara*ʿ) is to keep from committing anything that would result in consequences we would abhor.

For the generality of the faithful, this means avoiding what is forbidden or doubtful. For the elect, it means avoiding everything that troubles the heart and produces narrowness and obscurity, summed up in the words of the Prophet ﷺ "Leave what causes you doubt for what does not cause you doubt."[10] For the elect of the elect, it means refusing to become attached to anything other than God, closing the door of desire for anything other than God, keeping aspirations ever focused on God, and finding support only in God. This is the [state] which Ḥasan al-Baṣrī meant when he was asked: "What is the cornerstone of religion?" and he answered, "Scrupulousness." Then he was asked, "And what is the ruination of religion?" and he answered, "Covetousness (*ṭama*ʿ)."[11] The kind of scrupulousness that is the complete opposite of covetousness is that of the elect of the elect, and even the smallest amount of this

---

9. Forms of the root sh-k-r, "to thank," occur 75 times in the Qurʾān, including in the name of God *al-Shakūr*, the Grateful One. See also appendix II:4.
10. Ibn al-Athīr, *Jāmi*ʿ *al-uṣūl fī aḥādīth al-Rasūl*, ed. ʿAbd al-Qādir al-Arnāʾūṭ (Beirut: Dār al-Fikr, 1985), vol. 6, p. 444; Bayhaqī, *Shu*ʿ*ab al-īmān* (Beirut: Dār al-Kutub al-ʿIlmiyya, 1990), vol. 5, p. 52.
11. The saying "Scrupulousness is the central support of religion" is related in Bayhaqī, *Shu*ʿ*ab al-īmān*, vol. 5, p. 54.

is equivalent to thousands of [supererogatory] prayers and fasts.

Similarly, [al-Mursī] said in the *Tanwīr*, "It is not an abundance of formal knowledge nor constancy in supererogatory practices that shows a servant's understanding. What shows his light and understanding is that he finds his true wealth in God, keeps his heart [with God], rids his soul of covetousness, and becomes beautified by the jewel of scrupulousness."[12] The scrupulousness of which he speaks is that of the elect or the elect of the elect. And God most high knows best.[13]

9. Detachment (*zuhd*)

Detachment (*zuhd*) is to rid the heart of its ties to anything but the Lord. It is the heart's coolness toward the world and the ego's aversion to it.

For the generality, this means giving up possessions beyond what are absolutely necessary; for the elect, it means giving up everything that preoccupies them from approaching God in every state; for the elect of the elect, it means abstaining at every moment from beholding anything but God. In a word, it is a coolness in the heart toward all but God and toward desiring anything except the Beloved.

It is also the way to love, even as the Prophet ﷺ said, "Be detached from this world and God will love you. . . ."[14] It is both the means by which we journey and the arrival (*al-wuṣūl*). For a heart attached to something other than the Beloved, there is no journey.[15]

---

12. Abū l-Faḍl Ibn ʿAṭāʾ Allāh, *al-Tanwīr fī isqāt al-tadbīr* (Cairo: ʿAlam al-Fikr, 1998), p. 127. The wording there is, "It is not the abundance of his knowledge that shows a servant's true degree (*shiʿār*)."
13. Only one verbal form of r-w-ʿa is found in the Qurʾān (11:74), where it carries a meaning close to "fear": *When fear* (al-rawʿu) *had passed from the mind of Abraham and glad tidings had reached him, he began to plead with Us for Lot's people*. See also appendix II:5.
14. Abū Nuʿaym al-Iṣfahānī, *Ḥilyat al-awliyāʾ* (Beirut: Dār al-Kutub al-ʿIlmiyya, 1997), vol. 3, p. 289; Bayhaqī, *Shuʿab al-īmān*, vol. 7, p. 344, and elsewhere. The complete text is "A man came to the Prophet ﷺ and said, 'O Messenger of God, guide me to a practice through which God will love me and people will love me.' The Messenger of God replied, 'Be detached from this world and God will love you; be detached from what people possess and they will love you.'"
15. The verbal root z-h-d, "to be detached from," also includes the sense of "considering something to be of little or no value." This is the meaning

10. Dependence on God (*tawakkul*)

Dependence on God (*tawakkul*) [is when your] heart has such assurance in God that it ceases to rely on anything else; it is to be attached to God and reliant upon Him for all things, based on the knowledge that He is the Knower of all things and that what is in God's hand is more certain than what is in your own.

Its lowest degree is that you be with God like someone who has entrusted his affairs to a kind and caring confidant; its middle degree is that you be with God like a child with its mother who turns only to her for its every need; its highest degree is that you be like a body in the hands of the one who washes it for burial.

The first is for the generality, the second for the elect, and the third for the elect of the elect. For the first, there may still be glimmers of doubt. For the second, there is no longer any suspicion, but a child is only attached to its mother when there is a need. For the third, there is neither doubt nor attachment. Someone at this degree is effaced from himself, and sees at every moment what God is doing with him.[16]

11. Contentment and submission (*riḍā wa taslīm*)

Contentment (*riḍā*) is to meet tribulations with a smile on your face, to have joy in your heart as destiny unfolds, to leave the choice to God in all that He has planned and brought about, to feel relief in your breast, and to be without criticism for what comes from God, the One, the Overwhelming.

Submission (*taslīm*) is to serenely relinquish your self-direction and choice to the flow of divine decrees. It is synonymous with the third meaning of contentment, but contentment in its first two meanings is deeper than submission. It has also been said that contentment is at the moment [a divine decree] comes to pass, while submission is before it comes to pass. It is, in fact, identical to *tafwīḍ*, which means to leave your destiny wholly in God's hands.

---

expressed in its single Qurʾānic occurrence (12:20), in the story of Joseph: *And his brethren sold him for a paltry price, a few dirhams counted out; they held him in low esteem* (*kānū minhu mina al-zāhidīn*)." See also appendix II:6.

16. Forms of the verbal root w-k-l, which expresses the notions of trust, confidence, and reliance, appear 70 times in the Qurʾān, including in the divine name, *al-Wakīl*, the One in whom to place trust.

For both contentment and submission, the beginning is patience and spiritual effort, the middle is peace, even while some thoughts of annoyance and displeasure remain, and the end is happiness, peace, and the absence of these thoughts. The first, therefore, is for the generality of the faithful, the second for the elect, and the third for the elect of the elect.

An initial reaction [that lacks this virtue] is forgiven in all cases, for human nature is weak and no human being is entirely free of this.[17]

12. Vigilance (*murāqaba*)

Vigilance (*murāqaba*) is a permanent awareness that the Lord perceives us; or we could say that it is to observe what is due to God, both in public or private, free of illusions, and with sincere veneration.

Vigilance is the source of all good, and the degree to which we realize it will determine the degree of our contemplative vision (*mushāhada*, 15): if our vigilance is profound, so shall be our contemplative vision.

For people of the outward, vigilance means to guard the limbs of the body from slips. For people of the inward, it means to keep the heart from following every passing thought (*khawātir*, 44) and distraction. For people of the most profound dimension of the inward, it means to keep the innermost soul from reposing in anything but God.[18]

13. Self-reckoning and setting conditions (*muḥāsaba wa mushāraṭa*)

Self-reckoning (*muḥāsaba*) is to call ourselves to account for wasting our precious moments and "breath" (*nafas*, 73) in other than

---

17. There are just over 70 occurrences of variations on the root r-ḍ-y in the Qurʾān, with meanings that range from simply "human preference" to "divine pleasure." *Taslīm* comes from the root s-l-m, "to be at peace." Variations of this root, including those which refer to the religion of Islam, occur just over 150 times throughout the Qurʾān. *Al-Salām*, Peace, is one of the ninety-nine names of God.

18. *Murāqaba* is a nominative form of the root r-q-b, "to watch over" or "look out for." Variations of this root occur 14 times in the Qurʾān, including in the divine name, *al-Raqīb*, the Watcher or Guardian.

different sorts of devotions to God. [The time for] self-reckoning is usually at the end of a day.

At the beginning of the day comes the "setting of conditions" (*al-mushāraṭa*). This means that we say to ourselves, "Here is the start of a new day, a day that will bear witness for or against you. So make every effort to fill its hours with what brings you closer to God, for had you died yesterday, you would not have had the chance to achieve the good that might be your salvation today."

This self-reckoning should be done as night approaches and in the time before dawn as well, and you should maintain this practice until the presence of God is established in your soul. When this happens, time will be as one, immersed in the consciousness of God, and there will remain neither reckoner nor blamer. So, for as long as the journey lasts, the setting of conditions will come first, self-reckoning last, and vigilance, always. But upon arrival, neither the first nor second remains.[19]

14. Love (*maḥabba*)

Love (*maḥabba*) is the permanent inclination of an enraptured heart. It manifests itself first upon our limbs as service [to the Beloved], this being the station of the virtuous. Then it appears in our impassioned hearts as the process of purifying ourselves from vices and beautifying ourselves with virtue, this being the station of aspirants on the journey. Lastly, it appears in our purified souls and innermost beings as a stable and ongoing consciousness of the Beloved, this being the station of the gnostics. [We could also say that] at the beginning of the way, love appears as service (*khidma*), in the middle as intoxication and bewilderment, and in the end as calmness and lucidity in the station of gnosis.

For this reason, people have been grouped into three degrees: the people of service, the people of states, and the people of stations.

---

19. The root of *al-muḥāsaba*, ḥ-s-b, which carries the meaning of counting, numbering, or reckoning, appears in its verbal, nominative, and adverbial forms approximately 100 times in the Qurʾān, including in the divine name *al-Ḥasīb*, the Reckoner. A nominative form of *mushāraṭa*, sh-r-ṭ, "to make a pre-condition for something," occurs in (47:18): *Do they then only wait for the hour; that it should come on them of a sudden? But already have come some of its signs* (*ashrāṭuhā*, literally, "its pre-conditions").

[We could also say] that the beginning of love is methodic practice and service, the middle, attraction and effacement, and the end, lucidity and subsistence (*baqāʾ*, 54) in God.[20]

15. Contemplative vision and essential vision (*mushāhada wa muʿāyana*)

Contemplative vision (*mushāhada*) is to perceive the subtle essence in the places of Its epiphany in the formal world. It is thus the subtle returned to the dense. And if love [between the servant and the Lord] becomes ever finer, and the lights of the formal return to their subtle state, this is called "essential vision" (*muʿāyana*): the dense returned to the subtle. Essential vision is thus subtler and more complete than contemplative vision.

In other words, a vision of the essence is not possible except by the condensation of Its subtle mysteries in places of epiphany. As long as the subtle remains subtle, it is imperceptible.

Seeing epiphanies in formal manifestation is contemplative vision; seeing them as subsumed in the ocean of unity is essential vision.

Others, however, have said that these terms are synonymous.[21]

16. Gnosis (*maʿrifa*)

Gnosis (*maʿrifa*) is stability and perpetuity of the contemplative vision. It is the permanent consciousness of an enraptured heart witnessing only its guardian Lord, undistracted by anything else, yet all the while keeping its equilibrium and the commandments of the revealed law.[22]

---

20. The verbal root ḥ-b-b means "to love." Forms of this root can be found in 95 places in the Qurʾān. Although Sufic literature abounds in references to God as *al-Maḥbūb*, the Beloved, the divine name found in the Qurʾān is *al-Wadūd*, the One who loves, derived from the root w-d-d, nearly synonymous to ḥ-b-b. See also appendix II:7.
21. Words derived from the root of *mushāhada*, sh-h-d, "to witness," occur in the Qurʾān 160 times, including in the divine name *al-Shahīd*, the Witness. *Muʿāyana* is derived from the root ʿa-y-n, which may denote either an eye or a spring. In these two nominative forms it is found in 65 places in the Qurʾān.
22. *Maʿrifa* is a nominative form of the root ʿa-r-f, "to know something by direct experience or to be personally acquainted with something

Such is the extent of the stations of the way that end with gnosis. We will now proceed to the [terms designating] other essential truths frequently used both at the beginning of the way and at its end.

17. Piety (*taqwā*)

Piety (*taqwā*) is to keep the commandments and avoid transgressions both inwardly and outwardly. For the generality of the faithful, piety is to avoid sins; for the elect, it is to rid oneself of faults; and for the elect of the elect, it is to be absent from all but God by keeping the soul in the presence of the knower of the unseen.[23]

18. Integrity (*istiqāma*)

Integrity (*istiqāma*) is to put into practice what we know of the words, deeds, states, and virtues of the Prophet ﷺ, without going to excess, falling short, following every suggestion of the imagination, departing from the prescriptions of the law, or putting ourselves outside accepted norms. It is also to keep ourselves near God with true sincerity in all situations.

Integrity in speech means not to backbite; in practice, it means not to innovate; and in our general condition, it means not to depart from what the revealed law enjoins.

For the generality, integrity is to follow the [formal] sunna. For the elect, it is to realize in one's own character the virtues of the Prophet ﷺ. For the elect of the elect, it is to realize in one's own character the attributes of the All-Merciful by being immersed in His very presence.[24]

---

or someone." Forms of this root occur in the Qurʾān about 70 times, mostly as the nominative adjective *maʿrūf*, "something which is known by all" which by extension means "that which is good and fair." See also appendix II:8.

23. According to differing views of traditional Arabic grammarians, this word comes either from the root w-q-y or t-q-y. Both carry the meaning of "caution, taking precautions, or being protected against something." Verbal and nominative forms of this root occur about 260 times in the Qurʾān.

24. Based on the root q-w-m, "to stand, maintain, or establish," this word in its adjectival form, *mustaqīm*, "straight or upright" occurs nearly 40 times in the Qurʾān, first in *Sūrat al-Fātiḥa*. *Al-Qayyūm*, the One who maintains all, is one of the ninety-nine names of God. See also appendix II:9.

19. Purity of intention (*ikhlāṣ*)

Purity of intention (*ikhlāṣ*) is to rid our relationship with God, the Truth (*al-Ḥaqq*), of any concern about how we appear to people (*khalq*); it is to make God the sole object of our devotions, to empty our hearts of all but the Lord.

For the generality, this means to purify the deeds done for God from the desire to be seen; for the elect, it means to purify them from any desire for recompense in this world or the next; and for the elect of the elect, it means to see in oneself neither strength nor power other than the strength and power of God and to rid one's deeds and intentions from any desire to be seen by others until they become by God, from God, and to God, pure of all else.[25]

20. Sincerity (*ṣidq*)

Sincerity (*ṣidq*) is to remove all egoistic designs from our relationship with God, based on the coolness of certitude; or [we could say that] it is to be outwardly and inwardly the same in speech, words, and states; or to jealously conceal the mysteries of the All-Merciful. In a word, it is to purify ourselves inwardly from all other preoccupations.

The difference between sincerity and purity of intention (*ikhlāṣ*, 19) is that the latter concerns being free of both evident and hidden polytheism (*shirk*), while the former concerns being totally free of hypocrisy (*nifāq*) and duplicity (*mudāhana*). It is thus comparable to gold being refined of its dross: sincerity eliminates the remnants of hypocrisy from the soul and purifies it from the obscurities of imaginings. For a person may possess purity of intention and still be vulnerable to duplicity and finding excuses for egoistic passions, while the one who possesses sincerity is free from both. No one who is still subject to duplicity, either toward himself or others, in small matters or great ones, can smell the perfume of sincerity.

A sign of sincerity is that we are the same in public and private, untroubled that there could be something about us we would hate for people to know, unashamed that it might be made apparent to others, and content with the fact that God knows it.

---

25. Variations of the root kh-l-ṣ, "to render something pure, unmixed, clear of turbidity," appear about 30 times in the Qurʾān and the oft-repeated 113 *sūra* is called *al-Ikhlāṣ*.

For the generality of believers, sincerity is to purify deeds from the expectation of receiving something in return; for the elect, it is to purify one's inner states from being for something other than God; for the elect of the elect, it is to purify the drinking place of God's Oneness (*mashrab al-tawḥīd*) from distractions by what is other than God.

The one who attains the first station is called "sincere" (*ṣādiq*), while one who attains either the second or third station is called "utterly veracious" (*ṣiddīq*).

[Finally], contrary to what some *fuqarāʾ* of our time believe, to affirm God's existence or to affirm that God's saints possess special qualities and to venerate them on this account is not sincerity (*ṣidq*), but rather affirmation (*taṣdīq*), and while someone who is fervent in this affirmation is sometimes called "*ṣiddīq*," in truth this name should apply only to one who is profound both in his affirmation and sincerity.[26]

21. Serenity (*ṭumaʾnīna*)

Serenity (*ṭumaʾnīna*) is the tranquility of a heart that is turned toward God, free of troubles and agitation, trusting in [the divine] promise, a heart content with God's knowledge and deeply-rooted in gnosis.

This serenity may come to someone still veiled by way of sequential formal proofs and reflective thought, or by way of constancy in devotional practices and spiritual discipline. It may also come to someone for whom the veil has been lifted by way of stability in contemplation and deep-rooted gnosis.

In other words, there are people who find their serenity in the existence of God by way formal proofs and elucidations and there are others who find their serenity in the consciousness of God after He has manifested Himself to them by way of direct perception (*ʿiyān*). The first is the way of the learned, the second of the devotees, ascetics (*ʿubbād wa zuhhād*, 78), and virtuous, and third of the gnostics brought near.[27]

---

26. The verbal root ṣ-d-q can mean "to be truthful, sincere" and also "to give charity." With both meanings it occurs 150 times in the Qurʾān.

27. It may be that there is an omission in the original. The sense, referring back to the first paragraph, is that for the first type of person, serenity arises from logical proofs of the existence of God, for the second, from

22. Longing and ardor (*shawq wa ishtiyāq*)

Longing (*shawq*) is a heart's yearning to meet the Beloved, while ardor (*ishtiyāq*) is the joy it finds in being with Him. So while longing ends with vision and encounter, ardor is without end: the soul never ceases to crave ever greater unveilings and nearness.

The generality of the faithful long for the ornaments of Paradise; the elect long for God's contentment (*riḍwān*); the elect of the elect long for the supreme vision.[28]

23. Jealousy (*ghayra*)

Ghayra, jealousy, is the aversion you feel seeing the one you love with someone else, an aversion so strong that it impels you to vie for the exclusive possession of the beloved.

Al-Shiblī said, "Jealousy is of two sorts: human, which concerns people, and divine, which concerns hearts." This means that just as it is human nature to hate to see the one you love—your spouse, for example—with someone else, so too does God hate to see the hearts of those He loves attached to someone or something else. According to a *ḥadīth*: "No one is more jealous than God, and this is why He has forbidden lewdness (*fawāḥish*) both inward and outward."[29] There is, in fact, no jealousy in all of existence except the divine jealousy that pervades the places of His epiphanies.

For the generality, jealousy has to do with egos: to defend the sanctity of family and home. For the elect, it has to do with hearts: to be jealous if their hearts are drawn toward what is other than God, the Beloved. For the elect of the elect, it has to do with spirits: to be jealous if their spirits and souls become taken up by something other than the Beloved, or to be jealous if their Beloved inclines toward another.

It is in this highest sense that the servant has the right to be jealous, even as a poet has said:

---

devotional practices, and for the third, from contemplative or meditative vision.

28. See also appendix II:10.

29. Bukhārī, vol. 7, p. 35; Muslim, vol. 2, p. 1265. The *ḥadīth* continues, "And there is none who loves praise more than God."

> If I did not vie for Your love, and were I not jealous of You
> Then for whose love, I wonder, would I vie?
> Do not deem lowly my soul if You are its Beloved
> For each is drawn toward the one he is like.[30]

And it may be that God is so jealous of His friends (*awliyāʾihi*) that He exacts vengeance on foes who would harm them; and it may be that He is so jealous of them that He hides them from creation behind the veils of anonymity (*astār al-khumūl*), for they are the brides of His sacred presence.[31]

24. Magnanimity (*futuwwa*)

Magnanimity (*futuwwa*) is to prefer that others have what you love and to act with generosity and goodness toward them in what they love. For this reason, it has been said that perfect magnanimity exists only in the Messenger of God ﷺ, for in that place where all other creatures will be concerned with themselves, he will pray: "My people, my people!"[32]

It has also been said that magnanimity is never to see yourself as superior to another. This is why the one who realizes magnanimity has no adversaries.

It is generosity (*sakhāʾ*, 38), humility, and courage in the face of hardship. For the generality, this has to do with possessions, for the elect, with their own selves, and for the elect of the elect, with their souls: the gift of self for the sake of the Beloved.[33]

---

30. That is, "If my heart is drawn toward God, who is noble and beautiful, then it, too, must to some extent possess the qualities of nobility and beauty."
31. The word "jealousy," derived from the verbal root gh-y-r, "to be other," does not appear in the Qurʾān. As a grammatical marker of exclusion, however, the related word *ghayr* occurs with extreme frequency.
32. This is a reference to the lengthy and well-known *ḥadīth* describing the tribulations of the Day of Judgment when the Prophet will pray in prostration before God for the salvation of his community. Bukhārī, vol. 9, p. 146; Muslim, vol. 1, p. 107.
33. The root f-t-w, or according to some grammarians, f-t-y, carries the sense of "being or becoming a youth" and may be said of both genders. It came to express notions of magnanimity, chivalry, and selflessness as the virtues epitomizing the perfect young person. Nominative forms appear in the Qurʾān in 7 places, notably in the story of the youths

25. Will (*irāda*)

Will (*irāda*) is determination to reach the Beloved by way of spiritual effort, or the desire to become loveable to God by accomplishing what pleases Him. It is also giving spiritual counsel to the community with a pure intention, intimacy with God in solitude, and patience in the face of vicissitudes and adversity. It is to give preference to God's commandments, to feel shame beneath His gaze, to make the utmost effort for His sake, to use every means of reaching Him, to frequent those who guide to Him, to be content with anonymity, and to find true peace only upon arrival. Will is the first stage in the quest for God, the beginning of the traveler's path.

26. The aspirant (*al-murīd*)

The aspirant (*al-murīd*) is someone who wants nothing except his guardian Lord. There are three basic aspirations. [The lowest] is of those who aspire only to receive blessing (*tabarruk*) and sacred protection, whose motivation is weak or worldly attachments many. [At the second level are those who] are strong in their resolve to reach the divine presence and have left the workaday world. [At the third level are those who] aspire toward vicegerency (*khilāfa*) and the perfection of gnosis, whose intellects are manifest and merit complete and who are then proclaimed to be successors by a perfected shaykh or by way of a truthful inner voice.[34]

27. Spiritual combat (*mujāhada*)

Spiritual combat (*mujāhada*) is to wean the soul away from the things it is used to, to oppose its desires at every moment, and to break it of its habits in every state.

One of the Sufis has said, "Spiritual combat can be summed up in three rules: do not eat except if you are on the verge of starving; do

---

related in the chapter of the Cave: *We relate to you their story in truth: they were youths* (fityatun) *who believed in their Lord, and We advanced them in guidance* (18:13).

34. The terms *irāda* and *murīd* are both derived from the verbal root r-w-d (or according to some, r-ā-d) which originally meant "to walk in search of something." The Qur'ān contains approximately 150 occurrences of words derived from this root, almost exclusively related to the verb *arāda / yurīdu*, "to want, desire, intend."

not sleep except when weariness overcomes you; and do not speak except when it is absolutely necessary."

Spiritual combat ends with the contemplative vision (*mushāhada*, 15), after which there is no more combat, for the two of them do not coincide. Weariness ends when the journey is over. Upon arrival, there is but rest, contemplation of the Loved One, and maintaining the norms [of servanthood].

[It may also be said] that spiritual combat operates on three levels. There is the outward, which is to always accomplish [what the revealed law commands] and avoid what it prohibits; there is the inward, which to reject base thoughts and stay concentrated on the divine presence; and there is the spiritual combat of the innermost soul, which is to strive for a permanent consciousness of the divine, free of distractions from the One adored.[35]

28. Sanctity (*wilāya*)

Sanctity (*wilāya*)[36] is to reach intimacy with God after having borne hardships, to embrace the spirit after having gone through spiritual combat (*mujāhada*, 27).

Said otherwise, it to realize effacement (*fanā*ʾ, 54) in the Essence after the sensory world has disappeared: what had no existence passes away, and the One whose existence never ends remains.

Thus, it begins with effacement and ends in the realization first of subsistence (*baqā*ʾ, 54) and then of the subsistence of subsistence (*baqā*ʾ *al-baqā*ʾ), after which comes a perpetual ascent and expansion into what has no limit or end.

Ibrāhīm b. Adham once said to a man, "Do you wish to be a friend (*walī*) of God?" The man responded, "Yes." "Then," continued Ibrāhīm, "do not desire anything in this world and the next. Empty your soul for God, be He exalted, and turn your face toward Him. He will befriend you and take you into His protection and care."

Someone else said, "The saint is someone whose aspiration is God, whose occupation is God, and whose effacement is always in God."

[The term] *wilāya* can be applied on three levels. The first is general and means [all] the people of faith and piety, based upon

35. The root j-h-d, "to strive or make an effort," occurs in verbal and nominative forms 40 times throughout the Qurʾān.

36. This term may also be written *walāya.*

the words of God, *Truly, upon the friends of God* (awliyāʾ Allāh) *there shall be no fear nor shall they grieve: those who have faith and are among the pious* (10:62). Referring to the elect, [this term] means those who aspire toward knowledge through God, and referring to the elect of the elect, it means those who are established in gnosis by way of direct perception (*ʿiyān*).

It was asked of the Messenger of God ﷺ, "Who are God's friends?" and he answered, "Those who love one another for God's sake," and in another narration, "Those who behold the inner aspect of the world when the people are beholding its outer aspect."[37] This *ḥadīth* includes both the sanctity of the elect and of the elect of the elect. And God most high knows better.[38]

29. Freedom (*ḥurriyya*)

Freedom (*ḥurriyya*) is to purify ourselves inwardly of the love of what is not God, until nothing remains there that is not for Him. This acquired freedom may then predispose [us to receive] the freedom granted by the Lord: effacement in the places of divine epiphany, when the darkness of created things is subsumed in eternal light, the forms of servanthood effaced in the radiance of the epiphanies, and there remains only God, the Truth without the creation (*fa yabqā al-Ḥaqq bila'l-khalq*).

At that moment, a declaration of freedom is written for the servant so that thereafter his worship and servanthood become pure gratitude, free of constraints, even as the masters of the gnostics ﷺ said, "Should I not be a grateful servant?"[39] And the imam of the Sufis, al-Junayd, said, "For the gnostics, acts of devotion are crowns

---

37. This is quoted in the introduction of Abū Nuʿaym, *Ḥilyat al-awliyāʾ*, vol. 1, p. 41, and in Abū Ṭālib al-Makkī, *Qūt al-qulūb* (Beirut: Dār al-Kutub al-ʿIlmiyya, 1997), vol. 1, p. 205, as a saying of Jesus.

38. Nominative forms of the verbal root w-l-a, "to take charge or care of something for someone," occur in the Qurʾān about 100 times. Both *al-Walī* and *al-Mawlā,* the One who cares for and protects, are divine names. The plural form, *awliyāʾ*, which is sometimes translated as "saints," more literally means "protecting friends."

39. The words cited are the Prophet's response to his wife ʿĀʾisha when she asked him why he stood the night in prayer when God had forgiven him his past and future sins. Bukhārī, vol. 2, p. 50; Muslim, vol. 2, p. 1295.

upon their heads," which is to say the perfection of perfection.[40]

30. Servanthood (*'ubūdiyya*)

Servanthood (*'ubūdiyya*) is to maintain the comportment that is due to the Lord along with an awareness of our human weakness.

The Sufis have said, "Servanthood is to maintain completely the injunctions [of the revealed law] even while seeing that all our deeds fall short," or "It is to relinquish choice concerning what destiny makes clear to you," or "It is to recognize that in reality you have neither strength nor power nor plan, while acknowledging God's care of you and the blessings He gives you."

All this is summed up in the words of Ibn ʿAṭāʾ: "Servanthood means to respect God's limits, to fulfill your pledges, to be satisfied with what you have, and patient with what you lack."

To better understand this term, suppose you have bought with your wealth a slave. The way you would want this slave to be with you is how you should be with your guardian Lord. A slave owns nothing—neither possessions nor even his own self—and before the overwhelming power of his master, he has neither decision nor choice. He dons nothing but the garb of a slave ready to serve, ever at his master's command or prohibition. If he is attentive and understanding, he carries out what his master wishes before being told to do so, and understands his master's wishes from the slightest gesture. Such is the comportment of a mannered servant.

Abū ʿAlī l-Daqqāq 🙏 said: "Servanthood is more perfect than worship (*'ibāda*). The first stage is worship, then servanthood, then complete devotion (*'ubūda*). Worship is for the generality, servanthood for the elect, and complete devotion for the elect of the elect." I would add that complete devotion is synonymous with God-given freedom, and God most high knows better.[41]

31. Satisfaction (*qanāʿa*)

Satisfaction (*qanāʿa*) is to be content with our lot and not always looking for more, to find sufficiency in what is and stop seeking

---

40. Both *ḥurr*, "free," and *ḥarr*, "heat" arise from the verbal root ḥ-r-r. In its former sense, this root is mentioned 5 times in the Qurʾān, always in the phrase, *taḥrīr raqabatin*, "the freeing of a slave."

41. Forms of the verbal root ʿa-b-d, "to serve as a slave, to worship," occur 275 times throughout the Qurʾān.

what is not. It is the *wholesome life* and *goodly provision* mentioned in His words, *Truly God will provide them with a goodly provision* (22:58). This refers to those who immigrate for the sake of God: if they are slain or die, God promises to provide those who remain with a goodly provision. Satisfaction is one of the fruits of having found true wealth in God.

Wahb b. Munabbih said, "Honor and wealth went roaming and when they met satisfaction that is where they stayed."

The essence of satisfaction lies in closing the door of greed and opening the door of scrupulousness (*wara*, 8). It is desirable, however, only in respect to the matters of this world. In respect to the matters of the next world, or to increasing our knowledge, or deepening our gnosis, it is a fault, which is why it has been said, "To consider your relation to God satisfactory is a deprivation."[42]

32. Well-being (*ʿāfiya*)

Well-being (*ʿāfiya*) is the peace we find in our hearts when we are free from affliction, trouble, and agitation. If it arises from serenity and contentment in God, then it is perfect well-being (*al-ʿāfiya al-kāmila*), while if it arises from the flow of secondary causes in accordance [with our needs], then it is normal well-being.

In a *hadīth* it is stated, "After the gift of certainty, there is no better gift than well-being."[43]

For the generality, well-being is a feeling of reassurance concerning worldly means. If these means become straitened, however, their hearts may be troubled and agitated because they lack the light of certainty.

For the elect, well-being rests in the peace they have from the One who is the source of all means. Their well-being is thus permanent and if their worldly means are straitened, this may even increase their certitude. As one of them said, "We are like the stars: the darker it gets, the brighter our light." And Dhū l-Nūn said, "If the sky

---

42. That is, to become complacent in one's knowledge or relationship to God is to be deprived. The root q-n-ʿa, "to be content or satisfied with something," appears once in the Qurʾān as a noun in (22:36), speaking of the meat of camels offered as sacrifice, to *eat thereof, and feed the one who does not (beg not but) lives in contentment* (al-qāniʿ), *as well as the one who humbly begs.*
43. Ibn al-Athīr, vol. 4, p. 339, from Tirmidhī and Aḥmad.

were like glass and the earth like copper,[44] and all Egypt were my dependents, I would still not have the slightest worry about their sustenance."

As for the elect of the elect, their well-being resides in their consciousness of God, which removes them from concerns about having or not having worldly means. They are immersed in the ocean of unity and in the mysteries of uniqueness. Cares do not lodge in their courtyards; troubles do not cloud the waters they drink. May God make us among them! Amen![45]

33. Certainty (*yaqīn*)

Certainty (*yaqīn*) is the inner peace we find in God, arising from a knowledge that is unchanging, inalterable, and unaffected by transient events; it is the removal of doubts by a consciousness of the unseen.

The signs [of certainty in those who possess it] are three: they look beyond human beings when they are in need, they do not laud those who give to them, and they do not blame those who do not.

Certainty for the generality of believers rests in realizing the oneness of the divine acts so that they are at peace with God whether He gives or withholds. For the elect, it rests in realizing the oneness of the divine qualities such that they see creatures themselves as lifeless, without movement or rest except by God. For the elect of the elect, it is in realizing the oneness of God's essence so that they witness Him by all things and in all things, and do not witness anything else besides Him.

---

44. A more complete version of this saying adds here, "and not a thing would grow from the ground."

45. This term is derived from the root ʿa-f-ā which expresses meanings ranging from "erasing, effacing, or eliminating" to "pardoning, excusing, or forgiving," in the sense of erasing sins or faults. It may also express the notion of "being restored to health," in which case God effaces the illness. It appears in various forms throughout the Qurʾān 35 times, and *al-ʿAfū*, the One who pardons, is among of the ninety-nine divine names.

34. The knowledge of certainty, the eye of certainty, and the truth of certainty (*ʿilm al-yaqīn, ʿayn al-yaqīn, wa ḥaqq al-yaqīn*)

The knowledge of certainty arises from rational proof (*burhān*), the eye of certainty from unveiling (*kashf*) and experiential evidence (*bayān*), and the truth of certainty from consciousness and vision (*al-shuhūd wa-l-ʿiyān*).

The first is the certainty of those of the faithful in whom the mental or rational element prevails; the second, of the ecstatics in whom the intuitive element prevails; and the third, of those who attain depth and stability in the station of excellence (*maqām al-iḥsān*).

To illustrate this: someone who has heard of Mecca but has never seen it possesses the knowledge of certainty; someone who travels there and sees it from a distance but does not enter it possesses the eye of certainty; and someone who enters the city and becomes acquainted with its streets and locales possesses the truth of certainty.

Thus it is with people in their knowledge of God. Those who are veiled search for rational proofs and through these they gain certain knowledge of God's existence. Aspirants in the way seeking effacement in the divine essence are granted the eye of certainty when the lights of the spiritual world (*anwār al-maʿānī*) dawn for them and the darkness of the formal world recedes, except that they remain in the bewilderment of effacement and are not yet established in a permanent consciousness of the divine. Once they reach this, however, and find deep-rooted equilibrium in gnosis, they are granted the truth of certainty, and this is the supreme benefaction and summit of blessedness. May God, in His generosity and grace, make us among those who receive it! Amen![46]

35. Benefaction (*niʿma*)

By benefaction (*niʿma*), the Sufis mean lasting happiness, distance from sorrow, the attainment of goals, and a worldly lot that is beyond reproach.

---

46. *Yaqīn* is derived from the root y-q-n, "to know something with certainty." Forms of this root appear approximately 30 times throughout the Qurʾān, as in the oft-repeated phrase, *qawmun yūqinūn*: "a folk who are certain (in their faith)." See also appendix II:12.

In general, there are two kinds of benefactions: outward ones such as health, well-being, and a sufficiency of lawful provision; and inward ones, such as faith, guidance, and gnosis.

In respect to outward benefactions, people are of three sorts. There are those who are happy with the benefaction itself because of what they can do with it, but are veiled from the Benefactor; there are those who are happy with the benefaction because it is a sign of acceptance from the Benefactor and means that He has remembered them; and there are those who are happy only with the Benefactor, and nothing else beside Him: *Say, "Allāh!" and leave them to their vain chatter* (6:91).[47]

The gratitude of the first two increases if the benefaction increases and ceases if it ceases. As for the third group, their gratitude is constant both in ease and hardship. Such is the gratitude of the elect.[48]

36. Intuition (*firāsa*)

Intuition (*firāsa*) is a thought or inspiration that arises clearly in the heart and is seldom wrong if that heart be pure. According to a *ḥadīth*, "Beware of the believer's intuition, for he sees by the light of God."[49]

The accuracy of our intuitions depends upon our nearness to God and our gnosis. The nearer we are to God and the firmer in gnosis, the truer our intuitions will be, for when the soul approaches the

---

47. This largely paraphrases the second treatise in *K. al-ḥikam*. See Ibn ʿAṭaʾ Allāh, *The Book of Wisdom* (New York: Paulist Press, 1978), p. 114.

48. *Niʿma* is derived from the root n-ʿa-m, "to live in comfort and ease." Verbal and nominative forms of this root occur just over 120 times throughout the Qurʾān and include the divine name *al-Munʿīm*, the Benefactor. The transitive form, *anʿama* (*alā*), "to bestow comfort, favor, or grace (upon someone)," is part of *al-Fātiḥa*, in the verse, *Guide us to the straight path, the path of those upon whom You have bestowed grace.*

49. Ibn al-Athīr, vol. 2, p. 684, from Tirmidhī, and Suyūṭī, *al-Durr al-manthūr fī tafsīr bi-l-maʾthūr* (Cairo: Markaz Hajar, 2003), vol. 8, p. 639; Ḥakīm al-Tirmidhī, *Nawādir al-uṣūl fī aḥādīth al-Rasūl* (Beirut: Dār al-Jīl, 1992), vol. 3, p. 86; al-Ḥāfiẓ al-Ṭabarānī, *al-Muʿjam al-awsaṭ*, ed. Muḥammad al-Ṭaḥḥān (Riyadh: Maktaba al-Maʿarif li-l-Nashr wa-l-Tawzīʿ, 1995/1316), vol. 4, p. 160.

presence of the Truth, it is generally the epiphanies of the Truth which come to it.

There are three degrees of intuition. For the generality, it is an unveiling of people's thoughts or hidden aspects of their spiritual condition, and this can be a trial for someone who has not realized in his nature the attributes of the All-Merciful (*man lam yatakhallaq bi akhlāq al-Raḥmān*).[50] For the elect, it is an unveiling of the stations and stages of the way and knowledge of the mysteries of the dominions (*al-malakūt*, 58), and for the elect of the elect, it is an unveiling of the mysteries of the divine essence, the lights of the attributes, and being immersed in the mysteries of the omnipotence (*al-jabarūt*, 58).

To quote al-Kattānī, "Intuition is an unveiling of the truth and a vision of the unseen." And al-Wāsiṭī said, "It is the shining forth of the lights that have flashed in hearts, and it is to be firmly established in an intimate knowledge which bears secrets that exist in the realms of the unseen (*al-ghuyūb*) from one level to the next until one is able to perceive things the way God causes them to be perceived and then speaks of what is in people's minds."[51] I would say, however, that speaking (of what is in people's minds) is not a necessary condition to the intuition of the elect. And God most high knows best.[52]

---

50. This is a reference to Ibn ʿAṭāʾ Allāh, *K. al-ḥikam*, lithograph (Morocco, n.d.), aphorism 158: "Whoever is given knowledge of the secrets of servants without having realized the virtues of divine mercy will find his knowledge a tribulation and a means of drawing afflictions upon himself."
51. This saying appears in al-Qushayrī's *Risāla*, in the chapter on *Firāsa*, with some small but significant differences. In most of the editions of the *Miʿrāj* the word *ḥamalat* ("to carry or bear") has been mistakenly printed as *jumlata* ("the totality or whole of something"). We have followed the version in the *Risāla* because of its comprehensibility.
52. *Firāsa* is derived from the noun *fāris*, which originally meant "a Persian," and was then taken to apply to anyone who was a skilled horseman, the Persians being identified with equestrian skill. Gradually this term came to designate "someone who examines something carefully then acts." No forms of this word exist in the Qurʾān.

37. Character (*khuluq*)

Character (*khuluq*) is the faculty of the soul from which actions most easily proceed. If these actions [express virtues] such as clemency, pardon, generosity, and the like, then the character is said to be good, and if they [express faults] such as anger, hastiness, and miserliness, then it is said to be bad.

Wahb [b. Munabbih] said, "No servant acts according to a certain character for forty days except that God makes that character his nature." So good character is something to be acquired, and bad character something to be striven against until it disappears.

Good character is equal to fasting and night vigils and it is the fruit of Sufism. For anyone whose character does not improve, Sufism is a barren tree.

The essence of good character can be summed up thus: do not get angry, nor anger another; do not be miserly, nor harbor rancor. And in God is all success![53]

38. Munificence, generosity, and altruism (*jūd, sakhāʾ, wa īthār*)

Munificence (*jūd*) is the quality of one for whom it is easy to give in abundance. Someone who gives some of what he has but keeps most is said to possesses the virtue of generosity (*sakhāʾ*), whereas someone who gives most of what he has is said to possess the virtue of munificence.

As for the one who bears injuries and prefers others to himself, he is said to possess the virtue of altruism (*īthār*).

For the generality, generosity means to give of their possessions; for the elect, it is to give of themselves; and for the elect of the elect, it is to yield their spirits to death in spiritual combat (*mujāhada*, 27) that they might be brought back to eternal life in contemplative vision (*mushāhada*, 15).[54]

---

53. *Khuluq* is derived from the root kh-l-q, "to create or fashion," which occurs in various nominative and verbal forms in the Qurʾān 260 times, including in the divine name, *al-Khāliq*, the Creator. The plural form of *khuluq*, *akhlāq*, is generally taken to mean virtues or moral qualities.

54. Here he is speaking of *fanāʾ wa baqāʾ* (54). *Jūd* is derived from the root j-w-d, "to become good or excellent, to improve." It appears once in the Qurʾān in verse [38:31] in the noun *al-jīyād*, describing the "highest bred horses" that were presented to King Solomon. The gerundic

39. Spiritual poverty (*faqr*)

Spiritual poverty (*faqr*) is to withdraw your hand from the world and keep your heart from showing complaints. The marks of a true *faqīr* are three: he conceals his poverty, guards the secret [that exists between him and God], and maintains his religion.

Jaʿfar al-Khuldī said, "I served six hundred teachers and did not find one of them who could cure my heart of four matters until I saw the Messenger of God ﷺ in a dream and he said to me, 'Ask your questions.' I said, 'O Messenger of God, what is the intellect?' He answered, 'Its lowest degree is to abstain from this world and its highest is to abstain from reflection upon the divine essence.'

Then I said, 'And what is the affirmation of God's Oneness?' He said, 'It is to realize that our Lord is different from whatever your imagination presents to you or your understanding shows you.'

Then I said, 'And what is Sufism?' He answered, 'It is to give up pretense and to keep silent about meanings.'

Then I asked, 'And what is spiritual poverty?' He said, 'It is one of God's secrets which He places in those of His servants He will. Whoever conceals it will be made among its bearers, and God will increase him therein, while whoever discloses it will be deprived of its blessings.'"

I would add that the answer a person gets (to such a question) has to do with his spiritual degree, even as the Prophet ﷺ said, "Speak to people according to their understandings."[55] And so if [in the dream] he said that the highest degree of the intellect is 'to abstain from reflection

---

form *tajwīd* has come to mean the science of Qurʾānic recitation. *Sakhāʾ*, from the root s-kh-w, "to be generous," does not occur in the Qurʾān, where this action is usually expressed by a form of the verb k-r-m, "to be noble and generous," or m-n-n, "to show favor." *Īthār* is a nominative form of *āthara/yuʾthiru*, "to prefer something or someone," derived from the verbal root a-th-r, "to leave a mark upon something," as a nomad might do through the tracks of his camel (*āthar*) or by marking a preferred path in some other way. In its sense of "giving preference," it occurs 6 times in the Qurʾān, and as "traces or footsteps," 16 times.

55. The version of this *ḥadīth* in al-Daylamī, *Firdaws bi athūr al-khiṭāb*, (Beirut: Dār al-Kutub al-ʿIlmiyya, 1986), vol. 1, p. 398 reports Ibn ʿAbbās as having said, "I was ordered to speak to people according to the level of their intelligence (*ʿalā qadri ʿuqūlihim*)."

upon the divine essence,' it means reflection upon the ipseity of God, which is prohibited because it is beyond all human conception. But as for reflection upon the mysteries of His divinity and the lights of His attributes, there is no higher worship.

When he says, concerning the affirmation of God's Oneness, that God 'is different from whatever the imagination presents to you or the understanding shows you,' this means that the imagination, which can only conceive of the physical aspect of created things, is incapable of grasping the mysteries of God's Oneness, as is the understanding, without direct spiritual experience.

And when he says of spiritual poverty that 'whoever conceals it will be made among its bearers,' it means that he will be made one of the foremost (*al-sābiqūn*),[56] and God will increase him in mysteries and lights, these being the sweetness of interaction and gnosis.

It is related that Abū ʿAlī l-Daqqāq was sitting one day with some of his companions and lapsed into negligence such that he started complaining to them of his hard life. When his companions left him, one of them went to sleep and had a dream in which he heard a voice say to him, 'By God, convey to Abū ʿAbdallāh al-Daqqāq[57] what I say to you:

> Tell the little man of great standing:
> Poverty is the trait most becoming to the free.
> You who complain to people about the actions of your Lord—
> Why not complain instead of the many sins you bear?
> For the honored robes of piety you wear
> Could be stripped from you if your Lord so willed.'[58]

---

56. A term that appears in Q. 56:10, *And the foremost are the foremost! They are the ones brought near, in gardens of bliss. Many among the first and few among the last*. See our translation of Ibn ʿAjība's commentary of these words in *The Immense Ocean*, pp. 50–55.

57. It appears that Ibn ʿAjība or a scribe has mistakenly referred to al-Daqqāq as "Abū ʿAbdallāh."

58. *Faqr* is derived from the root f-q-r, which carries the basic meaning of being poor or in need. It is also related to the word *fiqrāt*, "the backbone." A possible ancient connection between the two ideas lies in the notion of "someone needing to be lent the back of a camel to ride upon." In the sense of neediness, this word appears 13 times in

40. Remembrance (*dhikr*)

Remembrance (*dhikr*) in its general sense refers to invocation [of God] with the tongue. It is one of the mainstays of the path toward union with God, and it is also the proclamation of sanctity. Whoever is inspired toward invocation is given this proclamation and whoever abandons it is excluded.

For the generality, remembrance is with the tongue; for the elect, it is with the heart; and for the elect of the elect, it is with the spirit and innermost being. This last [kind of remembrance] is none other than consciousness and vision, wherein we invoke God *in* everything and *through* everything, which is to say that we come to know Him in all things. At this stage, invocation with the tongue ceases—becomes, in fact, something feeble and purposeless—and [the invoker] is left in the silent wonder of direct contemplation. As the poet said:

> No sooner do I invoke you than do cares assail me—
> In my soul, my heart, and my spirit as they invoke You
> Until it is as if a watcher from You calls to me:
> "Beware and take care invoking, beware!
> Do you not see God's signs appearing to you
> And all His meanings united with yours?

This is the station which al-Wāsiṭī meant when he said, "The invokers in their remembrance of God are more forgetful than the forgetters in their remembrance, for His invocation is other than He."[59]

41. The moment (*al-waqt*)

The Sufis use the term "the moment" (*al-waqt*) to denote all that the servant presently finds himself in, be it contraction or expansion, sadness or joy.

Abū ʿAlī l-Daqqāq said, "The moment is whatever you are in presently. If you are in this world, your moment is this world and if you are in the final destination, your moment is the final destination." In other words, whatever prevails in our situation is our moment.

---

the Qurʾān, always in the noun form referring to those who are poor or needy (*faqīr*, pl. *fuqarāʾ*).

59. *Dhikr* is derived from the dh-k-r, "to recall, remember, or mention." Verbal and nominative forms of this root occur throughout the Qurʾān 292 times. See also appendix II:13.

Others have used this term to designate what is between the past and the future. They say, "The Sufi is the child of the moment (*ibn al-waqt*): he does not ponder about the future or the past. His concern is with what is now."

For every moment there is a desired comportment and if we fail to observe it, the moment is turned against us. This is why they say, "The moment is like the blade of a sword: if you handle it carefully, you are safe, but if you grab it, you get hurt." Handling it carefully means observing the comportment that is due. If the moment is one of divine rigor, the comportment due is contentment and submission beneath the flow of divine decrees; if the moment is one of divine beneficence, the comportment due is gratitude; if the moment is one of obedience, the comportment due is to see it as a gift from God; and if the moment is one of sin, the comportment due is repentance and conversion.[60]

42. State and station (*ḥāl wa maqām*)

A state (*ḥāl*) is an inward condition such as expansion or contraction, longing or agitation, awe or excitement, which comes upon the heart without effort, seeking, means, or merit.[61] Before an aspirant is granted equilibrium, the effects of a state may appear upon the limbs of his body in movements such as rocking to and fro, dancing, or roaming without direction. This, in fact, is what love does: first it moves you and then brings you to stillness and rest. As one of them has put it: "Its beginning is folly (*junūn*), its middle all kinds of movement (*funūn*), and its end repose (*sukūn*)."

A spiritual state may be acquired through certain kinds of actions such as taking part in circles of invocation or sessions of spiritual song (*samaᶜ*). It may require something which interrupts the soul's routine: when it grows cold, lukewarm, or lazy, some movement which will

---

60. *Waqt* is a nominative form of the root w-q-t, to assign a time to something. Forms of this verb occur in the Qurʾān in 13 places, often referring to the Hour of Judgment.

61. This part of the definition is quoted almost word for word from al-Qushayrī, *al-Risālat al-qushayriyya fī ᶜilm al-taṣawwuf*, ed. Maᶜrūf Muṣtafā Zarīq (Beirut: al-Maktaba al-ᶜAṣriyya, 2001), p. 57. This definition is also quoted word for word (without reference) in Ibn ᶜArabī, *al-Futūḥāt al-Makkiyya* (Cairo: Dār al-Kutub al-ᶜArabiyya al-Kubra, 1329/1911), ch. 73.

weigh upon it, break its routine, and warm it back up.

Sometimes the Sufis use [the word] *ḥāl* to mean "station" (*maqām*). For example, they might say about someone, "Contemplation has become his state (*ṣāra ʿindahu al-shuhūdu ḥālan*)." Thus, [ʿAbd al-Raḥmān] al-Majdhūb says:

> I made sure I could find none other than God
> And then passed the night at ease in my state.

As for station (*maqām*), this is what a servant realizes through spiritual degree, inward striving, and mastery in the stages of certainty that he has sought and acquired.

Our station is where we dwell. These begin as states that we are unable to master because they are ever changing. Once we achieve mastery of them, however, they become stations. Repentance, for example, may be reached and then lost until it becomes sincere repentance (*tawba*, 2), and so it is with all the other stations.

A condition of any station is that [the traveler] not go beyond it until its criteria have been met. So the station of conversion (*ināba*, 3) is not possible before repentance (*tawba*, 2), nor is the station of integrity (*istiqāma*, 18) before conversion, nor the station of detachment (*zuhd*, 9) before scrupulousness (*waraʿ*, 8), and so forth. However, someone who is the disciple of a perfected master may realize the first station by way of the second. Indeed, if the teacher sees that a disciple is worthy and gifted, he may fold up all the stations and bring him directly to effacement (*fanāʾ*, 54).

In general, however, we can say that states are given, stations earned. This is the meaning of the word *maqām* if pronounced with a *fatḥ* over the first *mīm*. If it is pronounced as *muqām*, however, it means "a stay," and no one stays at a given spiritual level except by seeing that it is God, the Truth, who has placed him there. As the *Ḥikam* states: "One of the signs of success in the end is to return to God most high in the beginning," and also, "Whoever's beginning is by God, his end will be to God."[62]

---

62. *K. al-ḥikam*, aphorism 26, and also the first treatise. *Ḥāl* is a noun form derived from root ḥ-w-l, "to change from one condition to another" or "to come between two things." Besides the present term, other words related to this root are *ḥawl* which means both "a year or complete cycle of seasons" and "power or strength"; *ḥīla*, "a way of accomplishing something or an artifice"; and *muḥāl*, "impossible." The

43. Contraction and expansion (*qabḍ wa basṭ*)

Contraction (*qabḍ*) and expansion (*basṭ*) are two states that come to those who have passed beyond the states of fear and hope. In the gnostic, contraction takes the place of fear for the novice and expansion takes the place of hope.

The difference between contraction and fear, on one hand, and expansion and hope on the other is that fear is connected to an external cause—losing what is loved, or being afflicted by adversity—while contraction may arise in the heart with or without a cause. Hope, likewise, can be the expectation of something we love in the future, whereas expansion is a state given us freely in the present moment.

Contraction is a pulling back and narrowness experienced in the heart which necessitates calmness and serenity, and expansion is a sense of release and broadening which necessitates movement and delight. For each of these states there is a comportment which has been described in longer treatises.[63]

44. Passing thoughts and intimate impressions (*khawāṭir wa wāridāt*)

Passing thoughts (*khawāṭir*) are inward discourses that may come to the heart either from an angel, a devil, or the ego. If the thought is from an angel, it is called "inspiration" (*ilhām*), if from a devil, "whisperings" (*waswās*), and if from the ego, "promptings" (*hawājis*).

The thoughts which come from an angel are those that conform to the truth and beckon us to follow it; thoughts which come from a devil conform to what is false and usually beckon us to sin, although the devil may also beckon us to obedience if this can be a way to sins

---

particle *ḥawla* "surrounding someone or something," is also derived from this same root. Forms of this root occur 25 times in the Qurʾān. *Maqām* is a noun of place derived from the root q-w-m, "to stand," explained in the note to term 18 above.

63. *Qabḍ* is derived from the root q-b-ḍ, literally, "to grasp or take a handful of something," and by extension "to contract." Forms of this root occur 9 times in the Qurʾān, notably in (2:245): *God is the One who contracts and expands and to Him you are returning*. Its opposite, *basṭ*, is a noun form of the root b-s-ṭ, "to spread out or open up," forms of which occur 25 times in the Qurʾān, often in reference to "expanding" one's provision in life. See also appendix II:14.

such as pretension or the love of praise. Thoughts emanating from the ego beckon us to follow our passions or to be lax [in spiritual practice].

Abū ʿAlī l-Daqqāq said, "Anyone whose sustenance is unlawful (*ḥaram*) will not be able to distinguish between inspirations and whisperings, and the same holds true for one whose provision is known (*maʿlūm*)."[64]

Al-Junayd distinguished between the promptings of the ego and the whisperings of the devil by the fact that the former will not leave you alone—they will keep returning unless (opposed) by great spiritual effort—while the latter will go away if they are opposed, but will return in a different form. Demonic whisperings may also be repelled by the formula of seeking refuge (*taʿūdh*) or others like it. Thus has it been said that the ego is more treacherous that seventy devils.

Intimate emotions (*wāridāt*) are powerful illuminations or salutary thoughts that come to the heart without effort. The difference between these and passing thoughts is that intimate emotions are general while passing thoughts are specific to the meanings they bear. Intimate emotions may be of joy, of sadness, of contraction, of expansion, of yearning, fear, and other such states, and some of them may [be so strong] that they rob the one who receives them of his senses, in which case they are very close in nature to a spiritual state (*ḥāl*, 42).

In some cases, an intimate emotion will bring with it some unveiling of the unseen, and if the one who receives it has a heart clear of obscurities, then he should accept [the unveiling] as true. And God most high knows better.[65]

---

64. That is, as compared to that of the wandering Sufi who is not sure where he will find his next meal.
65. The term *khawāṭir* (sing. *khāṭir*) is derived from the root kh-ṭ-t, "to raise or shake something (in order to call attention to it)," and by extension, "to come to mind, occur in one's thoughts." No forms of this root are found in the Qurʾān. *Wāridāt* (sing. *wārida*) is from the root w-r-d, "to come to a place or arrive," and in its most ancient sense, "to reach a place where animals may drink," as in Q. 28:23, which says of Moses, *When he arrived at* (warada) *the watering place of Madyan, he found a group of men watering their camels.* Derivations of this root occur in 10 other places in the Qurʾān. See also appendix II:15.

45. The ego, the spirit, and the innermost being (*al-nafs, al-rūḥ, wa-l-sirr*)

The ego (*al-nafs*) refers to the reprehensible aspect of our actions and character, the former being what we actively acquire—sins of omission or commission—and the latter what has become ingrained in our nature—pride, envy, anger, bad character, impatience, and the like.

The spirit (*al-rūḥ*) is the place of epiphanies where the lights of the dominions (*anwār al-malakūt*) are unveiled, and the innermost being (*al-sirr*) is where the mysteries of omnipotence (*asrār al-jabarūt*) are revealed.

The ego pertains most to the generality of believers, the spirit to the elect, and the innermost being to the elect of the elect; or [we could say] that the ego pertains most to the people of the world of the domain, the spirit to the people of the world of the dominions, and the innermost being to the people of the world of omnipotence. These three worlds are discussed later in this treatise.[66]

Are the ego, spirit, and innermost being separate and distinct entities or only names of the same entity at different levels of purity? [Concerning this], one of masters said, "The ego is a subtle entity placed in this corporeal mold and is the locus of all defective human traits. The spirit is also a subtle entity placed in this corporeal mold and is the locus of all laudable human traits. Both, however, share the same locus: the human being."

[According to this view] the ego and spirit are subtle entities, like angels and devils, which reside in the human being. They are the loci of a person's defects and virtues just as the eye is the locus of sight, the ear of hearing, and the nose of smell. As for the innermost being (*al-sirr*), it is also a subtle entity set in the corporeal mold[67] like the spirit but of a higher nature by virtue of its more perfect attributes.

Al-Sāḥilī said, "The ego, the heart, the spirit, the innermost being (*al-sirr*), and the interior dimension (*al-bāṭin*) are all names that designate the same thing: the subtle and divine entity (*al-laṭīfa al-rabbāniyya*) that makes a human being human. Differing names

66. See item 58.

67. The word here is *al-qalb*, "the heart" even in the manuscript version, but in the context, the correct word should almost certainly be *al-qālib*, "the mold," meaning the human form or the body.

reflect only differing traits: if it inclines in the direction of defects, it is called 'ego'; if it is purified enough to ascend from the station of surrender (*islām*) to the station of faith (*īmān*), it is called 'heart'; if it is further purified, but there still remain traces of defects like the scar left from a wound that has healed, it is called 'spirit'; and if even those traces disappear and it becomes totally pure, it is called 'innermost being'. If the question is [more] complex, then it is simply referred to as 'the interior dimension.'"

As for the spirit, the differing views concerning it are well-known. Some say it is life itself. Some say it is a sublime essence placed into this corporeal mold, since it is God's way to create life within a mold: as long as life is sustained in it, the human being lives by its life. The spirits placed in these molds, however, separate from them during sleep, ascend, and return. Also, it is by way of the spirit that the breath of life (*al-nafkh*) occurs.

As for the ego, it is created in the fetus before the spirit is breathed into it. It is by way of the ego that physical movement takes place, and so it is inseparable from the body until the moment of death. At that time, first the spirit leaves the body, then breathing ceases, and life comes to an end.

A human being is thus spirit, soul, and body and the gathering [of the Last Day] will be of all three, as will be the punishment and recompense of the next world.

[We may also add that] spirits are created before physical bodies and then infuse them like fire inside a glowing coal or sap inside a sapling.

As I said earlier, these entities are placed in the corporeal molds and are subtle, lordly, and divine. They are the entities which develop, and according to the level of their development, their names differ, as al-Sāḥilī said. But God most high knows better.

If it is said that they are created, that is in keeping with the doctrine of separation (*madhhab al-farq*), but according to the doctrine of unity, they are uncreated inasmuch as everything in existence is passing away. To quote al-Junayd: "When the contingent meets the eternal, the contingent is eclipsed and only the eternal remains." Thus, when I asked one of our brethren, a gnostic, whether spirits are created or eternal, he answered, "For the Sufis, even bodies are eternal!" By this, he was alluding to the station of effacement that I have just mentioned, but this is a mystery unspoken.[68]

46. Help, support, protection, guidance, direction, and firmness of purpose (*naṣr, taʾyīd, ʿiṣma, hidāya, rushd, wa tasdīd*)

Help (*naṣr*) is when God strengthens the limbs of our body to accomplish the good, and support (*taʾyīd*) is when God strengthens our inner vision (*baṣīra*). To be motivated inwardly is support; to have physical strength and be assisted outwardly in our worldly means (*asbāb*) is help.

Both these notions are contained in the terms "guidance" (*hidāya*), which is inner vision founded on the knowledge and discovery of the true nature of things; "direction" (*rushd*), which is the will to seek salvation; and "firmness of purpose" (*tasdīd*), which is the ability to direct one's movements toward a desired goal and be granted ease in doing so.

---

68. The word *nafs* is derived from the root n-f-s which carries two basic meanings: "to be highly esteemed, valuable, and desirable" (as in the adjective *nafīs*), and "to breathe," as in the verb *tanaffas*. Both these meanings appear to be included in the most common sense of the noun *nafs* (pl. *nufus*), "the individual self or ego" and in the pronoun forms *anfusukum*, *anfusunā*, etc. (yourselves, ourselves). In its simple nominative form this word appears in the Qurʾān approximately 150 times. The triad *al-nafs al-ammārtu bi-l-sūʾ* ("the soul which commands toward evil"), *al-nafs al-lawwāma* ("the soul which blames"), and *al-nafs al-muṭmaʾinna* ("the soul at peace"), comes from verses 12:53, 75:2, and 89:27. *Rūḥ* arises from the root r-w-ḥ, which includes in its scope of meaning the winds and breezes, the soul or spirit, and the experience of rest, comfort and invigoration. In the form of *rūḥ*, the "spirit," it appears in the Qurʾān in 24 places, including 5 references to *rūḥ al-qudus*, the "spirit of sanctity" or "holy spirit," which is usually taken to mean Gabriel, the angel of revelation. The root of *sirr*, s-r-r, expresses two main ideas: *surūr*, "lasting joy," and *sirr* itself, "a secret or mystery." A third nominative derivation, *sarīr*, "a bed or raised couch," and, by extension, "the dominion or authority of a ruler who sits on a raised throne," is said to be related to *surūr*, happiness. In its sense of "a secret or the concealment of something," this root occurs about 30 times in the Qurʾān, as "happiness," it occurs in 7 places, and as "raised couches," 6.

As for "protection" (*ʿisma*), its meaning is close to that of support. It refers to something divine which flows within a human being and by which he is given the strength to prefer good and avoid evil. It is like an inward barrier (between him and evil) of which he is not even conscious.

All this is according to al-Ghazālī.[69] These six essential notions—guidance, direction, protection, firmness of purpose, outward help, and inward help—I have understood from his words, ﵁. In actuality, guidance is what puts the servant on the path which will bring him to God (and here I refer only to its most literal meaning); direction is the heart's turning toward the path of salvation; firmness of purpose is strength to follow the way to goodness and avoid the way to evil; and protection is something divine, as has been already stated.[70]

47. Wisdom (*ḥikma*)

Wisdom (*ḥikma*) refers to the perfection and creation of something. In respect to knowledge, it means to realize [a teaching] and practice it. In discourse, it means to express something concisely and with fullness of meaning. In actions, it means to do something perfectly and completely.

It has been said that wisdom descended upon three peoples: upon

---

69. Abū Ḥāmid al-Ghazālī, *Iḥyāʾ ʿulūm al-dīn* (Samarang: Maktaba Keriyata, n.d.), vol. 4, pp. 105–106.

70. The root of the noun *naṣr*, n-ṣ-r, "to give help, especially in combat against an enemy," occurs in the Qurʾān in 33 places. *Taʾyid*, from the root a-y-d, also expresses help, but more in the sense of being strengthened. It occurs in the Qurʾān in its verbal form in 8 places. ʿa-ṣ-m, the root of *ʿiṣma*, expresses the notion of being defended or protected and occurs 13 times in the Qurʾān. *Hidāya*, from the root h-d-y, which means both "to give a gift to" or "to give direction to," occurs in 316 places in the Qurʾān. The root of *rashīd*, r-sh-d, also expresses the meaning of guidance and direction to what is right. It occurs in 19 places in the Qurʾān. Both *al-Hādī*, the Guide, and *al-Rashīd*, the One who shows the right way, are divine names. *Tasdīd* is a gerund derived from the verbal root s-d-d which, in its most ancient meaning, meant "to shoot an arrow so that it hits its target." Figuratively, then, it expresses singleness of purpose. In the expression *qawlan sadīdan*, "speech which is straight and to the point," it occurs twice in the Qurʾān.

the tongue of the Arabs, the hands of the Chinese, and the intellects of the Greeks. And God most high knows better.[71]

48. The intellect (*al-ʿaql*)

The intellect (*al-ʿaql*) is a light by which we may distinguish what is salutary from what is harmful. It therefore keeps the one to whom it is given from committing transgressions. It may also be defined as a spiritual light by which the individual soul may comprehend both practical and theoretical teachings, or the power by which we are receptive to knowledge.

It is called "intellect" (*ʿaql*) because it fetters (*yaʿqil*) the one who possesses it from doing what he should not do.

The intellect is of two sorts: the greater and the lesser. The greater intellect is the first light that God manifested in existence. It is also referred to as the supreme spirit (*al-rūḥ al-aʿẓam*) or the primordial Muḥammadin substance (*al-qabḍat al-muḥammadiyya*). From this light extends the lesser intellect, as moonlight extends sunlight, which continues to grow through acts of obedience, spiritual effort, and purification from passions until the servant enters the station of excellence (*maqām al-iḥsān*) where the sun of gnosis rises in the heart. Then is its light subsumed by the light of the greater intellect just as moonlight is subsumed by sunlight at dawn. When this happens, a human being will see mysteries and secrets which he had not seen before. For the light of the lesser intelligence is weak. It can discern that the work (*ṣanʿa*) of creation depends upon the Artisan (*al-Ṣāniʿ*), but nothing beyond that. The greater intellect, however, by its purity and brilliance, knows the Artisan both before and after His epiphanies.

In certain narrations it has been said, "The first thing that God created was the intellect. Then He said to it, 'Advance,' and it advanced, and He said to it, 'Go back,' and it went back, and He said to it, 'Be seated,' and it sat down, and He said to it, 'Arise!' and it arose. Then He said to it, 'By My majesty and might, I have not created any creation nor anything dearer to Me than you. By you

71. The root of *ḥikma*, ḥ-k-m, in its most ancient sense meant "to restrain or prevent someone from acting in a corrupt or evil fashion." By extension, it expresses judgment, rules, order, and wisdom and occurs 210 times in the Qurʾān. *Al-Ḥakīm*, the Judge or the One possessing wisdom, is among the ninety-nine divine names.

do I take and by you do I give," and in another version, "By you am I worshiped and by you am I disobeyed," or words close to this.[72] *Ḥadīth* speak of this as well.

The greater intellect is only attained by those beloved to God, those whom God has chosen to grant the gnosis of the elect. The lesser intellect, however, is given both to the generality and the elect and is of two types: innate and acquired. God has made the former as an instinct, while the latter is what comes through experience, spiritual effort, and trials.

Someone said, "The signs of the intellect are three: piety (*taqwā*, 17), honest speech, and ignoring what does not concern us." And the Prophet ﷺ said, "Among the signs of the intellect are a drawing back from this world of illusions, a turning toward the eternal abode, making provision for the grave, and preparation for the Day of Resurrection."[73]

A certain sage said, "The best thing a human being can be given is an intellect which will reproach him; if this is lacking, then a sense of shame which will restrain him; if this is lacking, then wealth by which he may make expiation; and if [all this is lacking], then a bolt of lighting which will strike him down so that the land and its people may be relieved of him!"

As for the question, "Are souls endowed with intellect before they enter the body?" the answer is that they possess an intellect kindled from the greater intellect. This is how they were able to acknowledge God's divinity before creation, and it is, in fact, an indication that

---

72. Ibn al-Athīr, vol. 4, p. 18, with no source; Tirmidhī, *Nawādir al-uṣūl*, vol. 2, p. 353; Bayhaqī, *Shuʿab al-īmān*, vol. 4, p. 154. Ṭabarānī, *al-Awsaṭ*, vol. 8, p. 119 and vol. 2, p. 503.

73. The wording quoted here appears in Ibn ʿArabī's *al-Futūḥāt al-Makkiyya*, vol. 4, p. 521. The better-known version is what is reported as a *ḥadīth* in Bayhaqī, *Shuʿab al-īmān*, vol. 1, p. 76, Tirmidhī, *Nawādir al-uṣūl*, vol. 1, p. 415, and by Ghazālī in the *Iḥyāʾ*, vol. 1, p. 76 with the wording, "The Prophet recited the verse *Whosoever God wishes to guide, He expands his breast to Islām* (6:125) and then was asked, "And what is this expansion?" He answered, "Verily, when light enters it, the breast expands and broadens to receive it." Then he was asked, "Are there any signs of this?" And he answered, "Yes. There is a drawing back from this world of illusions, a turning toward the eternal abode, and preparation for death before it befalls."

they possess the ability to know and understand all things, as Ibn al-Bannāʾ says.[74]

There is, in reality, neither gnosis nor comprehension except through the intellect. When [souls] are brought forth into this world of forms, God removes from them that intellect which came from the greater intellect, and when the fetus is formed in the womb, He causes the lesser intellect to grow within it. This continues to develop until puberty, or, according to some, until the age of forty. If, however, a servant becomes attached to a spiritual physician, this master will treat him until he is rejoined to the greater intellect and becomes thereby among the great saints. And in God is all success.[75]

49. The affirmation of divine unity (*tawḥīd*)

Affirmation of divine unity (*tawḥīd*) is of two sorts. One is by way of formal proof and affirms, through logical demonstrations, the oneness of God in His acts, attributes, and essence. The other is by way of essential vision and affirms that God alone exists, eternally without beginning or end.

To quote al-Junayd ﷺ "[*Tawḥīd*] is a spiritual reality (*maʿnā*) in which forms are effaced, all knowledge is contained, and God is as He ever was. It has five fundamental elements: lifting the veil of the contingent, realizing the utter singularity of the eternal, departing from brethren, leaving one's homeland, and forgetting both the known and unknown."

The "spiritual reality in which forms are effaced" refers to the

---

74. By which he means Ibn al-Bannāʾ al-Tujībī (see appendix III) in his poem on the fundamentals of Sufism, *al-Mubāḥith al-aṣliyya*. In part 1, section 3, on spiritual combat and breaking habits, he writes:

    And in every living soul there rests the knowledge of all things
    But the body, the lower soul, and the devil obscure it.

    Acknowledging God before creation refers to Q. 7:172: *And (remember) when your Lord brought forth from the children of Adam, from their reins, their seed, and made them testify of themselves, (saying): Am I not your Lord? They said: Yea, verily. We testify. (That was) lest you should say at the Day of Resurrection: Lo! of this we were unaware.*

75. The root of the term *ʿaql*, ʿa-q-l, in its most ancient sense expresses the act of tying or restraining a camel. This also came to signify blood money, paid in camels, in the case of having caused accidental death. As "intelligence" or "sense" it appears in the Qurʾān 49 times.

unveiling of the secrets of the divine essence. This unveiling takes place when an individual passes away from [perceiving] the physical shapes of existence—the containers of those secrets—and [is granted a vision of] God as the sole and eternally existing One: "God was, and there was nothing with Him and He is now as He ever was."[76] For when the veil of the contingent is lifted, the utter singularity of the eternal is realized. Those who are granted this taste depart from [all their] brethren except those who help them toward their Lord. They leave their homelands in search of the truth—for migration (*hijra*) is a sunna—and forget both the known and the unknown, passing away from them both before the treasure they have been given.

Al-Junayd was asked concerning *tawḥīd* [on another occasion] and said, "The color of the liquid is the color of the vessel." Here he meant that the sublime essence which is subtle, hidden, and luminous, when manifested through shapes and forms, takes on the hue of those shapes and forms. Understand this and accept it even if you have not tasted it.[77]

The stations of affirming God's oneness are endless, for they increase through unveilings and ascent. Above *tawḥīd* is *tafrīd*.

50. The affirmation of God's uniqueness (*tafrīd*)

The affirmation of God's uniqueness (*tafrīd*) is finer and more elevated than *tawḥīd*. This latter signifies the doctrine of oneness professed by the people of knowledge, while *tafrīd* is particular to the people of spiritual experience (*ahl al-dhawq*).[78]

Above *tafrīd* come:

---

76. *K. al-ḥikam*, aphorism 37.

77. *Tawḥīd* is a gerund form arising from the root w-ḥ-d, "to be one, or to be alone." Referring to the oneness of God, this occurs 27 times in the Qurʾān including as the divine name *al-Wāḥid*, the One. The phrase *lā ilāha illa Allāh* (There is no god but God) is called "the declaration of *tawḥīd*."

78. *Tafrīd* is a gerundic form arising from the root f-r-d, "to be or become single, alone, unique." In its adjectival form it occurs 5 times in the Qurʾān, three of which refer to coming to God on the Day of Judgment *farada*, often translated as *bare and alone*.

51. Supreme unity, unicity, singularity, unity, and exclusivity (*aḥadiyya, īḥād, fardāniyya, waḥdāniyya, wa infirād*)

I have arranged these terms in order of strength. Supreme unity (*aḥadiyya*) is the emphatic form of *waḥda*, unity. Unicity, *īḥād*, is the gerund form of the verb *awḥada*: "to make something one." Singularity (*fardāniyya*), unity (*waḥdāniyya*), and exclusivity (*infirād*) all signify that being belongs to God alone, after the ocean of unity subsumes the totality of existence so that absolutely nothing else is left in existence. This is experienced by the one who first tastes it and then drowns in it entirely, these being called the "solitary ones" or the "unique ones." Of them, al-Ḥātimī said that their knowledge of God is more perfect than that of the pole (*al-quṭb*, 79) and so they are outside the sphere of his authority.[79] But God most high knows better.[80]

52. The sublime essence (*al-dhāt al-ʿaliyya*)

The sublime essence (*al-dhāt al-ʿaliyya*) is perfect, eternal, subtle, and hidden. It reveals Itself in contours and forms, is qualified by the attributes of infinite perfection, one in eternity, without end. Such are its characteristics, but only God comprehends its actual nature.

53. The dark cloud (*al-ʿamā*)

The dark cloud (*al-ʿamā*) signifies the sublime essence in eternity before Its Self-revelation. Its reality was empty space, subtle, hidden, pure, and imperceptible, limitless above and below and in all the four directions, beginningless in its primacy and endless in its finality, free both of form and contour, and qualified by the attributes of perfection: power, will, knowledge, life, hearing, vision, and speech. This is what Ibn al-Fāriḍ alludes to in his lines:

> They say to me, "Describe it,
> For you are well-informed of its description."
> Indeed, I have some knowledge of its attributes:
> Purity, yet not water; subtlety, yet not air,

79. See Ibn ʿArabī, *al-Futūḥāt al-Makkiya*, vol. 1, p. 199.
80. Concerning the origin of these terms, see the notes for items 49 and 50 above.

Light, yet not fire; spirit, yet not body.
The tale of it told in eternity was more ancient
than all existing things
When there was neither shape nor trace.[81]

Then was it Self-revealed in contours and forms, the subtle becoming gross, the concealed becoming revealed, the unseen, perceived. Yet that which was in eternity before time is identical to that which is self-revealed in eternity after time. "God was, and there was nothing with Him, and He is now as He ever was."[82]

In a *ḥadīth* narrated by al-Tirmidhī according to Abū Razayn al-ʿUqaylī, it was asked of the Prophet ﷺ, "O Messenger of God, where was our Lord before He created His creation?" He answered, "He was in a cloud above which there was no air and below which there was no air."[83] That is to say, He was in a hidden and subtle mode with air neither above nor below. Rather, the infinitude of His essence enveloped all "above" and all "below" and all that was "air."

It was asked of our master ʿAlī [b. Abī Ṭālib], "O cousin of God's Messenger! Where was our Lord?" or "Did our Lord reside somewhere?" at which his face changed and he remained quiet for some time. Then he said, "Your words, 'where was God,' are a question about place. But God was, and there was no 'place.' Then He created time and space. And He is now as He was, without time or place."[84]

This is to say that God was, and there was nothing with Him, and He is now and there is nothing with Him. So understand this![85]

54. Effacement and subsistence (*fanāʾ wa baqāʾ*)

When the Sufis speak of "effacement" or "extinction" (*fanāʾ*), they are referring to effacement in the divine essence, meaning

81. Adapted from A. J. Arberry's translation in *Arabic Poetry: A Primer for Students* (Cambridge: Cambridge University Press, 1965).
82. *K. al-ḥikam*, aphorism 37.
83. Ibn al-Athīr, vol. 4, p. 16 from Tirmidhī, Ibn Mājah, and Aḥmad.
84. We were unable to find the source of this narration.
85. *ʿAmā* (which may also be written *ʿamāʾ*, that is, ending with a *hamza al-qaṭ*) is linguistically related to the root ʿa-m-ā, "he became blind." *ʿAmā* is thus defined as something which cannot be perceived either by the senses or the mind. Derivations from this root appear in the Qurʾān in 33 places, always in relation to blindness, either physical or spiritual.

the effacement of traces and forms in the consciousness of God, or the dissolution of the physical before the manifestation of the intelligible.

To quote Abū l-Mawāhib: "*Fanāʾ* is effacement, disappearance, leaving yourself behind, ceasing to exist as an individual entity." And Abū Saʿīd b. al-Aʿrābī said, "It is when the immensity and greatness [of God] appear to the servant causing him to forget this world and the next, states, degrees, stations, and invocations, effacing him from everything, from his own mind and individual self, and effacing him from this effacement, and effacing him from his effacement from effacement, as he is immersed in the divine immensity." This is to say that the majesty of the essence is revealed and effaces him from seeing created things, including his own self. Thus does he become essence itself, drowned in the ocean of unity.

They also speak of *fanāʾ* in respect to effacement in God's acts—that there is no Doer except God—and God's attributes—that there is no other One who is Able, no Hearer, and no Seer except God. [Whoever is granted this effacement] sees creatures themselves as being lifeless, powerless, unable to hear or see except by God. Then comes effacement in the essence, or as a poet has said:

> He is effaced, then effaced, then effaced
> And his effacement becomes his very subsistence

As for subsistence (*baqāʾ*), this is a return to consciousness of existent things after having passed away from it, to consciousness of the sensory (*al-ḥiss*, 57) after having passed away from it in consciousness of the intelligible, except that the servant then sees it as subsisting through God and as one of the lights of His epiphanies: were it not for the sensory, the intelligible could not be manifested, or [to paraphrase Ibn Mashīsh], 'were it not for the mediator (*al-wāsiṭatu*), the One for whom he mediates could not be known.'

God most high thus reveals Himself between two opposites: between the sensory and the intelligible, between power and wisdom (*qudra wa ḥikma*, 55), separation and union (*farq wa jamʿ*, 56). To be absented from one of these is effacement, while to see them both is subsistence. To be absent from the sensory, from divine wisdom, and from separation is effacement, while to perceive them both is subsistence.

Subsistence, therefore, encompasses effacement. [For the one who is granted this station], union does not veil separation, effacement does not veil subsistence, and the consciousness of divine power does not veil the consciousness of divine wisdom. Rather, "he gives to each that has a right its right," gives to each what is merited.[86]

The terms effacement and subsistence are also used to mean the process of "emptying and beautifying" (*takhliyya wa taḥliyya*) and so they may say, "He was effaced of his reprehensible traits and sustained in his praiseworthy traits." And God most high knows better.[87]

55. Power and wisdom (*qudra wa ḥikma*)

Power (*qudra*) refers to the manifestation of things in accordance with the divine will and wisdom (*ḥikma*) refers to their concealment by the intermediary and contingent. Power manifests, wisdom conceals. Power, however, does not occur independently of wisdom except in certain rare cases, such as the miracles of prophets, the charismatic deeds of saints, or the magic of sorcerers.

Power may also refer to the essence after its Self-revelation, using a quality to describe the One qualified. As for wisdom, it is the sensory world, human attributes, and laws of servanthood (*ʿubudiyya*) which conceal the essence.

In other words, the Self-revelation of God most high through His name the Outward (*al-Ẓāhir*) is called power, while His inwardness after this manifestation through His name the Inward (*al-Bāṭin*) is called wisdom; or the Self-revelation of God most high from the realm of the unseen to the realm of the seen is power, and His concealment in manifestation is wisdom.

---

86. This expression is part of a well-known *ḥadīth* in Bukhārī, vol. 3, p. 38 and vol. 8, pp. 32–33.

87. *Fanāʾ* is derived from the root f-n-y, "to pass away, die, vanish, become extinct," and occurs once in the Qurʾān in the verse quoted below. *Baqāʾ* is from the root b-q-y, "to remain or to last," forms of which appear 21 times throughout the Qurʾān, including the oft-quoted verse which combines them both: *All that is upon [the earth] is passing away* (fān) *and the face of your Lord remains* (yabqā) *full of majesty and generosity* (55:26).

To quote the *Ḥikam*:[88] "Glory be to the One who concealed the mystery of His specificity in the manifestation of the human nature, and revealed the grandeur of His lordliness in the manifestation of servanthood."[89]

56. Separation and unification (*farq wa jamʿ*)

Separation (*farq*) refers to consciousness of the sensory dimension of existence and to observing the rules and comportment appropriate to this consciousness: devotional practice and servanthood.

Unification (*jamʿ*) refers to consciousness of the intelligible dimension that is inherent in all things and continuous with the all-enveloping ocean of divine omnipotence (*al-baḥr al-muḥīṭ al-jabarūtī*). You could also say that separation is to perceive existence as molds (*qawālib*), while unification is to perceive it as places of divine manifestations (*maẓāhir*). The molds are where the prescriptions of the law are observed, while the places of manifestation are springs of the essential truth.

Abū ʿAlī l-Daqqāq said, "Separation is what is attributed to you; unification is what is removed from you." Separation without unification is immorality, formalism, and ignorance of God most high. Unification without separation—except in cases of [temporary] spiritual intoxication—is heresy and disbelief, because it disregards divine wisdom (*Ḥikma*, 55) and the laws which God's messengers have brought.

Since power is inseparable from wisdom, it is incumbent upon the servant of God to be unified in his separation and separated in his union, to witness unification within and to maintain separation without.[90]

---

88. *K. al-ḥikam*, aphorism 108.

89. Concerning the linguistic root of *ḥikma*, see the note for item 47 above. *Qudra* is derived from the root q-d-r, "to measure, determine, or decree." By extension, it carries the meaning of having the power to accomplish something. Nominative, verbal, and adjectival forms of this root occur 132 times in the Qurʾān, 37 of which are variations of the phrase, *that God, over all things, has power* (*anna Allāha ʿalā kulli shayin qadīr*), which could also be translated, *that God is the One who determines all things. Al-Qādir*, the One who possesses determinative power, is among the ninety-nine names of God.

90. The root f-r-q, "to make a separation or division between things," oc-

57. The sensory and the intelligible (*al-ḥiss wa-l-maʿnā*)

[The Sufis] use the term *al-ḥiss*, the sensory, to refer to the physical, opaque and solidified outward dimension of things, and the term *maʿnā*, the intelligible or "meaning," to refer to the subtle, interior dimension. Thus the sensory dimension of things is the vessels which bear their intelligible meanings. To quote al-Shushtarī ﷺ:

Regard not the vessels
But plunge into the ocean of their meanings
And then you might see Me!

The cosmos may thus be likened to snow which is outwardly ice, inwardly water. Outwardly, the cosmos is sensory, inwardly intelligible, and this intelligible aspect is none other than the mystery of the sublime and subtle essence inherent in all things. The intelligible flows through the vessels like water flowing through snow, even as the pole of all spiritual poles, the master al-Jilānī ﷺ said:

What is the cosmos except like snow
And You the water, its source.
And while snow and water in truth are one
The law bids we treat them as different.

The sensory cannot exist except by the intelligible and the intelligible cannot be manifested except through the sensory. The intelligible is subtle, fine, and unknowable except through the sensory dimension in the molds of existence. Its manifestation would be impossible without the sensory, but to see only the sensory without the intelligible is ignorance and darkness. Thus is it said in the *Ḥikam*: "The universe [in itself] is total darkness; only the light of God manifest therein illuminates it. . . ."[91]

God most high is not seen except through epiphanies in this world and the next, or as one of [the Sufis] said:

The essence is not reached save through Its epiphanies
Though man may be rent asunder in trying.[92]

---

curs 72 times in the Qurʾān, while j-m-ʿa, "to collect, gather, assemble, or unite" occurs 129 times, often as the qualifier, *jamīʿan*, "totally" or "all together," but also in the divine name *al-Jāmiʿ*, the One who gathers together.

91. *K. al-ḥikam*, aphorism 14

92. The notion of feeling or sensing is expressed by ḥ-s-s. It occurs in the

58. The domain, the dominions, and the omnipotence (*al-mulk, al-malakūt, wa-l-jabarūt*)

The domain (*al-mulk*) is the sensory dimension of existence, the dominions (*al-malakūt*) are its inward, intelligible dimension, and the omnipotence (*al-jabarūt*) is the all-enveloping ocean from which both pour forth. In other words, the primordial substance (*al-qabḍa*) which emerged from the vacuity of the dark cloud (*al-ʿamāʾ*, 53) is the "domain" in its outward, sensory aspect, and the "dominions" in its inward, intelligible aspect, while the all-enveloping ocean from which these both pour forth is the "omnipotence."

The mysteries of the intelligible are gardens for the gnostics, for that is where their souls roam freely, but the splendor of those realities appears only by way of the sensory realm, the domain. Also, the domain is related to our Prophet ﷺ inasmuch as it was manifested only for his sake, just as the mysteries of the divine essence poured forth only by way of his light.[93] This is what is meant by the words of the pole, Ibn Mashīsh, [in his prayer of blessing]: "The inner gardens of the dominions are adorned by the blossoms of his beauty," which refers implicitly to the domain, since it is in the sensory dimension that the beauty of those blossoms appears, "And the pools of the omnipotence overflow with the outpouring of his lights." Here he could just as well have said, 'The ocean of omnipotence overflows with the outpouring of his light,' to refer to the primordial substance emerging from the ocean of God's subtle light, but he chose [the word] "pools" (*ḥiyāḍ*) to rhyme with the word "inner gardens" (*riyāḍ*). Also, he referred to the primordial

---

Qurʾān in 5 places as a verb and once as a noun. The root of *maʿnā*, ʿa-n-ā, gives rise to the verb *ʿanā, yaʿnī*, "to concern (someone) or occupy someone's thoughts," as well as "to mean."

93. Besides referring to the *Ṣalāt al-Mashīshiyya*, Ibn ʿAjība is probably making a reference to certain narratives considered by some to be *ḥadīth* in which God says to Adam, 'Were it not for Muḥammad, I would not have created you.' See al-Bayhaqī, *Dalāʾil al-nubuwwa* (Beirut: Dār al-Kutub al-ʿIlmiyya, 1984), vol. 5, p. 479. This is also echoed in the thirty-third verse of Buṣīrī's famous ode, *al-Burda*, which refers to the Prophet's detachment: "How could poverty tempt him to worldliness, when but for him the world would have not been brought forth from the void?" Abdal Hakim Murad, *The Mantle Adorned* (London: Quilliam Press, 2009).

substance using the plural, "lights" (*anwār*), in order to evoke its multitudinous aspects, similar to how the word "worlds" (*ʿālamīn*) is used [in *Sūrat al-Fātiḥa*] even while the world is one. And God most high knows better.

The domain is thus what is known by way of the senses and the imagination, the dominions by way of knowledge and taste (*dhawq*, 61), and the omnipotence by way of unveiling and ecstacy.

Existence is one but our relationship to it differs according to our vision and spiritual level. For those who remain with the sensory aspect of creation which veils them from the intelligible, it is the "domain," for those who are granted consciousness of the intelligible, it is the "dominions," and for those who behold the source of the primordial substance, it is called the "omnipotence."

If branches are joined to their roots, and vessels turn subtle (*talaṭṭafat*) so that all becomes intelligible, and the cosmos is drowned in the ocean of absolute oneness, then all becomes omnipotence.

Each station veils what is before it: the dominions veil us from perceiving the domain and the omnipotence veils us from perceiving the dominions, except for those following the way methodically. And God most high knows better.[94]

59. Human nature, divine nature, and the realm of infinite mercy (*nāsūt, lāhūt, wa-l-raḥamūt*)

Human nature (*nāsūt*) is used to refer to the sensory dimension of the vessels (*al-awānī*), while divine nature (*lāhūt*) refers to the mysteries of [their] intelligible dimension. Thus, the former pertains

94. *Al-Mulk* is the title of the *sūra* 67 of the Qurʾān and appears in 27 other places. The term *malakūt* occurs once, in (6:75): *So too did We show Abraham the dominions* (malakūt) *of the heavens and the earth that he might be among those possessing certitude.* Both terms arise from the same verbal root, m-l-k, "to own or possess something." Other forms derived from this root occur in 90 places in the Qurʾān including in the noun *malāʾika* (angels) and the divine names *al-Mālik* and *al-Malik* (the Sovereign and the One who possesses). *Jabarūt* arises from the verbal root j-b-r, which expresses notions ranging from "restoring something to strength" to "exerting power over something." Although the term *jabarūt* itself does not appear in the Qurʾān, derived forms of the same root occur in 10 places, including in the divine name *al-Jabbār*, the One who is exalted in might.

to the domain, the latter to the dominions.

As for *al-Raḥamūt*, the realm of infinite mercy, this refers to the kindness and mercy of God that penetrate all things, be it in their rigor or in their beauty. "Whoever supposes that His gentleness is separate from His determinative power does so out of shortsightedness."[95]

60. Seeking ecstasy, ecstatic emotion, the ecstatic encounter, and pure ecstasy (*tawājud, wajd, wijdān wa wujūd*)

Seeking ecstacy (*tawājud*) means to outwardly show the signs of ecstatic emotion through sacred dance, rhythmic movement, and rising [for invocation], and to use it methodically. It is only permissible for the *fuqarāʾ* who have left the workaday world. For them, there is no harm in showing signs of ecstasy or a spiritual state. On the contrary, it is a balm for their souls.

While seeking ecstacy is generally a station of those who are weak, the strong may also practice it either to support [the weak] or simply for its sweetness.

It was once asked of Abū Muḥammad al-Jurayrī, "What is your

95. *K. al-ḥikam*, aphorism 106. *Nāsūt* is derived from word *nās*, "people," which itself is the plural of *insān*, "human being." Both these arise from the verbal root, a-n-s, which expresses the ideas of companionship, familiarity, intimacy, and happiness. The related verb ā-n-s means "to see something familiar," as in the words of Moses to his family in (20:10), *Stay here. Verily I have seen* (ānastu) *a fire*. The word *nās*, "people or human beings," occurs 241 times in the Qurʾān, ends five of the six verses of its final sura (114), and is thus the last word in the entire Qurʾān. Other variations of the root a-n-s can be found in over 95 places. The term *lāhūt* is said be derived from the verb *lāha*, "to shimmer or gleam," and originally described the appearance of a mirage on the horizon. According to some Arab grammarians this verb also means "to be hidden." The dictionary *Lisān al-ʿarab* mentions that Sībawayhi admits the possibility that the name *Allāh* is related to this verb. *Raḥamūt* is derived from the root r-ḥ-m, "to be compassionate and merciful," which in turn is said in a *ḥadīth* to be derived from the noun *raḥim*, "womb." Forms of this root occur in the Qurʾān 564 times, including in the two divine names, *al-Raḥmān* and *al-Raḥīm*, the All-Merciful and Compassionate, mentioned in the formula which begins all but one of the one hundred and fourteen *sūras*.

state during a session of spiritual song and invocation (*samᶜa*)?" He answered, "If there is someone present before whom I feel shy, I keep from showing the ecstacy I feel, but if I am alone, I give it free rein and express it."

As for al-Junayd, he was first among those who showed his ecstacy but later he would sit perfectly still. When someone then asked him, "Dear master, do you not experience anything in the sessions of spiritual song and invocation?" he answered [by quoting the Qurʾān]: *You see the mountains and you reckon them to be still, yet they are moving past like clouds* (27:88).

I myself have been present in sessions of invocation with our shaykh, al-Būzīdī ﵁ [and have seen him] swaying right and left, and someone who attended a session of invocation with his shaykh, Mulay al-ᶜArabī l-Darqāwī, said to me, "He stayed in the sacred dance until the entire session was finished."

No one denies the permissibility of these sessions except ignorant formalists who have no sense of the mysteries of divine reality.

Ecstatic emotion (*wajd*) is something that may come to the heart unexpectedly, without thought or effort, as either an ardent desire or unsettling fear (*shawqun muqliqun aw khawfun muzᶜijun*),[96] or it may come after seeking ecstacy.

It has been said that the experience of ecstacy is the fruit of efforts made in the mysteries of spiritual truths, just as the sweetness found in acts of obedience is the fruit of efforts made in outward devotions. The more effort we make in deepening our realization of the mysteries of spiritual truths and divine unity, the greater the experience of ecstacy, just as the more effort we make in acts of physical devotion, the sweeter they become.

The ecstatic encounter (*al-wijdān*) refers to the sweetness and prolongation of a contemplative state often accompanied by drunkenness and speechless awe. If this continues until the bewilderment and astonishment pass, and reflection and meditation become clear and lucid, it is called "pure ecstasy" (*wujūd*), referred to in the verse by al-Junayd:

96. This expression appears in a saying attributed to the Kufic traditionalist Yūsuf b. Asbāṭ (d. c. 195/810). "Only unsettling fear or a restless desire [for God] can erase passions from the heart," which is quoted nearly verbatim in *K. al-ḥikam*, aphorism 202, using the verb "expel" (*yukhrij*) instead of "erase" (*yamḥū*).

My ecstasy is to pass away from existence
By what is shown me in contemplation of the divine.

Abū ʿAlī l-Daqqāq said, "To seek ecstasy you must melt; to experience ecstasy you must drown; to find ecstasy you must perish." First behold the sea, then set sail upon it, and then drown it in.

Al-Qushayrī said: "Concerning this question, the order is: aspiration (*quṣūd*), then drinking (*wurūd*), then vision (*shuhūd*), then ecstasy (*wujūd*), then extinction (*khumūd*)." Aspiration is for those seeking ecstasy; ecstatic emotion and drinking is for those who experience ecstacy imbibing the wine; vision is for the people of intoxication in the ecstatic encounter; and pure ecstasy and extinction are for the people of sobriety. And God most high knows better.[97]

61. Taste, drinking, drunkenness, and sobriety (*dhawq, shurb, sukr, wa ṣaḥw*)

Taste (*dhawq*) comes after having acquired formal knowledge of the spiritual truth. It is a flashing of lights from the eternal essence upon the mind such that consciousness of the contingent vanishes. However, it is temporary: the light may shine forth brilliantly at one moment, and be hidden at another, so the one who experiences it goes in and out. When it shines, he may even lose his senses, but when it is hidden, he returns to them and to a consciousness of his ego.

Such is what the Sufis call a "taste." If, however, this light remains with someone for an hour or two, then it is called "drinking" (*shurb*), and if it continues beyond that, it is called "drunkenness" (*sukr*). Common to all these is that the forms of creation are effaced in a perception of the living, the eternal, and that there is a passing away from effects through witnessing the supreme cause, which is also

97. All four of these terms are derived from the same root, w-j-d, "to find, attain, discover, experience, or perceive something." Its relation to the terms above appears to be through the act of experiencing what is found or perceived. In its simple sense of "finding" there are 107 occurences of this verb in the Qurʾān and *al-Wājid*, the One who finds or perceives, is among the ninety-nine names of God, mentioned in (38:44) which says, referring to Job, *Verily, We found him steadfast: how excellent a servant!*

called "effacement" (*fanāʾ*, 54).

If the servant then returns to a consciousness of creation subsisting by God as light from the light of God, this is called "sobriety" (*ṣaḥw*), or "being quenched" (*rayy*). It may also be called "subsistence" (*baqāʾ*, 54), inasmuch as things, after having been effaced, then subsist by God, or "being effaced from effacement" (*fanāʾ al-fanāʾ*), since the one who experiences it realizes that nothing is effaced except illusion and ignorance, neither of which possesses true reality.

Al-Qushayrī said, "Know that sobriety is to the measure of intoxication. If our intoxication is real, our sobriety will be real; if our intoxication is tainted by egoism, our sobriety will be tainted by egoism. And whoever is genuine in his state will be protected in his drunkenness." He then adds, "And whoever's love is strong will drink eternally." Or as a poet said, may God bless him:

> Though I have drunk of love, cup after cup,
> The wine still flows and my thirst is yet unquenched.[98]

62. Erasure and affirmation (*maḥw wa ithbāt*)

Erasure (*maḥw*) is to pass away from created beings through extinction while affirmation (*ithbāt*) is to affirm their existence through subsistence.

These terms may also be used to refer to erasing the reprehensible traits in our character and affirming the praiseworthy ones.

In this sense, effacement has three stages: effacing outward faults, effacing mental heedlessness, and effacing weakness from one's innermost being. The first is accomplished by affirming repentance, the second by affirming wakefulness (*yaqaẓa*), and the last by affirming purity.[99]

---

98. *Dhawq* is derived from the root dh-w-q, "to taste or experience." Verbal and nominative forms of this root occur 63 times in the Qurʾān. Forms of sh-r-b, "to drink," occur 39 times, and of s-k-r, "to be intoxicated," 7 times. *Ṣaḥw* arises from the verbal root ṣ-ḥ-w, said of a clouded sky when it becomes clear and, by extension, of one who becomes sober after having been intoxicated. This word does not appear in the Qurʾān.

99. *Maḥw* is a nominative form of the root m-ḥ-w, which expresses the action of erasing or obliterating, its oldest usage in Arabic describes the action of the wind upon prints left in the sand. This root appears 3 times in the Qurʾān as a verb, in each case with God as the subject.

63. Covering and illumination (*sitr wa tajallī*)

By covering (*sitr*) the Sufis mean a state in which the servant is absent from the Lord, either because of having lapsed [in spiritual practice], or gone down [to a lower spiritual degree], or become taken by something [in the world]. By illumination (*tajallī*) they mean the unveiling of the Lord's resplendence and grandeur. Both these terms refer to states before an aspirant is firmly rooted [in direct knowledge of God]. Afterward, there is no longer any absence.

The generality of the faithful are perpetually covered; the elect are between unveiling and covering; and the elect of the elect are in perpetual illumination.

Though for the generality covering is a kind of punishment, for the elect it is a mercy, for without times when they are veiled from their Lord, they would be obliterated by the power of the supreme reality. But even as this reality is revealed to them, so too is it concealed from them. They are thus between stability and rapture:[100] in times of illumination, they are enraptured; in times of concealment, they return to themselves and regain stability.[101]

Ithbāt is derived from the root th-b-t, "to be established, firm, immoveable, or confirmed" and occurs 19 times in the Qurʾān both in verbal and nominative forms. Verbal forms of both these terms appear in (13:39): *God effaces what He wills and establishes (what He wills), and with Him is the Mother of the Book.*

100. The expression we have translated as "between stability and rapture"—*bayna ʿīsh wa ṭīsh*—literally means "between life and instability." Ibn ʿAjība uses it here in the sense of being between "ordinary everyday life and the state of intoxication." See also appendix II:17.

101. The root s-t-r, "to cover, veil or screen something," occurs 3 times in the Qurʾān, once as a verb, once a noun, and once an adjective. *Al-Sattār*, the One who covers (faults), is among the ninety-nine divine names. *Tajallī* is a gerundic form of the root j-l-w, which expresses the notions of revealing, manifesting, or making something clear and visible. In translating it here as "illumination," we are following Michon's word choice. Elsewhere in this work, however, we have used "epiphany" (also used by Michon) and "Self-revelation." The *tajallī* may be seen as an "event" akin to what is described in (7:143), in which Moses asks God to show Himself and is told: *You shall not see Me, but gaze upon the mountain! If it stand still in its place, then you will see Me. And when his Lord revealed (His) glory* (tajallā) *to the mountain He sent it crashing down. And Moses fell down senseless. And when he woke he*

64. Being present, discovery, and the intimate meeting (*muḥāḍara, mukāshafa, wa-l-musāmara*)

Being present (*muḥāḍara*) is the presence of a heart with the Lord from behind a veil of sequential proofs, discursive thought, or the overwhelming power of invocation.

After this comes discovery (*mukāshafa*), which is the presence of a heart with the Lord through some kind of clear proof, but without deeply pondering the formal evidence or seeking arguments. Although the veil remains, there is a kind of proximity characteristic of the station of vigilance. Discovery is particular to the devotees and ascetics (*ʿubbād wa zuhhād*, 78), and marks the limit of mysteries.

As for the notion of "discovering what is in the minds of people" (*mukāshafat ḍamāʾir al-nās*), this is by no means something the Sufis seek, but may occur even for those who have not reached this station.

After these two stations comes the intimate meeting (*al-musāmara*). This is when the mysteries of the essence appear and the servant passes away from awareness of himself and is plunged into the ocean of unicity for an hour or two, then returns to his consciousness and senses, like someone who has been swimming underwater for some time and then comes back up to the surface. It is here that the experience of ecstasy (*wijdān*, 60) and the glimmers of light from contemplative vision (*mushāhada*, 15) begin.

After this comes the contemplative vision itself, which is the ongoing and effortless consciousness of God, or the existence of God, free from doubt, even as al-Junayd said, "*Al-mushāhada* is when God is and you are not." This station has already been explained but I mention it here only to show its order with [the three terms] above.

Al-Qushayrī said, "Someone in the state of being present is tied to God's signs (*āyāt*); someone in the state of discovery is gladdened by God's attributes; someone in the contemplative vision is lost in God's essence." I would add that someone in the state of intimate encounter is at times like the former, at times like the latter. Al-Qushayrī then continues, "Someone in the state of being present

---

said: Glory to You! I turn to You repentant, and I am the first of (true) believers. It may also be seen as the presence of God inherent in all creation and perceptible to anyone granted spiritual vision.

is guided by the mind; someone in the state of discovery is brought near by knowledge; and someone in the contemplative vision is effaced through gnosis."

The most comprehensive thing ever said concerning the contemplative vision is that it is a succession of epiphanic lights in the heart, without veil or interruption, like ongoing flashes of lightning that turn a dark night into day. Such is the heart when the epiphanic illuminations continue and dispel its night, or as the Sufis chant:

> Even as darkness descends
> And people are wrapped in its veil
> Your face sets our night aglow
> And we stand in the light of day

And as al-Nūrī said, "When dawn arrives, lamps are no longer needed." As for the lines of the poet [quoted above], they mean, "The night of my existence is illuminated by the existence of Your essence: the darkness of my existence is subsumed in the day of Your being."[102]

65. Glimmers, flashes, and dawnings (*lawāʾiḥ, lawāmiʿ, wa ṭawāliʿ*)

These are three terms that are close in meaning and refer to the lights of perception which may shine forth and then disappear for those who are beginning in the way. First come glimmers (*lawāʾiḥ*), then flashes (*lawāmiʿ*), and then dawnings (*ṭawāliʿ*). Flashes are clearer than glimmers, and dawnings are clearer than flashes. Flashes may remain for two or three hours, whereas glimmers, which are much

---

102. The verbal root of *muḥāḍara*, ḥ-ḍ-r, means "to be present or to come to a particular place." There are 25 occurrences of words derived from this root in the Qurʾān. *Mukāshafa* is a noun form of the root k-sh-f, "to uncover or to remove something which veils something else," which has 20 Qurʾānic occurrences, as in (16:54), *Then when God removed* (kashafa) *the harm from them, behold, a group of them associated partners with their Lord.* The root of *musāmara*, s-m-r, is an ancient verb meaning "to spend the night talking with a companion." It is said be derived from the color *sumra*, reddish tan, the color of shadows cast by moonlight on sand. It occurs once in the Qurʾān as a verb in (23:67): *In their arrogant pride they would pass the night telling fables [about the revelation].*

weaker, vanish quickly, similar to what a poet said [about brief encounters]:

> For a year we were apart and when finally reunited,
> His greeting to me was only a farewell

Or as another has said,

> O you who came to visit but did not visit,
> You who hurried past my door,
> As if bearing a burning twig to light a fire—
> Would it have hurt to come in for a while?

Dawnings, for their part, are longer lasting and more powerful [than the first two]. They dispel darkness and doubt, but there is still the risk that they will disappear, for the one who has received them is not yet firmly established in the sunlight of gnosis. There are thus times when these lights burn brightly, and long periods when they are hidden, except that even when they are hidden, their traces will remain, and the one who has been granted them will live in the blessing of these traces until they return anew. Thus will it continue for him until the sun of his day arises, and he is standing firmly and fully in its light, and it never sets again:

> The sun of my Beloved arose one night,
> And illumined all and did not set.
> For while this world's sun goes down at dusk,
> The suns of hearts never set.[103]

66. Surprises and attacks (*bawādih wa hujām*)

Surprises (*bawādih*) are what unexpectedly take hold of your heart from the unseen world, provoking either sadness or joy. Attacks (*hujām*) are what come to your heart by the power of the moment without artifice or effort.

The inner states that may result from these will differ according to the power or weakness [of the one in whom they occur]. For some people, a "surprise" will completely alter them, and an "attack" will

103. The verbal roots l-ā-ḥ and l-m-ʿa have nearly the same meaning: "to appear, glitter, flash, shimmer, or glow." Neither of these roots occurs in the Qurʾān. Forms of ṭ-l-ʿa, "to ascend, rise like the sun or stars, reach a vantage point, or to look into something (including a book)," occur 19 times, both in the sense of "rising" and "looking into."

totally overwhelm them. For others, their spiritual state and strength are above being altered by a "surprise," changed by an "attack," disturbed by cares, or troubled by fears. Such are the masters of the moment (*sādāt al-waqt*), about whom the poet said:

> Vicissitudes of time do not overtake them
> If calamities befall, they hold the reins.

Such are the people of deep-rootedness and mastery. May God make us among them! Amen!

67. Change and stability (*talwīn wa tamkīn*)

Change (*talwīn*) is movement from one state to another or one station to another and the one who is subject to it may fall and stand back up, while someone who attains pure gnosis and a stable consciousness of God is said to possesses stability or mastery (*tamkīn*).

Those in the condition of change are constantly increasing, while those granted stability have arrived and are firmly established. The end of their journey comes with victory over the ego, a victory which marks the arrival at a stage where human qualities withdraw and the power of the supreme truth takes over. If this state continues for someone, he is called a "person of stability" (*ṣāḥib al-tamkīn*).

There may, however, be a kind of change after stability which is a descent (*nuzul*) through the spiritual stations comparable to the descent of the sun through its zodiacal stages (*burūjihā*). The gnostics evolve with God's decrees, turn with their turning, and change with the change of time. They are thus between contraction and expansion, strength and weakness, privation and giving, joy and sadness, and other such states. However, instead of being possessed by those states, they possess them. Vicissitudes of changing states do not alter them, nor do upheavals and calamities. And God most high knows better.[104]

---

104. *Talwīn* is a gerund form of the root l-w-n, "to take on a color," and by extension "to change in appearance." As "color" it occurs 9 times in the Qurʾān. *Tamkīn* is a gerund form of m-k-n, "to give a place or abode to something, to become steady or fixed, to enable, establish, or empower someone," which appears in the Qurʾān in various forms 18 times. See also appendix II:20.

68. Nearness and distance (*qurb wa buʿd*)

Nearness (*qurb*) refers to the proximity with God we may reach through acts of obedience and grace.

There are three degrees of nearness: through obedience [to God] and the avoidance of sin, through spiritual combat and striving against the ego, and through union and the contemplative vision. For the novices, nearness is largely through obedience; for the aspirants, it comes through spiritual combat; for those advanced in the way, through contemplative vision.

Distance (*buʿd*), by contrast, is first from grace, then from following the path, and then from realization.

In the sacred utterance (*al-ḥadīth al-qudsī*), God says, "Nothing brings those who seek to approach Me nearer than accomplishing what I have made obligatory on them. And a servant will continue to approach Me by voluntary devotions until I love him, and when I love him, I am his hearing and sight. . . ." And in another version, "When I love him, I am He."[105]

Our nearness to the Lord is when our hearts are ever ready to serve Him, while God's nearness to us is when He causes us to pass away from our illusory existence, raises the veil from before our inner vision, and lets us behold the truth nearer to us than anything else. Then is nearness subsumed in nearness, the One who is ever near united with the one who is drawing near, the lover with the Beloved. As one of them has said:

> I am the One I love and the One I love is I

Or as al-Shushtarī said:

> I am the Lover and the Beloved
> No second one is there.[106]

---

105. These are variations of the famous *ḥadīth qudsī* found in the collection of Bukhārī and others which begins, "To anyone who harms My friend, I announce war from Me. And My servant cannot approach Me by anything more beloved to Me than what I have made obligatory upon him, and My servant continues to approach Me by voluntary devotions until I love him. . . ." Bukhārī, vol. 4, p. 105.

106. The verbal root q-r-b, "to approach, come near," occurs 96 times in the Qurʾān, including in the divine name *al-Qarīb*, "the One who is near." Its opposite, b-ʿa-d, "to go far away," occurs 14 times in its sense

69. The law, the way, and the truth (*al-sharīʿa, al-ṭarīqa, wa-l-ḥaqīqa*)

The law (*al-sharīʿa*) is the responsibility required of us outwardly. The way (*al-ṭarīqa*) is the purification of our minds. The truth (*al-ḥaqīqa*) is to perceive God in His epiphanies. The law is [there] so that you may worship Him, the way, that you may journey to Him, and the truth, that you may witness Him.

At the moment that God, the Truth, manifested His light between the two poles [of existence] such that divine majesty illuminated the places of epiphany in the vessels of servanthood (*qawālib al-ʿubīdiyya*), the law and the truth were manifested. The truth is thus the consciousness of this majesty Itself, while the law is to maintain the norms which are fitting to the vessels through worship and servanthood. As for the way, it is to rectify our minds in preparation for the dawning of spiritual truths.

[Or it could be said that] the law is to rectify us outwardly, the way is to rectify us mentally, and the truth to beautify our innermost beings.

It has also been said that the law is the spring of the truth (*ʿayn al-ḥaqīqa*),[107] since it was made obligatory by God's command, and the truth is the spring of the law, since we were made responsible [for knowing God] even before the law was formulated.[108]

The Sufis may also use [the word] "law" to refer to all that leads to a certain thing or is a means of attaining it. All means are laws and all the ends to which they lead are truths. In this sense, the sensory world is the "law" of the intelligible world, since it is by the former that the latter may be grasped; spiritual combat is the "law" of contemplation; humility is the "law" of honor; spiritual poverty is the "law" of spiritual wealth, and so forth. Plowing and planting are the "law" of harvesting, and it has even been said, "Whoever sows the laws harvests the truths, and whoever sows the truths harvests the laws." That is, [if the truth is planted in your heart], it will bring you back to the law. Of this fact, a poet said:

---

of distance and over 200 times in its adverbial sense of "afterwards," as in *baʿda dhālik* ("after that").

107. The word *ʿayn* may also be used to mean "eye," "essence," or "something identical to something else."

108. See note 73 above.

The fruits you have sown are what you harvest.
Such is the way of time.[109]

70. The essence and the attributes (*al-dhāt wa-l-ṣifāt*)

Know that God, the Truth, be He exalted, is essence (*dhātan*) and attribute (*ṣifātan*), in pre-temporal and post-temporal eternity, which is to say before His Self-revelation and after it. His attributes are eternal by the eternity of His essence, since an attribute is inseparable from the one it describes (*al-mawṣūf*). Whenever the divine essence reveals Itself, the divine attributes are inherent to It and hidden therein; and whenever the attributes appear, the essence is inherent therein. The essence, therefore, is outward, the attributes inward.[110]

By "attributes" are meant the [seven] essential attributes as well as all other qualities of divine perfection.[111]

All that comes to pass in the process of Self-revelation and manifestation is between essence and attributes. The essence is inseparable from the attributes; the attributes are inseparable from the essence. This inseparability between them that infuses all being is what is meant by the one who said, "The essence is the spring of the attributes," that is, their place of theophany is one; or, as others

---

109. *Sharīʿa* comes from the verbal root sh-r-ʿa, which originally meant "to water animals by bringing them to the water." By extension, it refers to a wide, well-used path or way, and occurs 4 times in the Qurʾān. *Ṭarīqa* is a noun form of the root ṭ-r-q, "to follow a path, or to strike with a hammer in the way a blacksmith molds steel," forms of which occur 9 times in the Qurʾān. The root ḥ-q-q, "to prove to be true," occurs over 280 times, often as the noun *al-ḥaqq*, "the truth or right" which is also among the ninety-nine names of God.

110. Elsewhere, Ibn ʿAjība uses the image of the essence as a shoreless sea in which floats a piece of ice. The attributes, in this image, would be analogous to the inner surface of the piece of ice, and a tiny crystal in the center of that piece of ice would be the created world. See Jean-Louis Michon, *Le Soufi Marocain* (Paris: Vrin, 1973), p. 97.

111. Ashʿarī theology defines the essential attributes (here referred to as *ṣifāt al-maʿānī*, the substantial attributes) as seven: power, will, knowledge, life, hearing, sight, and speech, while the qualities of divine perfection include both the active forms of these seven—thus, God is willing, knowing, living, and hearing—as well as the attributes which describe His actions: creating, life-giving, and forgiving, for example.

have said, "The sensory world is the spring of the intelligible world," meaning that their place of manifestation is one. To quote a poet from the east:

O you who drink from the spring,
If you realize this truth, then doubt will vanish:
The essence is the spring of the attributes.
In these realities there is no doubt.

May the veil of the sensory that is spread over the face of spiritual realities not turn you away from perceiving the essence! This is something known by way of direct experience (*dhawq*, 61) and ecstatic encounter (*wijdān*, 60), not by way of logical argument or textual proof. As Ibn al-Fāriḍ so beautifully put it:

Beyond quotations from books and talks,
Dwells a knowledge so subtle it eludes the soundest minds

Know too that the essence does not reveal Itself except in places of epiphany, for if it were to be revealed without intermediary, all existence would be annihilated. It is in this sense that the Sufis say, "The revelation of the essence is majesty, the revelation of the attributes is beauty," for the revelation of the essence without intermediary would be annihilating and consuming, even as the *ḥadīth* states.[112]

The revelation of the attributes takes place through their "traces" (*athar*) in creation, and these may be accompanied by vision and gnosis, which pertain to divine beauty.

The Sufis may extend the use of these terms, however, and refer to everything pertaining to God's majesty as "essence," and everything pertaining to God's beauty as "attribute." So they say that spiritual poverty (*faqr*) is essence, spiritual independence attribute; that humility is essence, honor attribute; that silence is essence, speech

---

112. He is referring to a *ḥadīth* found in Muslim, vol. 1, pp. 96–97 and elsewhere: "Abū Mūsā l-Ashʿarī said, 'The Messenger of God ﷺ bade us to keep ever in mind five formulations: Verily, God does not sleep, nor should it be thought of Him that He sleeps. He lowers and raises the scales. The deeds of the night ascend to Him before the day, and the deeds of the day ascend to Him before the night. His veil is light and if He were revealed to you, the features of His face would burn the sight of any creature who gazed upon Him.'"

attribute, and so forth. Such is how the Shaykh of our Shaykh, Sīdī ʿAlī l-Jamal al-ʿAmrānī, used these terms in his book, and I do not know whether others before have done this or not.[113]

71. Lights and secrets (*anwār wa asrār*)

Lights (*anwār*) refer to the outward and dense aspects of God's epiphanies, while secrets (*asrār*) designate their inward and subtle aspects. Secrets are therefore subtler and finer than lights and pertain to the divine essence, while lights pertain to the divine attributes and are, in fact, their traces [in creation].

The essence in its self-revelation is between evident lights and hidden secrets, while as a "treasure" it was only secrets.[114] The omnipotence (*al-jabarūt*, 58) is totally secrets, the dominions (*al-malakūt*) are totally lights, and the domain (*al-mulk*) is obscurities and alterities.

Existence is one. Whoever beholds its inner dimension sees only secrets; whoever beholds its outer dimension with the eye of unification (*jamʿ*, 56) sees only lights, while whoever beholds its outer dimension with the eye of separation sees only alterities. Indeed, anyone who is turned away from God by turmoil and fear sees only obscurities.

If the epiphanies of the truth are here called "lights," this is by way of analogy: it is the nature of light to dispel darkness, just as these self-revelations dispel the darkness of ignorance and manifest the knowledge of God, even as they say, "Knowledge is light, ignorance darkness."

---

113. *Dhāt* is the feminine form of the pronoun *dhū*, used to show possession or quality, as in the Qurʾānic expression *God is the possessor of grace* (*Allāhu dhū l-faḍl*). *Ṣifa*, attribute, comes from the verb w-ṣ-f, "to describe or attribute to" and occurs 14 times in the Qurʾān as in the oft-repeated phrase, *Subḥāna Rabbika Rabbi-l-ʿizzati ʿammā yaṣifūn* (*Glorified be your Lord, Lord of honor, above what they attribute to Him*).

114. Ibn ʿAjība is referring to a saying that has been narrated as a *ḥadīth qudsī*: "God most high says, 'I was a hidden treasure and I loved to be known so I created the world and let them know Me.'" Ibn ʿArabī cites this saying several times in *al-Futūḥāt al-Makkiyya* and says concerning it, "It [is] authentic from the point of view of insight, not from the point of view of textual evidence" (vol. 2, p. 399).

As for the secret, it is something hidden and ungraspable [by the rational faculty]. The Sufis call the eternal wine and pre-temporal meanings (*al-maʿnī l-qadīma*) "secrets." They may also use this term to refer to the soul that has undergone the process of purification, for when this occurs, it returns to its origin which itself is a portion of the secret of the omnipotence. And should this purified soul come to prevail over the physical form, then all of it returns to the eternal. And God most high knows better.[115]

72. Consciences and innermost secrets (*ḍamāʾir wa sarāʾir*)

Some of the Sufis say that the terms "consciences" (*ḍamāʾir*) and "innermost secrets" (*sarāʾir*) are synonyms. Others say that innermost secrets are finer and purer than consciences, in the same way that the spirit (*al-rūḥ*) is finer than the heart (*al-qalb*). Consciences, they say, refer to all that is hidden within us, be it good or evil, while innermost secrets are only the beauties we contain.

In truth, both terms refer to one and the same thing: all the beliefs and all the intentions which we bear within us, based on the words of the Qurʾān, *On a Day when innermost secrets* (*al-sarāʾir*) *shall be brought forth* (86:9). And God most high knows better.[116]

73. Breath (*nafas*)

Al-Qushayrī says, "By 'breath' (*nafas*) the Sufis mean the repose which hearts find in the subtle emanations of the unseen (*laṭāʾif al-ghuyūb*). Someone who is granted breaths is at a higher level than someone granted a state (*ḥāl*, 42) or a moment (*al-waqt*, 41).

---

115. *Anwār*, the plural of *nūr*, is derived from the verbal root n-w-r, "to illuminate," forms of which occur 43 times in the Qurʾān, including in the divine name *al-Nūr*. The origin of *asrār*, s-r-r, has been mentioned under item 45 above.

116. The verbal root ḍ-m-r meant "to become thin and emaciated, shrink, withdraw to the point of not being visible." Related to this is the noun *ḍamīr*, "a valley or hollow." It occurs one time in the Qurʾān in (22:27): *They will come to you on foot and on every lean camel* (ḍamīrin), meaning "a camel which has grown thin from a long journey." *Ḍamīr* / *ḍamāʾir* is also the grammatical term for the pronoun: "That which stands for a noun which you do not see." *Sarāʾir* is yet another form of the root s-r-r mentioned in the note to item 45 above.

We could say that the one granted moments is at the beginning [of the way], the one granted breaths is at its end, and the one granted states is intermediary, [or that] 'moments' are for people of the heart, 'states' for people of the spirit, and 'breaths' for people of the innermost being."

A breath, then, is more delicate than a moment. Keeping moments from being wasted is for devotees and ascetics (*ʿubbād wa zuhhād*, 78), keeping breaths from being wasted is for gnostics who have reached the goal, and making use of states is for aspirants.

Keeping moments from being wasted means keeping the heart present with God. Keeping breaths from being wasted means keeping the soul present in the contemplative vision of the Truth. They might say about someone, "his breaths are pure," if his drinking from the spring of unity is clear of the turbidity of worldly vicissitudes.

When al-Qushayrī defines *nafas* as "a repose which hearts find," he means when they are released from the fatigue of being constantly on guard and constantly vigilant and find rest and relief in the contemplation of the subtle mysteries of unity they are shown and in the limitless expanse of spiritual vision.

Then al-Qushayrī says, "They say that the best form of devotion is guarding one's breaths," by which he means to be in perpetual reflection and contemplation, even as a poet said:

> Among the most beautiful doctrines: to be perpetually drunk!
> And most perfect desires: union without separation!

Abū ʿAlī l-Daqqāq said, "The gnostic is not allowed a breath," that is, to waste, "for there is no excuse which is valid for him. But for the one approaching God by the way of love, there must be a breath, otherwise he would waste away from lack of strength."

For the gnostic, guarding the breath becomes easier as his gnosis increases, for concentration becomes easier and his vision more firmly established. For the lover of God, on the other hand, the narrowness of his spiritual station prevents him from concentrating on his practice. Were he to be totally effaced in this practice and concentration came that much more easily, he might even risk losing his equilibrium. For this reason the Prophet ﷺ said, "Give rest to your hearts by permitted pleasures,"[117] and said to Ḥanẓala and Abū Bakr, "If you were to remain in the state you are in when you are with me, the angels would take you by the hand. But there is a time for this and a time for that."[118]

74. Meditation and introspection (*fikra wa naẓra*)

Meditation (*fikra*) is the heart's journey through divine epiphanies. In the *Ḥikam* it is called "the voyage of the heart in the domains of alterities."[119] Such is meditation for the novices, while meditation for those who have progressed in the way is the journey of the heart through the domains of lights, and for those advanced in the way, it is the journey of the spirit through the domains of mysteries.

Thus, as the *Ḥikam* continues, "There are two kinds of meditations: the meditation of belief and faith . . . and the meditation of contemplation and vision." The first is for the people of reflection from among the generality of the companions of the right, the second for the people of insight from among the most advanced of the aspirants and certain of the confirmed gnostics. [As the *Ḥikam* also states], "Meditation is the lamp of the heart. If it goes away, the heart has no illumination."[120] It is also the means by which we attain the "greater wealth" (*al-ghinā al-akbar*),[121] by which we realize the spiritual journey, and by which we reach its goal. For one without meditation, there is no journey, and if there is no journey, there is no arrival. Thus, my teacher, al-Būzīdī, used to say, "A *faqīr* without meditation is like a tailor without a needle!"

Introspection (*naẓra*) signifies something finer than meditation. It is on a higher level than meditation for it is the beginning of

---

117. This saying is found in al-Daylamī, *Firdaws*, vol. 2, p. 253 and with similar wording in Abū Nuʿaym, *Ḥilya*, vol. 3, p. 123 and is said to refer to such activities as listening to poetry or playing sports.
118. This *ḥadīth* appears in Muslim, vol. 3, pp. 1260–61. According to the version in Muslim, the Prophet repeated the advice at the end ("a time for this and a time for that") three times. The verbal root of *nafas*, n-f-s, has been mentioned in the note to item 45 above.
119. *K. al-ḥikam*, aphorism 263.
120. *K. al-ḥikam*, aphorism 262.
121. The "greater wealth" refers to a *ḥadīth* which states, "True wealth is not in having numerous possessions; truth wealth is the wealth of the soul." Bukhārī, vol. 4, p. 95 and Muslim, vol. 1, p. 464.

the contemplative vision. While meditation is a reflective journey through the created world and then its dissolution and sublimation, introspection is looking deeply into one's own soul or other epiphanies and then passing away from them in a vision of the Truth. If someone is granted stability in that vision and remains within it, it is called "retreat (*ʿuqūf*) in the divine presence."

They also say that the first station is remembrance (*dhikr*, 40), then meditation, then introspection, and then retreat in the divine presence. And God most high knows better.[122]

75. Witness (*shāhid*)

Of the term "witness" (*shāhid*), al-Qushayrī says, "Often one finds mention in the discourse of the Sufis that 'such and such person is by the witness of knowledge' (*fulān bi shāhid al-ʿilm*), or of ecstasy or of some spiritual state. By the word 'witness' in this context they mean what is most present in a person's heart or dominates his remembrance, such that it becomes like something he sees even if it is not physically present. If the remembrance of anything so dominates his heart, then he is said to be 'by the witness' of that thing, be it learning, ecstasy, or something else. In short, 'witness' means 'presence.' You are 'by the witness' of whatever is present in your heart."[123]

76. The wine, the cup, and drinking (*al-khamra, al-kaʾs, wa shurb*)

When the Sufis speak of the "wine" (*al-khamra*), they mean the sublime essence before God's Self-revelation (*tajallī*) and the divine mysteries inherent in all things after it. Thus, they say, "The eternal wine was unveiled in such and such a thing and through such and such a modality." By it do all things exist, veiling the secret of lordhood.

It was of this wine that Ibn al-Fāriḍ sang in his wine ode (*al-khamriyya*). They call it "wine" because if It is unveiled to people's hearts, they lose their senses like one who has drunk earthly wine.

---

122. Forms of the verbal root f-k-r, "to think, consider, reflect upon," occur 18 times in the Qurʾān, frequently in the construct *qawm yatafakkarūn*, "a folk who reflect." Forms of n-ẓ-r, "to look at, behold, or watch something," including *intaẓara* "to wait," occur 120 times.

123. The root of *shahīd*, sh-h-d is mentioned in the note to item 15 above.

They may also use the word "wine" to refer to spiritual drunkenness (*sukr*), ecstatic emotion, and pure ecstasy, saying, "We were in a mighty wine," to mean they had completely passed away from the sensory world. This is the state al-Shushtarī sings of in his verse: "Earthly wine falls far short of my wine: my wine is eternal," by which he means "the drunkenness of earthly wine pales compared to the wine that I have."

When the Sufis speak of the "cup" (*al-kaʾs*) from which this wine is drunk, they mean the radiance of epiphanic lights upon hearts filled with the fervor of love. The ecstasy that enters them is of such sweetness that they lose their senses, as may occur during a session of spiritual song (*samāʿ*), invocation (*dhikr*), or discourse (*mudhākara*).

It has also been said that the cup is the shaykh's heart; the hearts of spiritual teachers are cups filled with this wine which they give to all who sit with them and love them.

As for drinking (*shurb*), this means keeping your heart concentrated in meditation and reflection until you pass away from your individual being in God's being. It may also mean drunkenness itself, for spiritual drinking and drunkenness occur at the same time, unlike with earthly wine.

The pole Ibn Mashīsh said, "Love (*maḥabba*) is when God takes hold of the heart of someone who loves Him by unveiling the light of His beauty and the holiness of His majesty's perfection. And the wine of love (*sharāb al-maḥabba*) is an intermingling of Qualities with qualities, Character with character, Lights with lights, Names with names, Attributes with attributes, and Actions with actions—and God expands the vision of whomever He wills! Drinking is to quench the thirst of hearts, limbs and sinews with this wine. This is something done by practice and instruction and each is given to drink according to his capacity. So there are some who are given to drink with no intermediary—God most high takes over that for them," and I would say that this is rare. "Others are given to drink by way of intermediaries such as angels, the sages, or the great masters of the way who have been brought near to God . . . And the cup is the ladle by which God serves this pure and undiluted wine to those of His servants whom He chooses." I have further explained this passage in my commentary on the *Khamriyya*.[124]

124. *Khamra* is a noun form of kh-m-r, "to become veiled or concealed,"

77. The aspirant, the needy one, the person of blame, the one brought near (*al-murīd, al-faqīr, al-mulāmatī, wa-l-muqarrab*)

The aspirant (*al-murīd*) is someone whose will (*irādatuhu*) is attached to knowing God and for this purpose is receiving instruction from a spiritual teacher.

The one who is needy for God (*al-faqīr*) is someone who is independent of everything except God and has rejected all that would turn him away from God. For this reason, they say, "The *faqīr* does not possess nor is he possessed (*lā yamlik wa lā yumlak*)." He possesses nothing and nothing possesses him. The *faqīr* is thus more active than the aspirant and is at a higher spiritual level, for an aspirant may remain among the people of the workaday world. It is also said, "The *faqīr* is one whom neither the earth bears nor the sky covers," which is to say that the universe itself cannot enclose him because of the sublimity of his aspiration and the clarity of his vision.

A certain Sufi said, "The conditions for being a *faqīr* are four: high aspiration, beautiful practice, the veneration of sanctity, and firm resolve."

The person of blame (*al-malāmatī*) is someone who displays no good but contains no evil. Said otherwise, he is someone who conceals his sanctity and outwardly displays states which cause people to flee from him.

The one brought near (*al-muqarrab*) has realized effacement and subsistence (*fanāʾ wa baqāʾ*, 54).

One of them has said, "Spiritual poverty (*faqr*), the path of blame (*malāmata*), and way of approach (*taqrīb*) are varieties of Sufism as well as stages within Sufism." The Sufi, thus, is someone who is working to purify his time from all but God. If the world falls from his hands, he is someone needy of God (*faqīr*). If he is no longer preoccupied by people and ceases to show goodness outwardly or contain evil inwardly, he is on the path of blame (*malmātī*). If his states become perfected so that he is ever *by* his Lord and *for* his Lord, and receives no news except from God, and has no dwelling except with

---

which occurs 4 times in the Qurʾān in reference to wine. *Kaʾs* is said to be without a verbal root. It occurs in the Qurʾān, speaking of delights of heaven, 6 times. The root of *shurb*, sh-r-b, is mentioned in the note to item 61 above. See also appendix II:19.

God, then he is the one brought near (*muqarrab*).[125]

78. Devotees, ascetics, and gnostics (*ʿubbād, zuhhād, wa ʿārifūn*)

These are terms which are very close in meaning and contained within the [general] meaning of Sufism, which itself designates a firm orientation toward God most high. The one whose path is mainly by way of devotional practices, however, is referred to as *ābid*, that is, a devotee; the one whose path is mainly through renunciation is referred to as *zāhid*, an ascetic; and the one who has attained a contemplative vision of God and is firmly established therein is referred to as *ʿārif*, a gnostic.

God occupies the devotees and ascetics with His service, for they have not arrived at true knowledge of Him, while the gnostics He occupies with His love. *All do We aid—these as well as those—out of the bounty of your Lord. And the bounty of your Lord is not limited* (17:20).[126]

79. The virtuous, the saints, the substitutes, the front rank, the nobles, the stakes, and the pole (*al-ṣāliḥūn, al-awliyāʾ, al-budalāʾ, al-nuqabāʾ, al-nujabāʾ, al-awtād, wa-l-quṭb*)

The virtuous (*al-ṣāliḥūn*) are those whose outward actions are unblemished and whose inner states are upright.[127]

The saintly (*al-awliyāʾ*) are those who know God by way of direct perception. The name *walī* (the singular of *awliyāʾ*) is from *waly* which means "nearness" (*qurb*, 68). It has also been said that the saint

125. The verbal root of *murīd*, r-w-d, is mentioned in the note to item 26 above, and of *muqarrab*, q-r-b, under item 68. The root of *mulāmatī*, l-w-m, meaning "to find fault with or blame someone," occurs in the Qurʾān in various forms 14 times.

126. Here he is paraphrasing *K. al-ḥikam*, aphorism 68: "God makes some people remain in the service of Him and others He singles out for His love: *All do We aid—these as well as those—out of the bounty of your Lord. And the bounty of your Lord is not limited.*"

127. Forms of the root ṣ-l-ḥ, "to accomplish the good, improve, to be of use," occur in over 100 places throughout the Qurʾān, notably in the repeated phrase, *Those who believe and accomplish the good* (*al-ladhīna āmanū wa ʿamilū-l-ṣāliḥāti*).

is one for whom God has taken charge (*tawālat*) of his obedience, confirmed his nearness, and given perpetual help (*madad*).[128]

The substitutes (*al-budalāʾ*) are those who have replaced (*istabadalū*) vices with virtues and their own attributes with the attributes of the Beloved.[129]

The front rank (*al-nuqabāʾ*) are those who have pierced through the wall of existence and emerged into the limitless vision of the One who gives existence to all.[130]

The nobles (*al-nujabāʾ*) are the foremost in the journey to God by way of their diligence (*najāba*), the most fervent and gifted of the aspirants.

The stakes (*al-awtād*) are those who are deeply rooted in the knowledge of God (*al-rāsikhūna fī maʿrifati Allāh*). They number four and are the four supports of the universe.[131]

The pole (*al-quṭb*) is the one who safeguards the right of creation and the right of the Creator. This is a single person, but the term may also designate someone who has realized a certain station. For this reason, there may be "poles" existing at a single spiritual station or state or science, so that it may be said of someone, "He is a *quṭb* of knowledge, or a *quṭb* of states, or a *quṭb* in the stations of the way" if they are what prevail in his soul.

If I wish to refer to the rank which can only be occupied by a single person, however, I will use the word "help" (*ghawth*). The *ghawth* is the human being through whom spiritual support comes to the hierarchies of the saints—the nobles, front rank, stakes, and substitutes. He occupies the rank of the imam, heir [of the Prophet],

128. The root w-l-a is mentioned in the note to item 28.

129. Forms derived from the root b-d-l, "to change, or exchange one thing for another," occur 34 times in the Qurʾān.

130. The literal meaning of *nuqabāʾ* is "those who pierce the wall of a fortification." Forms of n-q-b occur twice in the Qurʾān, once in the literal meaning "to pierce" (18:97) and once in the figurative meaning "to travel or wander widely" (50:36). The relation between the two meanings is probably in the notion of wearing holes in the feet of camels from travel.

131. *Awtād*, the plural of *watad*, originally "the peg used to secure a tent," occurs 3 times in the Qurʾān, twice in reference to Pharoah, and once (77:7) in which the mountains are describe as "pegs" holding the earth.

and of esoteric succession. He is the spirit of the universe around whom its spheres revolve, which is why his place is likened to the place of the pupil in the eye. None knows [the *ghawth*] except those who have been apportioned something of the secret of subsistence in God. He is called the "help" because of the help (*ighātha*) he lends the worlds through his support and special rank.

There are signs by which this person may be known. Abū l-Ḥasan al-Shādhilī said: "The pole has fifteen distinctive signs. Let one who claims to possess this rank or some portion of it show that he has received, through divine support, (1) mercy, (2) protection from sin, (3) vicegerency, (4) delegation, and (5) the aid of the angels who bear the mighty throne. Let him show that (6) he has received illumination into the reality of the divine essence, and (7) comprehension of the divine attributes, (8) that he has been granted judgment and discernment between the two existences, (9) that he can distinguish the first from the first, (10) and what emanates from it to its furthest limit, (11) and what is established therein; [let him show] (12) [that he has been granted] judgment of what came before it, (13) and judgment of what came after it, (14) judgment of what has neither before nor after, (15) and knowledge of the beginning, which is to say the knowledge which envelops all knowledge and all things known and all that relates to it."[132]

The first of these signs means that the character of the pole expresses the attributes of divine mercy in accordance with the example of the one who bequeathed them, the Prophet ﷺ, whose character was one of clemency, sympathy, compassion, pardon, understanding, reflection, generosity, and courage.

The second sign means that the pole is supported by the grace of divine protection (*ʿiṣma*, 46) and lordly infallibility, as was the Prophet ﷺ, with the difference being that in the case of the prophets, protection from sin is an obligatory attribute, whereas in the case of the saints it is a possible attribute. When it occurs in this latter form, it is generally referred to as *ḥifẓ*, preservation, and the one to whom it is granted does not transgress any limit nor break any pact.

The third is vicegerency (*khilāfa*), meaning that he is the vicegerent of God on His earth, entrusted with the affairs of God's

132. This is quoted largely from the translation of Ibn ʿAṭāʾ Allāh, *Laṭaʾif al-minan*, by Nancy Roberts (Louisville, Kentucky: Fons Vitae, 2005) p. 112.

servants by way of the Prophet's vicegerency, with whom spirits vowed allegiance and bodies made a pact.

The fourth is delegation (*niyāba*), meaning that he is delegated by God to bring about the application of God's rules in conformity with divine wisdom (*Ḥikma*, 47, 55), even while in reality this is accomplished only by eternal power.

The fifth is that the pole receives aid in the form of strength and nearness (*qurb*, 68) from the bearers of the divine throne, for he is the bearer of the throne of created beings just as the angels are the bearers of the throne of the All-Merciful.

The sixth is that the reality of the divine essence is unveiled to him, which means that he is a gnostic by God, possessing the gnosis of direct vision (*ʿiyān*). Anyone who is ignorant of God has no share of the attributes of the pole.

Seventh is that there has been unveiled to him how the [divine] attributes envelop all beings, for there is no existent being except that it subsists through the attributes and the secrets of the essence. The knowledge which the pole possesses of the enveloping of the attributes is more complete than anyone else's, for it is experiential, not theoretical.

Eighth is that he has been granted judgment and discernment between the two existences (*al-wujūdayn*), meaning the first existence before God's Self-revelation, known as "pre-temporal eternity" (*al-azal*) or "the beginningless treasure,"[133] and the second existence in which God's Self-revelation took place. Discerning between these two entails knowing that the first is lordhood without servanthood, the intelligible without the sensory, power without wisdom, whereas in the second, there are both—lordhood and servanthood, the intelligible and the sensory, power and wisdom—in order that God's names the Outward and the Inward may be realized. The pairs of opposites, then, appear specifically in the primordial substance (*al-qabḍa*) through which God's Self-revelation takes place. The infinite majesty which envelops the primordial substance and subsists as the hidden treasure, however, remains eternally in its principial condition. Understand this.

Ninth and tenth are that the pole has been graced with the ability to distinguish the First from the first: to distinguish the Light of the

133. See note 113.

primordial substance from the Light of the eternal treasure which is the ocean of omnipotence (*baḥr al-jabarūt*). What proceeds from the primordial substance means its branching epiphanies to their limits at the present moment, for in respect to the future, there is no limit: divine epiphanies never cease. When the existence of this world is over, the epiphanies will continue through the existence of another world which has no end.

Eleventh is that the pole must know the positive qualities and miraculous gifts or their opposites manifested in existence in a distinctive mode. This, however, means knowing them in a global sense, for to know them in detail is exclusive to the divinity.

Twelfth is that he must know the character (*ḥukm*) of what comes before, that is, before God's Self-revelation. This character is none other than the absolute transcendence [of the divine essence] which remains eternally as the hidden treasure beyond all opposites.

Thirteenth is that he must know the character of what comes after [the Self-revelation], which is the law of responsibility incumbent upon those to whom God has made Himself known, maintaining the forms which arise from divine wisdom (*Ḥikma*, 55) and concealing the secrets which arise from divine power (*qudra*).

Fourteenth is that he must know that which is neither before nor after, which is to say that he must know What has no "before" and has no "after," this being the eternal wine and the principial essence of which Ibn al-Fāriḍ said:

> Before It, there is no 'before.' After It, there is no 'after.'
> The antecedence of the ages was the seal of its existence.

Fifteenth is that the pole must have knowledge of the beginning (*ʿilm al-badʾ*), by which is meant the divine pre-eternal knowledge that preceded all things in existence. This is the knowledge that envelops all other forms of knowledge as well as all things known, for there is naught which is beyond the divine knowledge. All knowledge and all the objects of knowledge relate to this knowledge. Such is the secret of destiny (*sirr al-qadar*).

Some portion of this knowledge may be granted the pole, but it is not a condition that his knowledge extends to the totality of things as well as their details, for this, again, is something exclusive to divinity.

God most high will endow him only with particular aspects of this knowledge. This is what Shaykh Abū l-ʿAbbās al-Mursī ﷺ was referring to when he said, "There is no saint, past or present, whom God most high has not made known to me by name, ancestry, and what he has received from God." And another of them said, "There is not a drop of seminal fluid that fertilizes a womb except that God most high brings to me knowledge of it and whether it will be born male or female."

Such are miraculous deeds (*karāmāt*) by which God most high has graced His saints. However, there may be a perfected pole who has not attained to any of these matters other than real and profound gnosis. If God most high wishes to make known to him something in His kingdom, He will make it known to him regardless of whether he had knowledge of it before. Thus did the Prophet ﷺ say concerning his she-camel when it had wandered off, "By God, I know only what my Lord has taught me."[134] He did not know where it had gone and some of the hypocrites began to speak against him. Then, however, God made known to him where it was.

So while knowledge of the unseen is among the miraculous gifts that may be given to God's saints, it is not an absolute condition, whether he be a pole or not. And God most high knows better.

May God bless our master Muḥammad and his people and Companions and give them salutations of peace.

This is the conclusion of what we have collected of the essential truths of Sufism and what we have commented upon. May God grant that this work be done sincerely for Him alone and may He allow its benefit to continue.

The one who collected these terms is
Aḥmad ibn Muḥammad Binʿajība al-Ḥasanī.
May God be kind to him in both worlds. *Āmīn!*
And our final prayer is,
Praise be to God,
Lord of the
Worlds!

134. Bayhaqī, *Dalāʾil al-nubuwwa*, vol. 6, p. 296.

Appendices

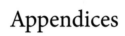

Appendix 1: The Station of *Tawba*

The excerpts below compare how five of the earliest Sufic lexicons defined the same station of the way, in this case, repentance (*tawba*).

1. *Kitāb al-ṣidq* (The book of truthfulness), by Abū Saʿīd al-Kharrāz (d. c. 287/900).

This book has the distinction of being the earliest extant work which attempts to systematize the Sufic path. For al-Kharrāz, anyone wishing to know God and dwell in greater proximity to Him needs to realize three fundamental virtues: sincerity (*ikhlāṣ*), patience (*ṣabr*), and truthfulness (*ṣidq*). These three, he explains, are so interrelated that no one of them can exist without the other two. Repentance is seen as the first step toward truthfulness. Following this come stations such as "knowledge of one's self," "knowledge of the devil," "knowledge of what is lawful and pure," "dependence on God," and so forth.

Al-Kharrāz's book is written in the form of questions which he, the seeker, asks an unidentified teacher. Thus, the singular "you" in the passage below may be taken as referring to al-Kharrāz himself.

Truthfulness (*ṣidq*) is a word with many meanings. The first stage of truthfulness is a servant's turning to God with sincere repentance, even as All-Mighty God says, *O you who believe, turn to God with sincere repentance* (66:8), and also, *And turn you all in repentance to God, O you who believe, that haply you may prosper* (24:31), and also, *God has turned toward the Prophet and the emigrants and the helpers* (9:118).

The beginning of repentance is to regret having fallen short in following God's commandments or prohibitions, to resolve not to repeat anything which is abhorent to God, to be constant in asking forgiveness, to restore any property wrongfully taken from God's servants, to acknowledge the sin to God and to [anyone who has been wronged], to continue in fear, sorrow, and grief that you might be proven insincere, to be fearful lest your repentance not be accepted, and not to feel safe [from the possibility] that God has seen you doing something He abhors and is angered with you [because of it].

Thus, Ḥasan al-Baṣrī said, "What could make me feel safe that God has not seen me engaged in something He abhors and has said, 'Do as you might, I will not forgive you?'"[1] and also, "I fear that He will cast me into the Fire and care not."

I have heard that one of the learned met a man and asked him, "Have you repented?" The man replied, "Yes." Then the learned man asked, "And do you know whether your repentance has been accepted?" The other said, "I do not." "Go then," rejoined the scholar, "and find out!"

Another said, "The grief of a bereaved mother passes away, but the grief of a penitent does not."

Also part of the truthfulness of repentance is that you give up any friends and boon-companions who had helped you transgress God's commandments, that you flee from them, and consider them your enemies unless they return to God. God says *Friends on that day shall be foes one to the other, save those who fear God* (43:67).

Truthfulness of repentance also demands that wickedness depart from your heart, and that you beware of secretly wishing to recall what turned you from God. God says: *And leave the outward part of sin, and the inward part thereof* (6:120). Know, too, that the sounder the believer's heart and the greater his knowledge of God, the stricter his repentance will be. For consider how the Prophet ﷺ said: "Verily my heart becomes clouded over and so I ask pardon of God and turn to Him a hundred times a day."[2]

2. *Manāzil al-ʿubbād min al-ʿibāda* (The devotees' stations of worship), Ḥakīm al-Tirmidhī (d. 320/932).

   Al-Tirmidhī's book is divided into two parts. In the first part, he describes seven stations of the way. In the second part, for each station he has described, he quotes the Qurʾānic verses

---

1. He is rephrasing a *ḥadīth* in which the Prophet said of the people who fought in the battle of Badr, "Perhaps God has said, 'Do whatever you will, I have forgiven you.'" Bukhārī, vol. 4, p. 59; Muslim, vol. 2, p. 1166.
2. Muslim, vol. 3, p. 1243.

and *ḥadīth* relating to it.

In al-Tirmidhī's definition, repentance is seen as starting from God's grace, which begins by showing a human being the ugliness of sin. The human response is then to rectify what is spoiled. Al-Tirmidhī also mentions some of the specific amends that have to be made, both to fellow creatures and to God.

God has devotees whom He looks upon with His mercy and graces with the gift of repentance. He opens the eyes of their hearts and shows them the ugliness of sin so that they behold the evil of how they have acted in respect to Him. There is also unveiled to them its outcome, the final destination of the sinful, that they might exert their utmost efforts to avoid it. Then does God strengthen their resolve and support them with His accord (*tawfīqihi*). Each time they rid themselves of a sin, their hearts become cleansed of the dark spot that the sin had made, even as the Messenger of God ﷺ said, "When the servant sins, a black spot forms upon his heart, but if he repents, and rids himself of the sin, his heart is polished clean."[3] Thus do they proceed until they gain firm footing at the door of repentance by purifying themselves of all the sins they were committing, making amends for what they had done in days past, and following [ṭheir repentance] by whatever corrections they can. They return what is due to any they have wronged, seek reconciliation, and strive to make up and complete whatever of the obligatory worship [*al-mafrūḍāt*] they had missed until they have achieved an amount such that their hearts are no longer disturbed by anything past or anything they are presently doing which might remove them from what God has enjoined upon them to the extent they are able. It is then that they may truly be called repentant (*tawwāb*) and reverent (*muttaqī*). This is the lowest of the stations of those who aspire to God and are traveling toward Him.

3. *Kitāb al-lumaʿ fi-l-taṣawwuf* (The book of flashes concerning Sufism) by Abū Naṣr al-Sarrāj (d. 378/988).

Al-Sarrāj's work contains the earliest mention of the levels or stages of different worshipers in respect to each station of the way. In addition, while al-Sarrāj quotes earlier Sufis, he does

3. Ibn al-Athīr, vol. 2, p. 425 from Tirmidhī, Ibn Mājah, and Aḥmad.

not use Qurʾānic verses in his definitions.

Abū Yaʿqūb Yūsuf b. Ḥamdān al-Sūsī said, "The first of the stations leading to God most high is repentance." When al-Sūsī was asked to define repentance, he said, "[It] is a return from what the teachings condemn to what they commend." When Sahl b. ʿAbdallāh [al-Tustarī] was asked to define repentance, he said, "It is that you do not forget your sin," and when al-Junayd was asked this same question, he said, "It is that you forget your sin."

The Shaykh (al-Sarrāj) said, "Al-Sūsī was speaking about the repentance of the aspirants (*murīdīn*) setting out in the path, the seekers and travelers who are at times for (themselves) and at times against, and Sahl b. ʿAbdallāh was speaking about this as well. Al-Junayd, however, who said that repentance was to forget your sin, was speaking about the repentance of the realized ones (*al-mutaḥaqqiqūn*) who do not remember their sins because the greatness of God and perpetual invocation have taken hold of their hearts. This is also what Ruwaym b. Aḥmad meant when he was asked about repentance and answered, "It is repentance from repentance." And when Dhū l-Nūn was asked, he said, "The repentance of the generality is from sins; the repentance of the elect is from heedlessness."

As for the words of the gnostics, the ecstatics, and the elect of the elect about the meaning of [this station], Abū l-Ḥusayn al-Nūrī said, "Repentance is that you turn away from everything other than God most high." This is also what was referred to by (Dhū l-Nūn) who said, "What is sin for those who have been brought near (*al-muqarrabīn*) is virtue for the conventionally good (*al-abrār*)," or as another has said, "What is ostentation (*riyāʾ*) for the gnostics is sincerity for the aspirants."

For the gnostic is someone who first approached God in the time of his seeking and the beginning [of his way] by accomplishing, through devotional practice, the means which would bring him near and, in that way, was granted realization. Then the lights of guidance encompassed him, providence reached him, divine care enveloped him, and he witnessed with his heart what he could of the immensity of his Lord, and meditated upon the artistry of His creation and His eternal goodness and generosity. Then he turned in repentance from both his speech and silence, and ceased to regard the devotions, good works, and practices he was wont to do in his time of seeking and beginning.

What a difference, then, between this penitent and that one: between someone who repents from sins and ill deeds, someone who repents from heedlessness, and someone who repents from regarding his good deeds and acts of worship.

4. *al-Taʿarruf li madhhab ahl al-taṣawwuf* (Introduction to the way of the people of Sufism) by Abū Bakr al-Kalābādhī (d. c. 380/990).

In al-Kalābādhī, the levels of aspirants within each station are further explained. Nearly the entire definition of the station of repentence is a compilation of sayings from earlier books.

Al-Junayd was asked, "What is repentance?" He replied, "It is forgetting your sin." When Sahl was asked the same question, he said, "It is that you do not forget your sin." The meaning of al-Junayd's statement is that the sweetness of the sinful act so completely leaves your heart that not a single trace of it remains and you become like someone who is absolutely unacquainted with it.

Ruwaym said, "The meaning of repentance is that you repent from repentance," which is like the saying of Rābiʿa, "I ask forgiveness from God for my lack of sincerity in saying, 'I ask forgiveness from God.'"

Ḥusayn al-Maghāzilī was asked about repentance and he said, "Are you asking about the repentance of conversion (*ināba*) or the repentance of response?" The questioner said, "What is the repentance of conversion?" He said, "It is that you fear God because of the power He has over you." Then he was asked, "And what is the repentance of response?" He answered, "That you are ashamed before God because of how near He is to you."

Dhū l-Nūn said, "The repentance of the generality is for sin; the repentance of the elect is for heedlessness, and the repentance of the prophets is for seeing that they are unable to reach what others have attained."

Al-Nūrī said, "Repentance is that you turn away from the remembrance of anything except God most high." And Ibrāhīm al-Daqqāq[4] said, "Repentance is that you be for God a face with no

4. We were unable to identify al-Daqqāq with the surname Ibrāhīm.

back, after having been for Him a back with no face."

5. From *Manāzil al-sāʾirīn* (The stages of the wayfarers) by ʿAbdallāh al-Anṣārī (d. 481/1088).

Of the early books describing the path and its stations, *Manāzil al-sāʾirīn* is probably the most complex in its arrangement and approach. The book is divided first into ten sections: "beginnings, character, states, gates, sources, sanctities, endings, interactions, valleys, and inner truths." Each of these, in turn, is divided into chapters. The chapter on repentance is the second of ten chapters which al-Anṣārī includes under "beginnings," the others being "awakening" (which precedes repentance), "self-reckoning," "conversion," "meditation," "remembrance," "protection," "fleeing," "spiritual exertions," and "audition." Each station is then defined in terms of its essential truths (*ḥaqāʾiq*), subtle meanings (*laṭāʾif*), and mysteries (*sarāʾir*), as well as in terms of what the station means for those at different stages of the way.

God most high says, *And one who does not repent is among the wrongdoers* (49:11), which means that the name "wrongdoer" is removed from the one who does repent.

Repentance is not possible except after having knowledge of what sin is. This means that you see in the sin three things: when you commit it, you do not have divine protection (*ʿiṣma*) and yet you are still content [with the sin], and would prefer to continue it rather than rectify it, even while you know that God beholds you.

The conditions of repentance are three things: that you feel remorse, ask for forgiveness, and rid yourself of the sin.

The essential truths of repentance are three things: that you realize the gravity of sin, are concerned about making repentance and having it accepted, and that you seek pardon from any of God's creatures (you have wronged).

The mysteries (*al-sarāʾir*) of these truths are three: that you distinguish true piety from [outward] respectability; that you forget the transgression [because the remembrance of God has overcome the heart]; and that you repent from repentance always, for in repenting you become one of those to whom God says, *And turn in repentance to God all together O you who believe* (24:31), which is a commandment to the repentant to repent.

The subtle meanings (*laṭāʾif*) of these innermost secrets are also three things. The first is that you look between the transgression and predestination and know God's purpose therein. For He has given you freedom (to act) and has allowed you to sin, and this may be for one of two reasons. One is that you might know His power and glory through [the irresistibility of] His decrees, know His goodness by how He [permits a sin] to be concealed, know His clemency by how He grants you time [to repent], know His generosity by how He accepts your excuses, and know His grace by how He forgives you. The second reason is that there might be proof of His justice if He punishes you.

The second subtle meaning is to know that if anyone who had true insight were to behold his ill-deeds, he would see that he really has no good deeds at all and would journey between witnessing divine grace and seeking [to rectify] the faults of his ego.

The third subtle meaning is [to know] that even if a servant is granted a vision of the divine order (*al-ḥukm*) and [his perception] ascends from [the diverse] meanings of all things to the one meaning of this order, this still does not remove from him the virtue of a good deed nor the vice of a bad one.

The repentance of the generality is through abundant acts of worship, which implies three things: an unawareness of [God's] grace to them in concealing [their sin] and granting them respite; or the illusion that they have some right over God; or that they are not in need [of God's forgiveness]. This is actually pride and injustice toward God.

The repentance of those midway [in the path] is for belittling their sins, which is actually [a kind of] hostility, challenge, and scorn that invites being cut off from God.

The repentance of the elect is for wasting time, for this abases them to the level of their shortcomings and flaws, extinguishes the light of vigilance (*nūr al-murāqaba*), and muddies the clear spring of companionship.

The station of repentance is not perfected unless it leads to repentance from all that is other than God, then seeing the defect of that repentance and repenting from that defect.

Appendix II: Correspondences

The passages below are excerpts from several of Ibn ʿAjība's other works in which he speaks more about some of the essential notions of Sufism.

1. The Sufi and the Four Elements

[In speaking of the Sufi], they have evoked the example of the four elements (*al-ʿanāṣir al-arbaʿa*) upon which the physical world is based: air, earth, water, and fire, also known as the four natures, and mentioned by Ibn Sīnā al-Ḥakīm[1] in the verses:

> What Hippocrates said of them was sound:
> They are fire, water, earth, and wind

And by "wind" he means "air."

All four of these elements can be found in [the nature of] the Sufi. He is like the air in the sublimity of his aspiration and rank. Also, air is hot and moist and so it is in the state of equilibrium which envelops all physical bodies, and in respect to which their perfections or deficiencies arise. Like the air, the Sufi is in equilibrium in respect to his actions: he neither falls short nor goes to extremes, but always seeks the middle way, "And in all matters, the middle way is best."[2] Because of his equilibrium, all creatures are at ease with him and return to him, and both actions and reactions happen through him by God's permission, while he, even as he intermingles with creatures, remains above them just as air mixes with both earth and water yet still rises above them.

At the same time, the Sufi is like the earth: lowly, humble, and easy. He is there for both the virtuous and sinful, both the small and the great, like the ground upon which they tread. One of my

1. See Ibn Sīnā, *Qānūn fī ṭibb*, as well as his *Risāla fī l-ḥudūd* which, in turn, is a transmission of Aristotle's definitions in *De Generatione et Corruptione* (II:3).

2. Bayhaqī, *Shuʿab al-īmān*, vol. 3, p. 402, narrates this saying as a *ḥadīth* with the wording "The best practice is the middle way." It is a frequently quoted saying in Moroccan speech to the present day.

teachers said, "We are like pathways: upon us pass the good people and the bad, the obedient and sinful, and we make no distinction between them."

Also, the nature of earth is cold and dry. By way of its coolness, it can be in contact with all the other elements. Were it hot and in contact with the air which is also hot, all that was upon it would be burnt up. And by way of its dryness, comes its stability.

This too is the way with the Sufi: by the coolness and suppleness of his actions, creatures may be in contact with him and derive benefit from him, and by his firmness in what is true, his sincerity is proven.

He has a heart, too, which is like the earth. All manner of vileness might be cast upon it, yet from it there comes forth only what is beautiful: the more the refuse, the richer its goodness. Also with the Sufi, the deeper you search, the greater the benefit and wisdom that will come to you. Thus our master Jesus (ʿĪsā) ﷺ said to his companions, "Where does a seed sprout forth?" They answered, "In the earth." He said, "So it is with wisdom: it does not sprout except in a heart that is like the earth." And Sahl ﷺ said, "This path of ours is for folk whose spirits have been swept up upon the rubbish heap."

The Sufi is also like fire in burning up blameworthy qualities, giving light, and in lighting the lamps in others' hearts.

Also, the nature of fire is heat and dryness, illumination and burning, and the Sufi is like this: there is an inward heat which never leaves him. The strength and warmth that arise from his awareness of his inner freedom burn up every egoistic trait which comes near him and allow him to look beyond it toward the gnostic truths and spiritual realities of existence.

The Sufi is also like water in the way he quenches the thirst of ignorance, and cools the heat of weariness that comes from being veiled from God. And even as the nature of water is cool and moist, so too is the Sufi's. In his coolness he does not seek victory for his ego and in his moistness he is never proud toward another, but quenches the thirst of all who need him.

al-Futūḥāt al-ilāhiyya fī sharḥ al-mubāḥith al-aṣliyya, p. 67.

2. Repentance

Commenting on the 197th aphorism of Ibn ʿAṭāʾ Allāh's *Ḥikam*—"Whoever finds it astonishing that God should save him from his passion or bring him forth out of heedlessness has underestimated the divine power: *And God, over all things, has Power* (18:45)"—he wrote:

Without a doubt, nothing is beyond the power of God, may He be exalted. He is the overwhelming one in His command. The hearts of His servants are in His hand and He directs them however He wills and He turns them[3] whenever He wills. Even someone totally engrossed in heedlessness and drowning in the seas of his passions should not be astonished that God can deliver him from his heedlessness and remove him from his passions: to believe otherwise would be to underestimate his faith.

Why should you find this surprising when our Lord most high says, *And God, over all things, has power* (18:45) and you are one of those things! And He says to the sinner, *O My servants who have wronged their own souls, never despair of the mercy of God. Truly God forgives all sins* (38:53) and also, *Whosoever repents following a wrong he has committed and sets it aright, verily God will turn to him in forgiveness* (5:39), and there are so many other verses [with the same import]. And the Prophet ﷺ said "If your sins were to fill the sky and you turned to God in repentance, God would forgive you."[4]

Recall, too, the heedless and sinful ones of the past who became people of contemplation and insight! Bandits (*luṣūṣ*) who became saints (*khuṣūṣ*)! People like Ibrāhīm b. Adham, Fuḍayl b. ʿIyyāḍ, Abū Yaʿzā and so many others whose transgressions were pardoned. Al-Qushayrī, in fact, begins his treatise[5] by mentioning those saints who had started out as profligates in order to strengthen our hope in God. Recall, too, the [*ḥadīth*] about the man who had killed ninety-nine people and then went to a hermit to ask whether repentance

3. The verb, *yuqallibuhā* (He turns them), is from the same root as the Arabic word for heart, *qalb*. In his commentary on the prayer of blessing by Ibn Mashīsh, he notes that the heart (*qalb*) is so named because, "It turns back and forth (*taqallab*) between negligence and presence, sin and obedience." Ibn ʿAjība, *Kitāb sharḥ ṣalāt al-quṭb ibn Mashīsh*, ed. ʿAbd al-Salām al-ʿUmrānī (Casablanca: Dār al-Rashād, 1999), pp. 29–30.

4. Ibn al-Athīr, vol. 8, p. 30, cites this as a *ḥadīth qudsī* from Tirmidhī, and Ṭabarānī, *al-Awsaṭ*, vol. 5, p. 163.

5. See Abū l-Qasim al-Qushayrī, *al-Risāla* (Cairo: Dār al-Maʿārif, 1995), vol. 1, p. 35ff.

was possible for him. When the hermit answered it was not, he slew him as well and completed one hundred. Then he went to a sage and asked the same question. The sage instructed him to repent, to depart for a land where the people worshiped God, and to remain there. On the way [to that land], the man died, and the angels of mercy took his soul. This *ḥadīth* in its entirety is in the collection of Bukhārī.[6]

Similar to this is the tale of the man who had been a thief and asked an ascetic whether there was any repentance for him. In mockery, the ascetic took a withered date frond and said, 'Take this frond! When it turns green, your repentance will be sincere!' The former thief took the frond and with the intention [of repentance] set about worshiping God, and he would look upon the frond [from time to time], and behold, one day it became a tender sapling ready to be planted.

I have come across people drowning in heedlessness, people who had stopped praying, who no longer had the slightest knowledge of the common religion let alone the Sufic path, and yet they turned their lives around, and became among the elect of the gnostics! And I have come across people who were engrossed in sin, drowning in disobedience to God and wrong to their fellow man, and they became among the greatest of the pious!

I have seen Christians near the citadel of Sebta who came to stand near a circle of invocation and were seized by such ecstasy that when we left that place, they followed us right to the border, and had they found some way, they would all have become Muslims on the spot.[7] And I knew a man from among our brethren who used to say concerning his ego and how impossible it seemed that he would

6. Bukhārī, vol. 2, p. 184. When the angels of mercy and the angels of chastisement measure the distance between the sinful land he was leaving and virtuous land to which he was heading, they find that he is closer to the latter by a single handspan, or in other versions, by a single joint of his finger, and thus he is forgiven.

7. Sebta, or Ceuta as it is referred to in European tongues, was taken by the Portuguese in 1415 and in 1580 passed into Spanish control. Although on Morocco's Mediterranean coast, it remains Spanish territory to this day along with the enclave of Melillia. The incident Ibn ʿAjība refers to here is also mentioned in his *Fahrasa*. See Michon, *Fahrasa*, p. 85.

ever be delivered from his heedlessness: "My heart is a brass cannon! Nothing can get to it!" And yet he was taken out of that state and I have seen him since, wandering ecstatic in God, bareheaded and barefoot, and today he is one of the greatest of the saints.

Īqāẓ al-himam, pp. 272–273.

3. Patience

In his commentary on Q. 2:45–46—*Seek help through patience and prayer—and truly this is hard except for the humble, those who know they will meet their Lord and that unto Him they are returning*—he wrote:

O you who long to enter the divine presence, be humble and lowly before God's saints and drink deeply of patience that you might be brought thence. As a poet has said:

> Be humble toward the One you love—love is never easy!
> But if the Beloved be content with you, you will surely be united.

And if the love of power and worldly rank is what is keeping you from this, *then seek help through patience and prayer*, for patience is the basis of all success, and prayer repels lewdness and iniquity. Keep knocking on this door until you enter among the beloved friends.

Constancy in the prayer is *hard except for* those who approach it with the sincere desire to commune with God most high, to realize the encounter of contemplation and vision, and to return to their guardian lord at every moment. Then will the prayer be one of the things in which they find the coolness of their eyes. And with God is all success, and He is the guide to the fairest of paths.[8]

al-Baḥr al-madīd, vol. 1, p. 102.

4. Gratitude

In his commentary on the 64th aphorism of the

---

8. In his words "the coolness of their eyes" is a reference to the famous saying of the Prophet Muḥammad, "[Those things] made loveable to me in this world are women and fragrances, and the coolness of my eye has been placed in the prayer." Ibn al-Athīr, vol. 4, p. 766 from Nasāʾi and Aḥmad; Ṭabarānī, *al-Awsaṭ*, vol. 6, p. 361.

Ḥikam—"Whoever is not thankful for graces runs the risk of losing them, and whoever is thankful fetters them with their own cord"—he wrote:

The sayings of the wise are all in agreement with the meaning of this [*ḥikma*]: that gratitude will bind God's graces to us and prevent their loss, and that if we are given a grace for which we are not grateful, it will be taken away from us without our even knowing that it is lost. . . .

Thus does God most high say, *Verily God does not alter what is with a folk until they alter what is in themselves* (13:11), which means God does not change the benefactions which He has bestowed upon a people unless they change the gratitude in themselves, and to change the gratitude in themselves means to become engrossed in sin and rejection. . . .

Abū Ḥāzim was asked, "What is the gratitude of the eyes?" He answered, "When you see something good with them, mention it, and when you see something bad, conceal it." Then he was asked, "And what is the gratitude of the ears?" He said, "If you hear something good with them, take it to heart, and if you hear something bad, bury it." Then he was asked, "And what is the gratitude of the hands?" He answered, "That you do not use them to take what is not yours, nor keep them from giving what belongs to God." Then he was asked, "And what is the gratitude of the stomach?" He said, "That its lower part be patience and its upper part be knowledge." They then asked, "And what is the gratitude of the sexual organs?" He answered, "It is as God says: *And those who guard their chastity* (23:5). . . ." Then he was asked, "And what is the gratitude of the feet?" He said, "It is that when you see something that may lead to your salvation, you use them to get there, and when you see something that may lead to your perdition, you keep them from going there."[9]

Īqāẓ al-himam, pp. 116–117.

5. Scrupulousness

In his commentary on the 62nd aphorism of the *Ḥikam*—"When you stop hoping [to possess something], you are free, but as long as you covet it, you are a slave"—he wrote:

9. This saying also appears in Abū Nuʿaym, *Ḥilya*, vol. 3, p. 279.

It has been said that the most lawful of lawful provision (*aḥalla al-ḥalāl*) is what comes to you without your having ever thought about it and without your having asked either woman or man. And Shaykh ʿAbd al-ʿAzīz al-Mahdawī ﷺ said, "Scrupulousness means that you neither move nor stay still without seeing God in that movement or stillness, and when God is seen therein, the movement and stillness vanish and you remain with God. (Indeed, movement is contingent upon a mover.[10]) He also said, "I do not see anything without seeing God therein, and when I see God therein, I am no longer there." And also, "All the learned agree that the only absolutely lawful provision is what is taken from the hand of God without intermediary. That is the station of complete dependence upon God (*tawakkul*, 10)." Or as yet another of them has said, "The lawful (*al-ḥalāl*) is that in which God is not forgotten. . . ."

Īqāẓ al-himam, p. 114.

6. Detachment

Commenting on the 45th aphorism of the *Ḥikam*—"No deed arising from a renouncing heart is small; no deed arising from an avaricious heart is fruitful"—he wrote:

For the Sufis, detachment (*zuhd*) means an aversion toward everything that distracts them from God and keeps them from the divine presence.

Their detachment will first be in respect to wealth, and its sign is that gold and dust, silver and stones, wealth and poverty, and withholding and giving will be equal in their eyes.

Second, it will be in respect to position and rank, and its sign is that honor and lowliness, fame and obscurity, praise and blame, elevation and abasement will be equal in their eyes.

Third, it will be in respect to attaining spiritual stations, miracles, or special gifts, and its sign is that hope and fear, strength and weakness, and expansion and contraction will become equal, so that they will journey in one state as they do in another, and know God in one state as they know Him in another.

Last, it will be in respect to all existence through a permanent

10. Movement implies time and place, and God is beyond both.

consciousness of the One who is the source of existence and of His command.

When an aspirant realizes these levels of detachment or most of them, all his deeds become great in substance before God, even if they appear small to people. This is, in fact, the meaning of the Prophet's saying ﷺ, "A little practice following the sunna is better than a lot of practice following innovation (*bidʿa*)."[11] For what innovation is worse than to love this world and to pursue it with body and soul? This did not exist in the time of the Prophet ﷺ nor in the time of the Companions; it did not exist until the appearance of pharaonic rulers who built great edifices and adorned them with all manner of ornament. Such, in fact, is truly reprehensible innovation: grand in form, paltry in substance. Indeed, the true measure is not in the movement of forms but rather in the humility of souls.

The worship of the *zāhid* is by and for God, while the worship of someone attached to the world (*rāghib*) is by and for the ego. The worship of the *zāhid* is alive and eternal, while the worship of someone attached to the world is dead and passing away; the worship of the *zāhid* is constant and ongoing, while the worship of someone attached to the world is cut off and incomplete; the worship of the *zāhid* is in the mosque of the presence *which God has permitted to be raised up*[12] while the worship of someone attached to the world is on the trash heap of impurities which God has permitted to be abased. . . .

And I heard our Shaykh (al-Darqāwī) say, "Someone attached to the world is heedless of God even if he is constantly saying, 'Allāh, Allāh,' for the measure is not by the tongue, while the *zāhid* is remembering God always, even if the invocation by his tongue is little."

Īqāẓ al-himam, pp. 94–95.

7. Love

Commenting on Q. 2:168—*Yet of mankind are some who take unto themselves rivals to God, loving them with a love that is*

---

11. Daylamī, *Firdaws*, vol. 3, p. 41.
12. This paraphrases Q. 24:36, *In houses God has permitted to be raised up in which His name is invoked. He is glorified therein both morning and evening.*

God's alone, while those who believe are stauncher in their love for God—he wrote:

Know that the love we have for God may come to us in two ways. One is when we behold His generosity and grace toward us and our hearts are drawn to [God] as they are to anyone who treats us well. This is called "selfish love" and it is something acquired. God showers us with blessings and lets us see them as such. And each time we behold one of God's countless gifts, it becomes like a seed planted in the pure soil of the heart. We continue to see blessing upon blessing, and each one is greater than the one before, for each time we perceive a blessing, our heart receives light and our faith increases. We see the intricacies and mysteries of grace which were not evident to us before, and so our love becomes ever greater.

The second [way God's love comes to us] is when the veils are lifted and the obstacles removed from our heart's vision and we behold His beauty and perfection, for beauty, by its very nature, is loveable.

These are the two modes of love which Rābiʿa al-ʿAdawiyya spoke of, saying:

> I love You with two loves: one is a selfish love
> And the other a love that is worthy of You.
> The selfish love is when I am busy with Your remembrance
> To the exclusion of all others.
> The love that is worthy of You
> Is when You raise the veils that I might see You.
> And in neither this love nor that is any praise mine.
> In both this love and that, the praise is totally Yours.[13]

. . . When she says, "And in neither this love nor that is any praise mine," she means that both of these loves, in their deepest reality, are from God, to God, and by God. There is no question of her "possessing" either of them, for in respect to the supreme reality, God is the praiser and God is the praised (*al-ḥāmid wa-l-maḥmūd*).

al-Baḥr al-madīd, vol. 1, pp. 194–195.

13. Based on the translation in Margaret Smith, *Rābiʿa the Mystic* (Cambridge: Cambridge University Press, 1984), p. 102

8. Gnosis

Commenting on the 94th aphorism of the *Ḥikam*—"Deprivation hurts you only because of your lack of understanding of God therein"—he wrote:

Understanding of God necessitates gnosis, and gnosis is not complete until the one to whom it is granted knows God both in majesty and beauty, in His giving and withholding, in contraction and expansion. To know God only in beauty is the knowledge of the generality of people who are enslaved by their egos, pleased if they receive, but angered if not. Among the fruits of gnosis are contentment and submission to what is destined, and among the fruits of love is patience in the face of hardship and tribulation:

You claim the way of love but then complain.
Tell me, then, where is love in your claim.
Had we found you one who patiently endures
All that you had hoped for would be yours.

The lover is not sincere in his love, nor the gnostic sincere in his gnosis until God's giving and withholding, contraction and expansion, poverty and wealth, honor and lowliness, praise and blame, loss and gain, sorrow and happiness are equal in his eyes. Then does he know His beloved in all things—as someone said, "My friend and my beloved in every state!"—and is content with Him and submits to Him in all things. If he does not find [all these conditions] to be equal, then he should not claim the station of passion and love. Let him know his limits, and not exceed them, for he who claims what is not really his risks being tested therein.

Īqāẓ al-himam, p. 157.

9. Integrity

Commenting on the 179th aphorism of the *Ḥikam*—"It may be that a miracle (*karāma*) is given to someone who has not been given integrity (*istiqāma*)"—he wrote:

Shaykh Abū l-ʿAbbās al-Mursī said, "It does not matter that someone can 'fold up' (*taṭwī*) [distances upon] earth so that, suddenly, there he is in Mecca or some other distant place. What matters is that he can 'fold up' his egoism so that, suddenly, there he is in the presence of his Lord!" Indeed, the real miracle is integrity in your faith and to attain complete certitude. As for paranormal powers, however, if the person who has them also has inward and outward integrity, then he is worthy of esteem, and such powers only testify to the perfection of his state. But if they are not accompanied by integrity, they have no real meaning. Indeed, for most of the people of the inward, miracles are inward: to have the veil removed [between them and God]; to be increased in faith; to be granted the gnosis which comes from contemplation and vision.

Similarly, the punishment which befalls those who would seek to harm [God's saints] is usually something inward and even unperceived: hardness of heart, falling ever deeper into sin, becoming heedless of God, and being distant from His presence. Such punishments are undoubtedly worse than any physical affliction.

Īqāẓ al-himam, p. 255.

10. Longing and Ardor

Commenting on the 169th aphorism of the *Ḥikam*—"His providential care of you is not due to anything coming from you. Where were you when He confronted you with His providence or met you face-to-face with His care? Neither sincerity of deeds nor existence of states has any being in His eternity. Instead only pure bestowing and divine giving are there"—he wrote:

For some of them, longing and ardor have overwhelmed their souls. Thus, one of them said, "Among the signs of the gnostic is to be in [the station of] subsistence (*baqāʾ*) and long for the meeting (*liqāʾ*)." The world and all it contains is too narrow for such a one. Sarī (al-Saqaṭī) said, "The greatest of the stations of gnosis is yearning."

[It is narrated that] God most high said [to one of His saints]: 'There are among My servants those whom I love and they love Me; I yearn for them, and they yearn for Me; I remember them and they remember Me; I look toward them and they look toward Me. Whosoever walks their path, that one do I love; whosoever spurns them, that one do I abhor.' [The saint asked], 'O Lord, what are the signs by which we may know them?' And [God] answered, 'They watch the shadows [for the approach of night] like a caring shepherd watches his sheep, and they long for sunset like a bird longs to return to its nest. When night falls, and darkness fills the sky, when pallets are placed on the ground and beds are stood up, and every lover is with his beloved, they rise to stand [in prayer], and place their faces upon the ground [in prostration]. They speak to Me with My speech, and implore Me for My grace. And some of them cry out, and some of them weep, and some of them moan, and some voice their plaints, and some of them stand, and some of them sit unable to stand, and some of them bow, and some of them prostrate, and I see what they bear for My sake and hear their plaints for My love. The first thing I give them is My light which I cast into their hearts so that they speak of Me as I speak of them. The second is that if the heavens and earth and all they contain were placed in their scales, I would consider it paltry. And third is that I turn to them with My face, and what I give to that one to whom I turn with My face, no one else can know.'

It is also narrated that Ibrāhīm b. Adham ﵁ said, "One day, I was overwhelmed with longing for God, and I said, 'O Lord, if ever You have given any of those who love you what would calm their hearts before they meet You, please give that to me, for truly I suffer from longing!' That night I saw in a dream that it was as if God had placed me before Him and said, 'O Ibrāhīm! Are you not ashamed to ask Me to give you what will calm your heart before you have met Me? Can anything calm the heart of the yearning one before he has met his beloved?' And I said, 'O Lord, I was confused and I knew not what I was saying. Forgive me and teach me what to say.' And God answered him, 'Say: O God, make me content with Your decrees, patient with Your trials, and grateful for Your blessings!'"[14]

Īqāẓ al-himam, pp. 245–246.

14. *Allāhumma, raḍḍinī bi qaḍāʾik, wa ṣabbirnī ʿalā balāʾik, wa awziʿnī shukra niʿmāʾik.* This prayer echoes several recorded in *ḥadīth* as well as the words of Solomon in Q. 27:19, *My Lord, grant that I may be grateful for* (awziʿnī an ashkura) *Your benefaction with which You have favored me and my parents, and to do the good that is pleasing to You, and make me among Your righteous servants.*

11. Servanthood and Freedom

Commenting on the 100th aphorism of the *Ḥikam*—"The best of your moments is when you witness your actual neediness and are thereby brought back to your actual lowliness"—he wrote:

Witnessing your neediness is the best of your moments in two respects. The first is that it is a realization of [your] servanthood and veneration for [God's] lordliness and in this lies your dignity and perfection, for it is to the degree that you realize servanthood outwardly that you venerate the consciousness of God's lordliness inwardly. Or you could say that your inward freedom is in proportion to your outward servanthood; or that your inward dignity is in proportion to your outward lowliness; or that your inward exaltation is in proportion to your outward humility. Whoever humbly deems himself to be lower than he actually is, God will exalt higher than he actually is. Look, too, at the most noble of God's creation, the prophets, and how God refers to them by [their] servanthood: *Glory be to the One who caused His servant to journey by night* (17:1). . . . *And mention Our servants Abraham, Isaac, and Jacob* (38:45) . . . *and mention Our servant David, endowed with might* (38:17) . . . *and mention Our servant Job* (38:41). And when our Prophet ﷺ was offered the choice between being a prophet-king or a prophet-servant, he chose the latter.

All this indicates that servanthood is the most noble of human conditions, and that to the degree we realize it outwardly, we are made great within. Conversely, when we leave this state outwardly by showing our freedom, a divine decree will come to correct us, return us to our original state, and show us what we [really] have and do not have.

Īqāẓ al-himam, pp. 163–164.

12. The Degrees of Certainty

Commenting on Q. 2:260—*And remember when Abraham said (to his Lord): My Lord! Show me how You give life to the dead, He said: Do you not believe? Abraham said: I do, but (I ask) in order that my heart may be at ease. (His Lord) said: Take four of the birds and cause them to incline to you, then place a part of them on each hill, then call them, they will come to you in haste. And know that God is Mighty, Wise*—he wrote:

God, the Truth, says, '*And remember*, O Muḥammad, or any who may be listening, *when Abraham said, My Lord! Show me how You give life to the dead,* that is, 'Let me see with my own eyes the way in which You revive the dead.' Here, his wish was to be taken from the knowledge of certainty to the eye of certainty. . . .

And God answers him with a question, *Do you not believe* that I have the power to revive the dead and restore life and order? It has been said that God asked Abraham this not because He did not know the surety of his faith, but rather in order that Abraham would answer Him as He answered him and that those who were listening would know why. And Abraham answers: *Indeed I do* believe that You have power over all things, *but (I ask) in order that my heart may be at ease*, for one who knows by having heard cannot compare to one who knows by having seen (*laysa l-khabīr ka-l-ʿiyyān*);[15] that is, the knowledge of certainty cannot compare to the eye of certainty. Abraham wished to add vision and perception to revelation and logical proof.

Then God says to him: *Take four of the birds*, and it has been related that these were the peacock, the rooster, the crow, and the pigeon, though some say the fourth was the eagle. *And cause them to incline to you,* that is, hold each in your hands that you might look upon it carefully and know its characteristics and not be confused concerning them after they are revived. *Then place a part of them on each hill. . . .* It has been said that he was ordered to slaughter the birds, pluck their bodies, cut them into pieces, and intermingle the pieces of flesh. Then he was to distribute the pieces upon the mountains but to keep the heads with him, and then call them. When he did this, each piece flew to one like it and they bound themselves together and reformed the birds' bodies. These then flew

15. This saying is a version of the phrase *laysa l-khabr ka-l-muʿāyana*, "Word-of-mouth is in no wise like eye witnessing," which has become an expression used by Sufis and others and is said to have its origins in the *ḥadīth* "God most high told Moses that his people had fashioned the calf, but it was not until he saw this with his own eyes that he cast down the tablets." Daylamī, *Firdaws*, vol. 3, p. 399, Ṭabarānī, *al-Awsaṭ*, vol. 1, pp. 45–46, and elsewhere.

to Abraham and to each he gave its head, and the birds flew off into the air. So glory be to the One who is not incapable of anything, and from whose knowledge nothing is hidden!

If we wish for our spirits to be revived with infinite life and to travel from the knowledge of certainty to the eye of certainty, our egos must die four deaths: they must die to the objects of their desires and love for the ornaments of this world, such being the attribute of the peacock; they must die to their lust for control and egoistic power, such being the attribute of the rooster; they must die to their vileness, meanness, and lack of hope, such being the attribute of the crow; and they must die to their desire for height and speed in the air, such being attribute of the pigeon.

When we slay these attributes of the ego, our spirit is given life and our ego becomes tame and obedient. Whenever we call it, it hastens to us, even as Abū l-Ḥasan al-Shādhilī says in the words in *al-Ḥizb al-Kabīr* (Greater litany), "Make for us of our minds a helper, of our souls a guardian, and over our egos, control, *That we might glorify You in abundance and invoke You in abundance. Truly You are ever seeing us* (20:33–35)."

al-Baḥr al-madīd, vol. 1, p. 294.

13. Remembrance

> Commenting on the 47th aphorism of the *Ḥikam*—"Do not abandon the invocation because of your lack of presence with God in it; for verily your negligence *of* the invocation is worse than your negligence *in* the invocation. And it may be that God will raise you from invocation with negligence to invocation with vigilance, and from invocation with vigilance to invocation with presence, and from invocation with presence to invocation with absence from everything except the One invoked. *And that is not difficult for God* (14:20)—he wrote:

Invocation (*dhikr*) is a powerful mainstay of the Sufic path and the most excellent of spiritual practices. God has said: *Remember Me; I shall remember you* (2:152) and also *O you who believe, invoke God with abundant remembrance* (33:41), and *abundant remembrance* is not to forget Him ever.

Ibn ʿAbbās said, "For every devotional practice that God has ordained, He has designated a special time and has excused His servants from offering it at other times, except the remembrance. God has not limited it any particular time but has said, *Invoke God with abundant remembrance*, and also, *When you have completed the prayer, remember God standing, sitting, and lying on your sides* (4:103).

A man once said to the Prophet ﷺ, "The rules of Islam have become too many for me! Give me one thing by which I can catch up to what I have missed and surpass it." And he answered, "Let your tongue be ever moist with the remembrance of God."[16]

He also said ﷺ, "If there were a man who had dirhams in his room and spent them [in charity] and another who invoked God, the invoker would be the more excellent of the two."[17]

And also, "Shall I not inform you of the best of your practices, the most purifying before your Lord, and the most elevating in rank, better for you than spending gold and silver, better for you than meeting your foes in battle that you might strike at their necks and they at yours?" They said, "And what is that, O Messenger?" He said, "The remembrance of God."[18]

And ʿAlī, may God honor him, said, "O Messenger of God, which is the shortest path to God, the easiest for His servants, and most excellent before Him?" He answered, "O ʿAlī, I urge you to invoke Him unceasingly." He answered, "All people invoke God," He said, "O ʿAlī, the hour shall not be arise until there is no one left upon the face of the earth who says, *Allāh*." He then asked, "How do I invoke, O Messenger of God?" He answered, "Close your eyes and listen to me three times, then say as I say." And ʿAlī said, "Then I listened, and he said, *Lā ilāha illā Allāh* three times, his eyes closed," and [ʿAlī] said it the same way. Thereafter, he conveyed this to Ḥasan al-Baṣrī, and from Ḥasan to Ḥabīb al-ʿAjamī, and from Ḥabīb to Dāwūd al-Ṭāʾī, and from Dāwūd to Maʿrūf al-Karkhī, and from Maʿrūf to al-Sarī, and from al-Sarī to al-Junayd and thereafter, it was conveyed to all the masters of spiritual training.[19]

16. Bayhaqī, *Shuʿab al-īmān*, vol. 1, p. 393.
17. Ṭabarānī, *al-Awsaṭ*, vol. 6, p. 451; Daylamī, *Firdaws*, vol. 3, p. 364.
18. Mālik, *al-Muwaṭṭaʾ*, vol. 2, p. 160; Bayhaqī, *Shuʿab al-īmān*, vol. 1, p. 394, Ibn Athīr, vol. 9, p. 515, from Tirmidhī.
19. This is narrated in *Rayḥān al-qulūb fī tawaṣṣuli ilā al-maḥbūb* by Yūsuf b. ʿAbd al-Salām al-ʿAjamī (d. 768).

Indeed, there is no entrance to God except through the door of remembrance, and so a servant's hours should be immersed in it and therein should he make the utmost effort.

The invocation is, in fact, the proclamation of sanctity (*manshūr al-wilāya*) and is absolutely essential both in the beginning and end of the path. Whoever is given the invocation has been given this proclamation, and whoever abandons it is excluded from it. Thus do they chant:

> Invocation is the greatest gate.
> You enter it for God,
> So make for it with guarded breaths.

To the extent that we are effaced in the divine name, we are effaced in the divine essence, and to the extent that we fall short of effacement in the name, so too do we fall short of effacement in the essence. Thus, the aspirant should persevere in [this practice] in every state and not give up invoking with the tongue because his heart lacks concentration during it. Rather, he should invoke God with his tongue even if his heart is distracted, for his "neglect *of* the invocation is worse than his neglect *in* the invocation," because the former means to leave it totally, while the latter means that he is at least involved to some degree. Even if only the tongue is invoking, it still means that at least one of the limbs of the body is being beautified by obedience to God, while if that is lost, it invites transgression. Thus, when one of the Sufis was asked, "Why should we invoke God with our tongues if our hearts are distracted?" he answered, "Thank God that He has allowed your tongue to invoke Him, for if He had left it to backbiting instead, what would you do?"

So we should invoke with the tongue until God opens the way toward invocation with the heart. And it may be that He will take you from invocation with negligence to invocation with vigilance, which means He makes you conscious of the meaning of what you are invoking as you invoke, and from invocation with vigilance to invocation with concentration on the invoked One so that [the invocation] becomes inscribed in the imagination such that your heart finds serenity therein and becomes concentrated in perpetual invocation. Such is the invocation of the elect, while the former is the invocation of the generality.

Then, if you persevere in invocation with presence, God will raise you to invocation with the absence of all else except the invoked One, such that light floods your heart. Indeed, it may be that the proximity of the light of the invoked One becomes so strong that you drown in it and pass away from all else. The invoker becomes the Invoked, the seeker becomes what is sought, and the one seeking union is united. *And that is not a difficult thing for God*: to raise you from the lowest rung to the highest rank where invocation ceases with the tongue and moves to the heart.

Īqāẓ al-himam, pp. 97–98.

14. Contraction and Expansion

Commenting on the 80th aphorism of the *Ḥikam*—"He expanded you so as not to keep you in contraction; He contracted you so as not to keep you in expansion; and He took you out of both so that you not belong to anything apart from Him"—he wrote:

Know that contraction and expansion each has its own comportment (*ādāb*) and if one fails to observe that comportment, he is put out the door, left to deal with beasts. In the state of contraction, the comportment required is serenity, dignity, calmness in confronting the flow of divine decrees, and a return to the One, the irresistible. For contraction is a kind of night, just as expansion is a kind of day, and when night falls, it is time for rest, calmness, silence, and care. Be patient, dear aspirant, and calm through the darkness of this night of contraction until the suns of the day of expansion dawn in your heart. Night must follow day, just as day must follow night, for *God causes the night to pass into the day and the day to pass into the night* (22:61, 31:29, 35:13, 57:6).

Such is the comportment required by contraction when you do not know its cause. In the case when you do know the cause, you should return from the cause to the One who is the Cause of all causes, and draw near to the most generous of givers. Has He ever shown you anything but goodness or bestowed upon you anything but favor? The One from whom these decrees have reached you is the same One who has always shown you the best of choices. The One who has sent down the illness is the One in whose hand is the cure! O you who are burdened with cares for you own soul, if you were to give it to God, you would find rest! The sadness that hearts go through is because they have been kept from the vision and consciousness of [the divine]. In a word, the cause of contraction is looking toward others and neglecting the Lord. As for the people of clarity, they witness nothing but the pure.

For this reason did the Prophet ﷺ say concerning someone afflicted by cares and woes, 'Let him say, "Allāh! Allāh! I associate none with Him!" and God will remove his cares and woes,' or words close to these, and this is an authentic *ḥadīth*.[20] See, then, how the Prophet ﷺ directed the person in that state of contraction to the remedy, which is to bear witness to God's oneness (*tawḥīd*) and pass away from associating any others with Him. He instructed him to a saying, but, of course, what was intended is the meaning of that saying: 'Know God and affirm His absolute oneness and He will turn your contraction into expansion and your grief into grace.'

Similar to this is what is narrated in another *ḥadīth*: "There is none who says, 'O God! Truly, I am Your servant, and the child of two of Your servants. My forelock is in Your hand, Your judgment and decree have come to pass within me, and I ask You by every one of the names which You have called Yourself, or revealed in Your book, or made known to any one of Your creatures, or have chosen in the knowledge of the unseen, that You make the Qurʾān the verdure of my heart, the light of my vision, the dispeller of my sadness, and the remover of my cares,' except that God will remove his cares and woes and replace them with happiness and joy."[21]

As for the state of expansion, among the actions it requires is to keep the limbs of your body from excess and above all, from the wounds that the tongue can inflict. For when your soul experiences the happiness of expansion, it may become overly exuberant, overly energetic, too light, and in this state you may say something [to another] without thinking about it, and fall into an abyss of separation by this rudeness.

So expansiveness can be a stumbling block. When the aspirant senses this state, the best thing he can do is rein in the soul with silence, don the raiment of calmness and dignity, go to a secluded

20. Abū Dāwūd; Bayhaqī, *Shuʿab al-īmān*, vol. 7, pp. 257–258. Ṭabarānī, *al-Awsaṭ,* vol. 6, p. 141, and vol. 9, p. 216, where the wording is "Allah! Allah is my Lord. I associate none with Him!" (*Allāh, Allāhu Rabbī! Lā ushriku bihi shayʾan*).

21. Daylamī, *Firdaws*, vol. 1, p. 466.

place, and stay there for a time. The *faqīr* in the state of expansion is like a cooking pot on the fire. If you just leave it there, it will boil over and all the broth will be lost, but if you put out the fire, the broth will remain savory and in tact. Such is the *faqīr* in the state of energy and expansion: his light intensifies and heart is collected, but if he then begins to move, and becomes excessively active, and follows his energy wherever it leads him, he will grow cold and be returned to his weakness. This is only because of his poor comportment toward God, and God most high knows better.

Īqāẓ al-himam, pp. 141–142.

15. Passing Thoughts and Intimate Impressions

Commenting on the 216th aphorism of Ibn ʿAṭāʾ Allāh—"When an intimate impression comes to you, your everyday habits are broken: *Truly, kings, when they enter a town, bring it to ruins*" (27:34)—Ibn ʿAjība writes:

An intimate impression (*wārid*) is an intense experience of longing, desire, love, fear, awe or majesty that God produces in your heart and which shakes you to the core of your being and inspires you to make renewed efforts toward your guardian lord. It is something that takes you out of your ordinary habits, your appetites and desires, and sets you on the path toward deeper knowledge of your Lord and what is pleasing to Him. And it may happen that the lights of that love and yearning shower down upon you with such intensity that you pass away completely from the sensory, this [being called] *jadhb*, divine attraction. Intimate impressions expressing such love and yearning are referred to in the plural since it is only when they are abundant and increasing that they can break through the habitual.

Intimate impressions have also been called 'breezes of the spirit' (*nafaḥāt*), about which [the Prophet] ﷺ, said, "Verily God has breezes of the spirit so be open to His breezes."[22] If these intimate

22. Bayhaqī, *Shuʿab al-īmān*, vol. 2, p. 42, Tirmidhī, *Nawādir al-uṣūl*, vol. 2, p. 293. The wording is "Verily, your Lord has breezes of the spirit through the days of your life, so be open to these breezes that perchance He might send one to you and that thereafter you may never suffer again," or "Seek goodness your entire life and be open to the breezes of God's mercy, for truly, God has breezes from His mercy

impressions do not come to you, you may still be opened to them by way of love for the gnostics, the people of the "elixir" which can transform your nature. And if you keep company with them and the intimate impressions still do not come, then you should break the habits of your ego outwardly in order that this might lead you to what is inward.

[Whatever the means], when intimate impressions do come to you, they overturn your everyday habits and bring them to ruins. Your honor will be turned into abasement, your wealth into poverty, your high rank into obscurity, your place in the world into lowliness, your speech into silence, your cuisine into feed, your repletion into hunger, your many words into silence, your destination and dwelling into wandering and travel. Such is the nature of *wāridāt*, bringing the habitual to ruins, like a mighty king with a fierce army who enters a township or city and levels its buildings and landmarks, even as God most high says, *Verily, kings, when they enter a town, bring it to ruins* (27:34). They tear it down, bring low its dignitaries, and subordinate its leader. Such is what they do because such is their nature, and so the use of this verse to explain [this process] is entirely fitting.

Īqāẓ al-himam, pp. 293–294.

16. The Two Oceans

Commenting on the words of the *Ṣalāt al-Mashīshiyya*, "O First, O Last, O Outward, O Inward," he wrote:

I shall mention to you something about the ocean of power (*qudra*) and the ocean of wisdom (*ḥikma*) in order to show you how they differ even while their abode is one.

We say, and all success is with God, that the ocean of power is abounding, and its nature overwhelming. It is beginningless and endless. It manifests and absorbs, moves and is still, contracts and repels, gives and withholds, raises up and brings low. In its hand is the determination of all things and about its axis revolve the heavenly spheres. It is the root of all branches, the branches of all roots, the end of all arrivals, and to it the hearts of the yearning ones fly.

---

which He sends to whomever He will. And ask God to cover your shame and still your fear."

The spirits of travelers (*sālikūn*) float in its shallows while the souls of those who have arrived (*al-wāṣilūn*) plumb its depths. Even the gnostics' hearts know not the mysteries of its infinitude: their uttermost limit is but wonder and awe, and then solitude in the sacred presence.

As for the ocean of wisdom, it too is a limitless ocean, but relating only to what is outward. It manifests intermediary causes and maintains the veil by the bonds of rules. It determines revealed laws and religions, covers with its cloak whatever emerges from the element of power, and veils the mysteries of lordhood with majesty. It illuminates the way and protects the supreme truth. It manifests servitude (*ʿubudiyya*) and conceals freedom (*ḥurriyya*). One who stops with this ocean is veiled, one who penetrates it to the ocean of power arrives ravished by the divine attraction, while one who [is permitted] to witness them both is complete, beloved, and by providence blessed.

Know too that these oceans call to one another by the tongue of their states. Power says to wisdom: 'You are under my compulsion and my will. Do naught save what I will for you, nor let there arise in you aught save what I desire. For if you oppose me, I will reject you, and if you seek to outstrip me, I will overwhelm you.'

And wisdom says to power: 'You are subject to my judgment, my orders and my prohibitions. If you disobey me, I will discipline you and perhaps even slay you.'

If a manifestation of power is in harmony with wisdom, that is a sign of divine beauty, either now or hereafter, but if a manifestation of power is in opposition to wisdom, that is a sign of divine rigor, either now or hereafter. For wisdom is at the source of the revealed law (*al-sharīʿa*), while power is at the source of the essential truth (*al-ḥaqīqa*). Essential truth which is not in accord with the revealed law is sin and the object of divine rigor and punishment sooner or later, while essential truth which is in harmony with the revealed law is obedience and the object of divine beauty and grace, sooner or later.

The human being, then, is between [the poles of] power and wisdom, the revealed law and the essential truth. And God most high knows best.

Sharḥ ṣalāt al-quṭb ibn Mashīsh, pp. 36–37.

17. Illumination

Commenting on Q. 7:189—*God is the One who created you from a single soul and therefrom did make his mate that he might take rest in her*—Ibn ʿAjība quotes Ruzbihān al-Baqlī as having said:

Adam ﷺ [after his creation] found nothing in the Garden except the brilliance of God's illumination (*tajallī*) and was almost annihilated by light which would envelop him layer upon layer. And God, be He glorified, knew that Adam could not bear the weight of this illumination, knew that he would melt in the light of its beauty, for all that was in the Garden was drowned in it. So He added to it the radiance of the omnipotence and the dominions (*ḍaw al-jabarūt wa-l-malakūt*) and from it created Eve, that Adam might find in her times of rest from the overwhelming power of divine illumination. Thus, too, would our Prophet ﷺ say to his wife ʿĀʾisha ﷺ "Speak to me, O rosy-cheeked beauty![23]

al-Baḥr al-madīd, vol. 2, pp. 293–294.

18. Nearness and Distance

Commenting on the 73rd aphorism of the *Ḥikam*—"If you want to know what your standing is with God, then look toward what God has placed you in"—he wrote:

God most high in His wisdom has made two kinds of human beings: the blessed and the wretched. Of the blessed, too, He has made two kinds: the people of nearness and the people of distance, or you could say, the people of the right hand, and those brought nigh, who are [also called] the foremost. If you wish to know where you yourself stand among these, whether you are among the blessed or the wretched, then look into your heart. If you affirm the existence of your Lord, and know Him as One in His sovereignty, and if you have found guidance in following the one who made your Lord known to you—and that is His Messenger ﷺ—then you are among those for whom 'the good [from God] has gone before them.'[24] If, however, you find denial or doubt, or if

23. This *ḥadīth* is mentioned by al-Ghazālī in the *Iḥyāʾ*, vol. 3, p. 98.

24. He is paraphrasing Q. 21:101: *Those for whom the good (record) from Us has gone before will be far removed [from the suffering of hell].*

you join to your Lord partners in your belief, or you do not accept the guidance of the one who made God known to you, then you are among the wretched.

And if you have found yourself to be among the blessed, and wish to know whether you are among the people of nearness or the people of distance, then behold: if you are guided by creation to the Creator, then you are among the people of distance, among the companions of the right hand; and if you are guided by God to all else, then you are among the people of nearness, from among those brought nigh. If you know yourself to be among the companions of the right hand, and wish to see if you are among those who are honored with your Lord or those who have been abased, then behold: if you find yourself fulfilling His commandments and avoiding His prohibitions, hastening toward what is pleasing to God, loving God's saints and friends, then you are among the honored and esteemed, and if you find yourself belittling God's commandments, taking excessive license concerning His prohibitions, lazy in fulfilling acts of obedience to God, disrespectful of what He has sanctified, and feeling enmity toward His saints, then, by God, you are among the lowly and deprived, those who have been placed far away, unless providence overtakes you from the lord of the worlds.

And if you affirm that you are among the people of nearness and have reached the station of vision by which you are guided by God's existence to all else, then you will not perceive other than Him. If you are near to what is intermediary between you and God, have affirmed divine wisdom (*ḥikma*) and you 'give to each that has a right its right,'[25] then you are among those brought nigh and those who are complete. And if you reject divine wisdom and have passed away from perceiving an intermediary, then if you are among the divine fools, overwhelmed by your state, in this state you are deficient, and if you are among the people of sobriety (*al-ṣaḥw*), then you have failed (in the way) unless a realized teacher or a perfected gnostic take you by the hand.

And here is yet another criterion by which you may know whether you are among the people of nearness or distance: if you have found

25. *An tuʿaṭī kulla dhi ḥaqqin ḥaqqahu.* Variations of this expression occur in several sayings of the Prophet and are often quoted by the Sufis to express the middle way between formalism and intoxication.

a shaykh to teach and instruct you and God has revealed to you his lights, and shown you the particular qualities of his secrets, then you are assuredly among the people of nearness, either in fact or possibility, following the words of the Shaykh [Ibn ʿAṭāʾ Allāh]: "Glory be to the One who has made guidance to His saints none other than guidance to Himself, and never unites anyone with one of His saints unless He wishes to unite that one to Himself."[26]

And if you have not found a master to teach you, and are deluded by the words of those who say that God's existence is separated [from our own], then you are assuredly among the people of the right hand, the generality of Muslims. This is usually true, and the rare exception cannot be used as the basis of judgment, but God most high knows better.

In a *ḥadīth*, the Prophet ﷺ said, "God, be He blessed and exalted says, 'I am *Allāh*. There is no god but Me. I created good and evil. So blessed be the one whom I created for good, and by whose hand I bring it forth, and woe be to the one whom I have created for evil and by whose hand I bring it forth.'"[27] And in another *ḥadīth*: "One who wishes to know what God has to do with him, let him behold what he has to do with God," and in another narration, "Let one who wishes to know his place with God behold where he has placed God in his heart. For God most high places the servant wherever the servant has placed Him in himself,"[28] or as His words attest, *So as for the one who gives in charity, has reverent fear, and affirms the good, for him will We smooth the way to bliss* (92:5–7). And God most high knows better."

Īqāẓ al-himam, pp. 131–132.

19. The Wine, the Cup, and Drinking

In his commentary on *al-Khamriyya* (The wine ode) of Ibn al-Fāriḍ, Ibn ʿAjība wrote:

The Shaykh begins his ode:

---

26. *K. al-ḥikam*, aphorism 156.

27. Ṭabarānī, *al-Muʿjam al-kabīr* (Mosul: Maktaba l-ʿUlūm wa-l-Ḥikam, 1983), vol. 12, p. 173.

28. Ṭabarānī, *al-Awsaṭ*, vol. 3, pp. 243–244, with the wording, "Let him look at where he has placed God in his soul, for verily God most high gives a servant the place the servant give Him in his soul."

We drank to the remembrance of the Beloved
a wine that made us drunk before the creation of the vine

. . . Here he says that following the invocation of the Beloved, we drank with our hearts and spirits a pure wine in the station of clarity. And we became drunk from this wine and passed away from our senses, so that we saw the lights of the beloved *in* everything, and *with* everything, and *before* everything, and *after* everything, and in our drunkenness were taken out from the darkness of the created world and allowed to gaze upon the lights of the One without beginning and without end. As I have written in an ode ending in *ʿayn*:

Our understandings were made drunk by the splendor of His
beauty,
We passed from our senses and the light shone forth
The sun appeared on the horizon, and then it rose
And starlight vanished with the dawn.

He also says that our drunkenness from this eternal spiritual wine happened before the vine, that is, before the source of earthly wine, also referred to by al-Shushtarī in his lines:

Not the drink from the vine: that is something earthly!
That is not my wine! My wine is eternal!

. . . To lose oneself in God is called drunkenness (*sukr*), for like physical drunkenness it entails losing the senses, which become covered by layer upon layer of spiritual lights which take hold of them from the eternal wine. . . .[29]

He then says:

The full moon is its cup

This eternal wine has a cup, and that cup is the full moon of oneness (*badr al-tawḥid*) as understood in its deepest sense. Anyone who associates partners with God by claiming the existence of another besides Him, or by seeing created things alongside the guardian

29. Ibn ʿAjība follows here with a description of taste (*dhawq*), drinking (*shurb*), drunkenness (*sukr*), sobriety (*ṣaḥw*), the sensory and the intelligible (*al-ḥiss wa-l-maʿnā*), power and wisdom (*qudra wa ḥikma*), ecstatic emotion, ecstatic encounter, and pure ecstacy (*wajd, wijdān, wa wujūd*), and unitive and separative consciousness (*jamʿ wa farq*) using much the same language as the *Miʿrāj*.

lord will not drink from the wine of love. Or we might also say that anyone whose heart is weighed down by the love of things or tempted by the world will taste nothing of this wine.

> And it is a sun surrounded by a crescent

This wine itself is the sun of gnosis. When it dawns on the horizons of hearts, it covers up the existence of created things; with the passing away of individual entities direct vision occurs. Then the crescent moon of beatitude envelops the drinkers and their aspirations rise.

> And how much more appears
> when the stars are intermingled.

The pure wine is finally drunk, intoxication with the world vanishes, and nothing remains in the gaze of the beholder save the lights of the living and eternal. When this [vision] is then intermingled with sobriety and method, the aspirant is whole and perfected. Then how many stars of doctrine become clear for him, how many treasures of understanding are opened for him, and if he is given permission to speak of the spirit, his expressions fall upon attentive hearts and his allusions are clear.

Among the things that Shaykh Abū l-Ḥasan [al-Shādhilī] said concerning love are these words:

"The drink (*al-shurāb*) is the radiant light that comes from the beauty of the beloved. The cup (*al-kaʾs*) is the kindness which brings that drink to the mouths of hearts. The winepourer (*al-sāqī*) is the One who is in control of this for the greatest of His elect and His saints from among His servants—and He is Allah, the knower of all that has been decreed and all that is best for His servants. If this beauty is unveiled to someone or he is given a glimpse of it for even a moment or two, and then the veil returns, he is a yearning taster (*al-dhāʾiq al-mushtāq*); and if for an hour or two, he is a true drinker (*al-shārib ḥaqqan*). If he is overwhelmed by the vision, and his drinking lasts until his veins and sinews are replete with the treasure of God's light, then he is one whose thirst is quenched. And it may happen that he loses his senses and does not know what is said to him or what he says, and that is what is called drunkenness (*sukr*). Then after many cups are passed among them, and many spiritual states befall them, they are brought back to invocation and worship and are not veiled from the divine attributes even if the exigencies of worldly life crowd upon them. This is the time of their sobriety when their view grows ever vaster, and their knowledge increases. The stars of doctrine and moon of oneness guide them through their nights; the suns of gnosis light their days. *They are the party of God. Is not the party of God the successful ones?* (58:22).

Sharḥ ṣalāt al-quṭb ibn Mashīsh, pp. 109–112.

20. Transformation and Stability

In his spiritual allusion on Q. 5:3—*This day I have perfected for you your religion and completed My grace upon you, and have chosen for you Islam as your religion*—he wrote:

When the aspirant attains to the mysteries of divine oneness (*tawḥīd*), and plunges into the oceans of divine uniqueness (*tafrīd*), and tastes the sweetness of spiritual meanings, and passes away from a perception limited to sensory forms, and is then granted deep-rootedness and stability in all this, the devil and anything else that would block his path despair of [making him fall], and he ceases to fear anyone except God or rely upon anything other than God, and is largely safe from being turned back in the way except by an overwhelming command: *And God was overwhelming in his life* (12:21). Thus, one of them has said, "By God, no one who has ever turned back has turned back from anything except having traveled the path. Those who arrive do not turn back."

And arrival means reaching stability and permanence in all that we have mentioned above. If [the traveler] attains to complete gnosis, and comes to stand firmly upon the knowledge of gnostic truths, his religion is perfected, his life is set aright, his lights appear, his innermost secrets are confirmed, and there remains only an ascent through ever greater mysteries, ceaselessly and forever. The journey through the spiritual stations thus becomes like the journey of the sun through its stages. He is transported from station to station in accordance with what emerges from the element of divine power. At times there will emerge what requires fear, at times what requires hope, at times what requires contentment and peace, and at times what requires complete trust in God. Thus is he transformed with every station, maintains what is due it, and ceases to stop at any one station or at any one state, for he is then truly God's vicegerent upon earth, and God most high has said, *Every day He is in some task* (55:29).

This is the meaning of transformation after stability, and God most high knows better.

al-Baḥr al-madīd, vol. 2, p. 8.

Appendix III: Biographical Listings

Biographical index of persons, excluding prophets, mentioned in the text of *Miʿrāj al-tashawwuf* or in appendices I or II. Numbers refer to item numbers. The *ṣaḥāba* are the Companions who saw the Prophet; *tābiʿī* are the Followers, those of the next generation who met the *ṣaḥāba*; a *muḥaddith* is a narrator or collector of *ḥadīth*; a *mufassir* is a commentator on the Qurʾān.

Abū Bakr al-Ṣiddīq b. Abī Quhāfa al-Taymī (d. 13/634)—73. Among the greatest of the *ṣaḥāba* and the first of the rightly-guided caliphs. Upon assuming his role as caliph, he is reported to have said to the people, "I have been made your leader, though I am not the best of you. If I do what is right, help me. If I err, set me straight (*in aḥsantu, faʿīnūnī, wa in asaʾtu, fa qawwamūnī*)." His reign lasted just over two years before he succumbed to an illness. His tomb is next to that of the Prophet and ʿUmar b. al-Khaṭṭāb in Medina.

Abū l-Mawāhib, Abū Ḥāmid Abū ʿAbdallāh (d. c. 850/1446)—54. Egyptian Sufi of the Shādhilī lineage noted for his visions and states of intoxication. He is reputedly the author of *Qawānīn ḥikm al-ishrāqī fī qawāʾid al-ṣūfiyya ʿalā l-iṭlāq*, a book presenting fundamental notions of Sufism in the form of maxims, translated into English as *Illumination in Islamic Mysticism*. His tomb is in Cairo.

Abū Ḥāzim, Salma b. Dīnār al-Madanī l-Aʿraj (d. c. 135/752)—II:5. *Tābiʿī, muḥaddith*, scholar, known for his asceticism and virtue. He is quoted in scores of *ḥadīth* in Bukhārī and Muslim and his sayings on living a virtuous life are quoted extensively in the *Ḥilyat al-awliyāʾ*.

Abū Yaʿzā Yallanūr (sometimes rendered Abū Yiʿzzā Yalannūr) (d. 572/1177)—II:2. Known in Morocco to this day as Moulay Bouʿazza, he was the near-legendary illiterate Berber Sufi who was one of the teachers of Abū Madyan. It is said that he spent years of his youth wandering the mountainous regions of Morocco living off wild plants. His tomb is on the site of the *zāwiya* he built in the Middle Atlas Mountains near the town of Azrou.

al-ʿAjamī, Abū Muḥammad al-Baṣrī (d. c. 140/757)—II:13. One of the earliest Baghdad Sufis who is said to have received the teachings of Sufism from Ḥasan al-Baṣrī and who taught, in turn, Dāwūd al-Ṭāʾī.

ʿAlī b. Abī Ṭālib (d. 40/661)—53. Among the greatest of the *ṣaḥāba*, he was the cousin and later son-in-law of the Prophet through his marriage to Fāṭima. He was also the first male to accept Islam, the fourth caliph, and (according to Shīʿī doctrine), the first Imam. ʿAlī (and Fāṭima) became the model of austerity, piety, and chivalry (*al-futūwa*).

al-ʿAmrānī, ʿAlī b. ʿAbd al-Raḥmān b. Muḥammad (d. 1193/1779)—70. Known in Morocco as Sidi ʿAlī l-Jamal ("The Camel") because of an incident that happened in his youth when he lifted a young camel out of a public road in Fes. He was the spiritual master of Mulay al-ʿArabī l-Darqāwī, who was in turn the master of Ibn ʿAjība's shaykh, Muḥammad al-Buzīdī. Sīdī ʿAlī authored one work, a collection of insights into the way called *Naṣīḥa al-murīd fī ṭarīq ahl al-sulūk wa-l-tajrīd* (see bibliography). Another Moroccan Sufic master, Sīdī ʿAbd al-Wāḥid al-Debbāgh, said concerning him, "No one knows Sīdī ʿAlī l-Jamal except the one who is Sīdī ʿAlī l-Jamal!"

al-Anṣārī, Abū Ismāʿīl b. Abī Manṣūr Muḥammad ʿAbdallāh al-Hararī (d. 481/1089)—I:5. One of the greatest of the Sufis of Khurasan, he lived and died in Herat, Afghanistan, followed the Ḥanbalī school, and authored several works in Persian and Arabic, including his *Munājāt* (published in English as *Intimate Conversations*) and *Manāzil al-sāʾirīn* (The abodes of the wayfarers), upon which Ibn Qayyim al-Jawziyya based his well-known and voluminous commentary, *Madārij al-sālikīn*. His tomb is just outside of Herat.

Baqlī, Rūzbihān b. Abī l-Naṣr al-Faswī l-Shīrāzī l-Gāzrūnī (d. 606/1209)—II:17. A Persian Sufi, *muḥaddith*, scholar and author of several unique works, including an esoteric commentary on the Qurʾān, *ʿArāʾis al-bayān fī ḥaqāʾiq al-Qurʾān* from which Ibn ʿAjība quotes extensively throughout his own Qurʾānic commentary, *al-Baḥr al-madīd*, mistakenly referring to its author as "al-Wartajibī," possibly the name of a scribe who copied the manuscripts of this *tafsīr* that were available in Morocco in Ibn ʿAjība's time. Only parts of this *tafsīr* still exist.

al-Būzīdī, Muḥammad b. Aḥmad al-Slimānī l-Ghomāri (d. 1229/1813)—60. Sufi shaykh. He was born and raised in the village of Benslimān, in the Ghomāra region of Morocco near Tetouan. After some years of spiritual wandering around Morocco, he met and became of the disciple of Mulay al-ʿArabī l-Darqāwī (see below) and was eventually put in direct charge of Ibn ʿAjība's training in the path. During his life, Mulay al-ʿArabī designated al-Būzīdī as his successor, but the latter's death pre-dated his shaykh's by ten years. His tomb is in Tijīsas, Ghomāra, not far from Tetouan.

al-Daqqāq, Abū ʿAlī (d. c. 412/1021)—30, 41, 44, 56, 60, 73. One of the renowned Khurasanī Sufis and an Ashʿarī theologian, he was both father-in-law and shaykh of al-Qushayrī (see below).

al-Darqāwī, Abū ʿAbdallāh Muḥammad al-ʿArabī (d. 1238/1823)—60; II:5. Sufi shaykh. Founder of the *ṭarīqa* al-Shādhiliyya al-Darqāwiyya which continues to exist in Morocco and elsewhere. He is also the author of a collection of letters pertaining to the spiritual path which has been translated partially into English and in their entirety into French (see bibliography). His tomb and original *zāwiya* are in the Banī Zarwāl region of the Rif Mountains in northern Morocco.

Dāwūd al-Ṭāʾī b. Nuṣayr Abū Sulaymān (d. 165/781–2)—II:13. One of the earliest of the Baghdad Sufis. He is said to have been one of the first to receive the teachings of Sufism. He is reputed to be among those who buried his books, presumably out of fear that they contained misinformation or what might be misunderstood. He is buried in Kufa.

Dhū l-Nūn al-Miṣrī, Thawbān (d. 245/860)—I:4. Born in Upper Egypt, he was one of the most renowned of the early Sufis and reputedly the first to systematize the *maqāmāt*, the stations of the spiritual path. His tomb is in Cairo.

al-Fuḍayl b. ʿIyyād (d. 187/803)—II:2. As a youth he had been a thief and is said to have repented while he was climbing a wall in order to get into a house and heard someone reciting the verse *Is it not time for the hearts of the faithful to grow humble at the remembrance of God?* He became, thereafter, one of the greatest of the early Sufis, studying *ḥadīth* with Abū Ḥanīfa.

al-Ghazālī, Abū Ḥamīd Muḥammad b. Muḥammad (449–504/1058–1111)—46. Sufi, scholar, prolific author and known as *Ḥujjat al-islām* ("The Proof of Islam"). He was born and died in Ṭūs, in Khurasan. After an illustrious career as teacher and lecturer, he renounced his position around the age of forty and took up the life of a wandering dervish. The fruits of both his scholarship and efforts in the spiritual path form the basis of his most famous work, *Iḥyāʾ ʿulūm al-dīn* (The revival of the religious sciences). His works are said to have influenced St. Thomas Aquinas and numerous other western philosophers.

Ḥanẓala b. Rabīʿa al-Usayyidī l-Tamīmī (d. c. 52/672)—73. *Ṣaḥāba* and among those who recorded the revelation of the Qurʾān in writing for the Prophet. He is principally remembered for the *ḥadīth* quoted by Ibn ʿAjība.

al-Ḥasan al-Baṣrī (d. 110/728–9)—8; I:1; II:13. *Tābiʿī* and also considered one of the earliest Sufis. He was born in Medina the son of a slave who had been freed by Zayd b. Thābit, one of the scribes of the Prophet. After taking part in the conquest of eastern Iran, he moved to Basra, where he spent the remainder of his life teaching to great multitudes. His tomb is found in that city.

Ibn Adham, Abū Isḥāq Ibrāhīm (d. c. 161/777)—28; II:2; II:10. He is reputed to have started life as a member of royalty (acccording to some, a king) in Balkh (in present-day northwest Afghanistan). After a transformative spiritual experience, he renounced his former life and lived as a wandering ascetic. During his life he kept company with Sufyān al-Thawrī and Fuḍayl b. ʿIyyād. His tomb is in the town of Jabala in Syria.

Ibn al-Aʿrābī, Abū Saʿīd (d. c. 340/952)—54. *Muḥaddith* and linguist. Originally from Basra, he figures in the chains of *ḥadīth* transmission in the *Sunan* of Abū Dāwūd, Bayhaqī's *Shuʿab al-īmān*, and others. He died in Mecca.

Ibn ʿAṭāʾ, Abū l-ʿAbbās (d. c. 309/921 or 311/923)—30. One of the Baghdad Sufis contempory to al-Junayd and among those who became embroiled in the controversy surrounding al-Ḥallāj. When Ibn ʿAṭāʾ was summoned before the vizier Ḥamid b. al-ʿAbbās, his defense of al-Ḥallāj and condemnation of the vizier's policies led to his execution.

Ibn al-Bannāʾ, Abū l-ʿAbbās Aḥmad b. Muḥammad b. Yūsuf al-Tujībī l-Sarqusṭī (d. ca. 850/1446)—48. A Moroccan Sufi and scholar who figures in the Shādhilī lineage and is known principally for his poem on the fundamentals of Sufism, *al-Mubāḥith al-aṣliyya*, upon which Ibn ʿAjība wrote his commentary, *al-Futūḥāt al-ilāhiyya*. Although he is referred to as Ibn al-Bannāʾ, he should not be confused with the famous mathematician and astonomer by that name who is buried in the city of Marrakesh. The tomb of Ibn al-Bannāʾ al-Sarqusṭī is in Fes.

Ibn al-Fāriḍ, ʿUmar b. ʿAlī (576–632/1181–1235)—53, 70, 76, 79; II:19. The renown Egyptian Sufi poet known as *sulṭān al-ʿāshiqīn* ("the sultan of the lovers") of God. His father gained the name al-Fāriḍ as a religious judge who specialized in rulings in inheritance cases (*al-furūḍ*). ʿUmar grew up in Cairo and studied traditional knowledge, then turned toward the Sufi path. A visionary experience led him to Mecca where he spent a considerable length of time in a valley not far from the city and where, it is said, much of his poetry was written in an ecstatic state. After fifteen years in the Hijaz, he returned to Egypt where he gained considerable fame as well as numerous detractors.

Ibn Mashīsh, ʿAbd al-Salām (d. c. 565/1355)—54, 58, 76. He was the near-legendary spiritual master of Abū l-Ḥasan al-Shādhilī. What is known of his teachings arises from the sayings recorded in the early books of the Shādhiliyya order, notably *Laṭāʾif al-minan*. He is reputed to be the author of a famous prayer of blessing upon the Prophet although there is no direct evidence of this in those books. His tomb atop Jabal ʿAlam in the Rif Mountains of northern Morocco is one of the most venerated shrines in the country.

Ibn Sīnā, Abū ʿAlī (known in the west as Avicenna) (d. 428/1037)—II:1. Persian philosopher, scientistic, doctor, and mystic born in Central Asia. He is famous for his *Qānūn fī l-ṭibb* (Canon in medicine), an encyclopedia of practically everything known about medicine from both Islamic and Greek sources.

al-Jilānī, Muḥyī l-Dīn Abū Muḥammad ʿAbd al-Qadir (d. 561/1166)—57. After studying Ḥanbalī law in Baghdad, he became the disciple of Abū l-Khayr al-Dabbās and lived for years in seclusion. In 521/1127, however, he began to preach. It is said that his sermons drew such crowds in Baghdad that it was difficult to find venues large enough. Several treatises on the Sufic path bear his name, including *Fatḥ al-ghayb*, *al-Ghunya li ṭālib ṭarīq al-ḥaqq*, and others. The Qadiriyya *ṭarīqa*, found all over the Muslim world, traces its beginnings to him. His tomb is in Baghdad.

al-Junayd, Abū l-Qāsim b. Muḥammad (d. 277/910) 1, 8, 29, 44, 45, 49, 60, 64; I:3; I:4; II:13. His family origins were Persian although he was born in Baghdad and is possibly the most famous of the Baghdad Sufis. He kept company with his uncle Sarī l-Saqaṭī (see below), al-Ḥārith al-Muḥāsibī, and ʿAlī l-Qaṣāb among many.

al-Jurayrī, Abū Muḥammad (d. 311/923–24)—60. He was originally a disciple of Sahl al-Tustarī in Basra, but upon the death of his shaykh, he traveled to Baghdad, studied with al-Junayd, and, according to some views, became al-Junayd's successor as the principle Sufic master of Baghdad after the latter's death.

al-Kalābādhī, Abū Bakr b. Abī Isḥāq Muḥammad b. Ibrāhīm b. Yaʿqūb al-Bukhārī (d. c. 380/990), I:4. He is principally remembered as the author of *Kitāb al-taʿarrūf*, one of the earliest works on the Sufi path and its practioners. His tomb is in Bukhara in present-day Uzbekistan.

al-Kattānī, Abū Bakr Muḥammad b. ʿAlī b. Jaʿfar (d. 322/934)—36. Originally among the Baghdad Sufis, he studied with al-Junayd, al-Kharrāz, and al-Nūrī and then traveled to Mecca where he is buried.

al-Kharrāz, Aḥmad b. ʿĪsā Abū Saʿīd (d. 277/890)—I:1. One of the Baghdad Sufis. He was a companion of Dhū l-Nūn al-Miṣrī and Bishr al-Khāfī, disciple of Sarī l-Saqaṭī and one of the teachers of al-Junayd. He is especially remembered as the author of *The Book of Sincerity* (*Kitāb al-ṣidq*), one of the earliest works on Sufi doctrine and practice. Among his many quoted sayings, "The saying 'No!' is not in the character of a believer, for when he regards the generosity that exists between him and his Lord, he is embarrassed to say 'No' to anyone."

al-Khuldī, Jaʿfar b. Muḥammad b. Nuṣayr (d. 348/959)—39. He was among the Baghdad Sufis in the circle of Ruwaym, al-Junayd, al-Nūrī, and Sufyān al-Thawrī. His aphorisms appear in many of the later books on Sufism. He is buried in Baghdad.

al-Mahdāwī, ʿAbd al-ʿAzīz (d. 621/1224)—II:6. A Tunisian Sufi. Little is known about him except that he was a student of Abū Madyan and one of the principle teachers of Ibn ʿArabī, who mentions him in the introduction to *al-Futūḥāt al-Makkiyya* as one of those for whom the book was written. He is buried in the city of Tunis.

al-Maghāzilī, Ḥusayn (d. ?)—I:4. A Baghdad Sufi contemporary with Bishr al-Ḥāfī.

al-Majdhūb, ʿAbd al-Raḥmān b. ʿIyyād b. Yaʿqūb b. Salāma al-Ṣinhājī (976/1568)—42. He was born in Azemmour on the Atlantic coast of Morocco during the early years of the Saadi dynasty but traveled to Meknes where he lived most of his life and is buried. He is known throughout Morocco as the author of a small book of poetry written in Moroccan Arabic and containing popular wisdom, an attribution which may or may not be correct. His lines of mystical poetry, however, are quoted extensively both in the letters of the Shaykh al-Darqāwī and by Ibn ʿAjība.

Maʿrūf al-Karkhī, Abū Maḥfūẓ b. Fayrūz (d. 200/815)—II:13. One of the earliest Baghdad Sufis, known for his life of asceticism. His father was probably Persian and he himself was born either a Zoroastrian or Christian and then converted to Islam in his youth with ʿAlī b. Mūsā l-Riḍā, considered the eighth imam by Shīʿī Muslims. Maʿrūf studied with Dāwud al-Ṭāʾī and figures among the teachers of Sarī l-Saqaṭī. He spoke extensively on the love of God and many Sufic orders trace their lineage back through him. He is buried in Baghdad.

al-Mursī, Aḥmad b. ʿUmar al-Anṣārī Abū l-ʿAbbās (d. 686/1286)—8, 79; II:9. Sufi, Malikī scholar and successor of Abū l-Ḥasan al-Shādhilī as the shaykh of the Shādhiliyya order. As his name indicates, he was born in Murcia, in Andalus, and then traveled to Alexandria where he became a disciple of al-Shādhilī. Most of what is known concerning his teachings comes from the *Laṭāʾif al-minan* by Ibn ʿAṭāʾ Allāh, his student and successor.

al-Nūrī, Abū l-Ḥusayn Aḥmad b. Muḥammad (d. 295/908)—64; I:3; I:4. One of the renowned Baghdad Sufis, a contemporary of al-Junayd and student of Sarī l-Saqaṭī. He was the author of one of the earliest treatises on Sufism, *Maqāmāt al-qulūb* (The stations of hearts), a work often attributed to al-Ḥakīm al-Tirmidhī.

al-Qushayrī, Abū l-Qāsim ʿAbd al-Karīm b. Hawāzin, al-Nisapūrī (376–465/986–1072)—60, 61, 64, 73, 75; II:2. Sufi, scholar, *mufassir*, known as the master of Khurasan of his age. Ascetic, and learned in all the religious sciences, he lived his whole life in Nishapur and died there. His best known works are his treatise on Sufism, *al-Risāla*, which has been published many times in Arabic, and his Qurʾānic commentary, *Laṭāʾif al-ishāra*.

Rābiʿa al-ʿAdawiyya (d. 185/801)—II:7. The most famous woman Sufi saint in Islamic history and one of the Basra mystics. She associated with and taught Ḥasan al-Baṣrī, Mālik b. Dīnār, and Shaqīq al-Balkhī. Both her mystical poetry and devotions place the love of God above all else.

Ruwaym b. Aḥmad, Abū Muḥammad (d. 303/915)—I:3; I:4. One of the Baghdad Sufis, a teacher of the Qurʾān, and companion of al-Junayd. He left no writings but his sayings are quoted extensively in the early books of the Sufis.

al-Sāḥilī, Muḥammad b. Ibrāhīm al-Anṣārī (d. 754/1353)—45. Sufi and scholar. He was born in Andalus, in the coastal town of Malaga where he eventually became the Friday preacher of the city's largest mosque. He traveled both to Morocco and the east and later returned to Malaga where he died. He is the author of a number of treatises including *Baghīyat al-sālik fī ashrafi al-masālik* and *al-Nafḥa al-qudsiyya*.

Sahl b. ʿAbdallāh (see al-Tustarī)

Sarī l-Saqaṭī, Abū l-Ḥasan (d. /253/867)—II:10; II:13. One of the Baghdad Sufis. He is reputed to have received the fundamental teachings of Sufism from Maʿrūf al-Karkhī, eventually becoming the teacher of many important Sufis, including al-Junayd and al-Kharrāz. None of his writings are extant, but are known from many quotations in the books of the Sufis; he downplayed the role of asceticism as a mode of living, emphasizing instead the love of God and neighbor.

al-Sarrāj, Abū Naṣr ʿAbdallāh b. ʿAlī (378/988)—II:3. He was a native of Ṭūs, near present-day Mashhad in Iran, which is where he is buried. He is known principally as the author of *Kitāb al-lumaʿ* (The book of flashes), one of the earliest lexicons of Sufism. Judging from the meetings with Sufis recorded in it, he must have traveled to

Basra, Baghdad, Damascus, Cairo, Tustar, Tabriz, and other centers of learning. He is considered one of the shaykhs of ʿAbd al-Raḥmān al-Sulamī.

al-Shādhilī, Abū l-Ḥasan ʿAlī b. ʿAbdallāh (591–656/1195–1258)—79; II:12; II:19. The founder of the Sufic order which bears his name. He was born in the Ghomāra region of Morocco near Chefchaouen and studied in Fes. After a discipleship with Mulay ʿAbd al-Salām b. Mashīsh atop Jabal ʿAlam in the Rif Mountains of Morocco, he took his spiritual teachings first to Tunisia and then Egypt, where he spent the rest of his life. He died en route to one of the several pilgrimages he made during his life and was buried on the old pilgrims' route, near the Red Sea.

al-Shushtarī, Abū l-Ḥasan (d. 668/1269)—57, 68, 76; II:19. Sufi poet. He was born in Grenada, according to some into royal lineage. He eventually came under the influence of the esoteric doctrines of Ibn Sabʿīn and taught these in Meknes. Toward the end of his life, he traveled to Egypt and died there. His tomb is in Damietta (near Alexandria), Egypt.

al-Sūsī, Abū Yaʿqūb Yūsuf b. Ḥamdān (d. c. 280/893)—I:3. A contemporary of al-Junayd whose sayings appear in nearly all the classic works of Sufism.

al-Thawrī, Sufyān b. Saʿīd b. Masrūq (d. 161/778)—2. *Tābiʿi*, *ḥāfiẓ*, scholar, and founder of the Thawrī *madhhab*. He figures in the chains of transmissions of *ḥadīth* in all of the six principle collections and a *tafsīr* of the Qurʾān bearing his name exists to this day.

al-Tirmidhī, Abū ʿAbdallāh Muḥammad b. ʿAlī l-Ḥakīm (d. c. 295–300/905–910)—II:2. Originally from Tirmidh on the right bank of the Oxus River in what is now Uzbekistan, he was the son of the famous *muḥaddith* ʿAbī b. al-Ḥasan. He was accused of heretical views at one point in his youth but was eventually exonerated. His prolific writings influenced many mystics who came after him. The best known include *Nawādir al-uṣūl* (The rarest of sources) a collection of *ḥadīth* organized around 257 fundamental questions, or "sources" (*uṣūl*), *Khatim al-awliyāʾ* (also known as *Ṣirāṭ al-awliyāʾ*), and *Kitāb manāzil al-ʿubbād min al-ʿibāda*. His tomb is in Tirmidh.

al-Tustarī, Sahl b. ʿAbdallāh (200–283/815–896)—1; I:3; I:4; II:1. One of the early Sufis. He was born in Tustar, in Khurasan. For a time, he was one of al-Ḥallāj's teachers and the latter accompanied him to Basra where he spent most of his life. Al-Tustarī's doctrine, however, was probably better represented by his student Ibn Sālim (d. 296/909) founder of the Sālimiyya school to which Abū Ṭālib al-Makkī, the author of *Qūt al-qulūb*, belonged. A mystical commentary on parts of the Qurʾān is attributed to al-Tustarī.

al-ʿUqaylī, Laqīṭ b. ʿĀmr b. Ṣabra Abū Razayn (d. ?)—53. *Ṣaḥāba*. He figures in the transmission of scores of *ḥadīth*.

Wahb b. Munabbih b. Kāmil (d. 110/728–9)—31, 37. *Ṭābiʿī*, originally from Yemen, possibly of Persian descent. He is the source of a number of narratives of Jewish origin that appear in many books of Qurʾānic commentary.

al-Wāsiṭī, Muḥammad b. Mūsā (d. 331/942)—36, 40. One of the greatest of the early Sufis, and foremost of the followers of al-Junayd. He was born in Farghana (in present-day Turkistan) and journeyed to Khurasan where he spent the remainder of his life. Shaʿrānī said of him, "No one has spoken as he has about the principles of Sufism." Among his sayings: "We are tried by living in an age in which there is neither the manners (*adab*) of Islam, nor the virtues of the Jāhiliyya, nor the dreams of the chivalrous."

Bibliography

Manuscripts

Ibn ʿAjība, Aḥmad. *Miʿrāj al-tashawwuf ilā ḥaqāʾiq al-taṣawwuf*. Rabat: Municipal Library, ref. 1974 d, dated 1305.

———. *Miʿrāj al-tashawwuf ilā ḥaqāʾiq al-taṣawwuf*. Rabat: Royal Library, ref. 12433, n.d.

Works in Arabic

Abū Dāwūd, Sulaymān b. al-Ashʿath al-Sijistānī. *Sunan*. Riyadh: Bayt al-Afkār al-Dawliyya, n.d.

Abū Nuʿaym al-Iṣfahānī. *Ḥilyat al-awliyāʾ wa ṭabaqāt al-aṣfiyāʾ*. Beirut: Dār al-Kutub al-ʿIlmiyya, 1997.

ʿAmrānī, ʿAlī b. ʿAbd al-Raḥmān b. Muḥammad al-. *Naṣīḥat al-murīd fī ṭarīq ahli al-sulūk wa-l-tajrīd, aw al-yawāqīt al-ḥisān fī taṣrīf maʿānī l-insān*. Beirut: Dār al-Kutub al-ʿIlmiyya, 2005.

Bayhaqī, Aḥmad b. al-Ḥusayn al-. *Dalāʾil al-nubuwwa*. Beirut: Dār al-Kutub al-ʿIlmiyya, 1984.

———. *Shuʿab al-īmān*. Beirut: Dār al-Kutub al-ʿIlmiyya, 1990.

Bukhārī, Muḥammad b. Ismāʿīl al-. *al-Jāmiʿ al-ṣaḥīḥ*. Jeddah: Dār al-Minhāj, 1422/2001.

Darqāwī, Mulay al-ʿArabī al-. *Majmūʿa rasāʾil*. Edited by Muḥammad Bassām Bārūd. Abu Dhabi: Cultural Foundation Publications, 1999.

Daylamī, Abū Shujāʿ Shīrawayh b. Shīrawayh al-. *al-Firdaws bī athūr al-khiṭāb*. Beirut: Dār al-Kutub al-ʿIlmiyya, 1986.

Ghazālī, Abū Ḥāmid Muḥammad b. Muḥammad al-. *Iḥyāʾ ʿulūm al-dīn*. Samarang: Maktaba Keriyata, n.d.

———. *Maʿārij al-quds fī madārij maʿrifat al-nafs*. Beirut: Dār al-Kutub al-ʿIlmiyya, 1988.

———. *Miʿrāj al-sālikīn* (in *Majmuʿat al-rasāʾil al-Imām al-Ghazālī*). Cairo: al-Maktabat al-Tawfiqiyya, n.d.

Harawī, Abū Ismāʿīl ʿAbdallāh b. Muḥammad al-Anṣārī al-. *Manāzil al-sāʾirīn*. Cairo: Muṭbaʿa Muṣṭafā al-Bābī l-Ḥalabī, 1966.

Ibn ʿAbbād, Abū ʿAbdallāh Muḥammad b. Ibrāhīm. *Ghayth al-mawāhib al-ʿaliyya fī sharḥ al-ḥikam al-ʿaṭāʾiyya*. Edited by ʿAbd al-Ḥalīm Maḥmūd. Cairo: Dār al-Maʿārif, 1993.

———. *Rasāʾil al-kubrā*. Edited by Kenneth Honerkamp. Beirut: Dār al-Machreq, 2005.

Ibn ʿAjība, Aḥmad. *al-Baḥr al-madīd fī tafsīr al-Qurʾān al-majīd*. Cairo: Ḥassan ʿAbbās Zakkī, 1999–2001.

———. *al-Fahrasa*. Cairo: Dār al-Ghadd al-ʿArabī, 1990.

———. *Futūḥāt al-ilāhiyya fī sharḥ mabāḥith al-aṣliyya*. Beirut: Dār al-Kutub al-ʿIlmiyya, 2000.

———. *Īqāẓ al-himam fī sharḥ al-Ḥikam*. Beirut: Dār al-Kutub al-ʿIlmiyya, 1996.

———. *Kitāb sharḥ ṣalāt al-quṭb ibn Mashīsh*. Edited by ʿAbd al-Salām al-ʿUmrānī. Casablanca: Dār al-Rashād, 1999.

———. *Miʿrāj al-tashawwuf ilā ḥaqāʾiq al-taṣawwuf*. Tetouan: Muṭabʿa al-Marīnī, 1982.

———. *Miʿrāj al-tashawwuf ilā ḥaqāʾiq al-taṣawwuf*. Cairo: Maktab Umm-al-Qurā, 2002.

———. *Miʿrāj al-tashawwuf ilā ḥaqāʾiq al-taṣawwuf*. Edited by ʿAbd al-Majīd Khiyyālī. Casablanca: Markaz al-Turāth li Thaqāfī l-Maghribī, 2004.

Ibn ʿArabī, Muḥyī l-Dīn. *al-Futūḥāt al-makkiyya*. Cairo: Dār al-Kutub al-ʿArabiyya al-Kubra, 1911/1329.

———. *al-Isrāʾ ilā al-maqām al-asrā aw kitāb al-miʿrāj*. Beirut: Dandara li al-Ṭibāʿat wa-l-Nashr, 1988.

Ibn ʿAṭāʾ Allāh, Abū l-Faḍl Aḥmad b. Muḥammad. *Kitāb al-ḥikam* (lithograph). Morocco, n.d.

———. *Laṭāʾif al-minan*. Cairo: Dār al-Maʿārif, 1992.

———. *al-Tanwīr fī isqāt al-tadbīr*. Cairo: ʿAlam al-Fikr, 1998.

Ibn al-Athīr, Muḥammad al-Jazrī. *Jāmiʿ al-uṣūl fī aḥādith al-Rasūl*. Edited by ʿAbd al-Qādir al-Arnāʾūṭ. Beirut: Dār al-Fikr, 1985.

Ibn Qayyim al-Jawziyya, Muḥammad b. Abī Bakr. *Madārij al-sālikīn*. Edited by Ḥassān ʿAbd al-Mannān al-Tībī and ʿAṣam Fāris al-Hurstānā. Beirut: Dār al-Jīl, 1994.

Ibn Qunfudh, Ibn al-Qusanṭībī Abū l-ʿAbbās Aḥmad b. al-Ḥusayn. *Uns al-faqīr wa ʿizz al-ḥaqīr*. Edited by Abū Sahl Najāḥ al-ʿAwḍ. Cairo: Dār al-Muqṭam, 2002.

Jurjānī, ʿAlī b. Muḥammad al-Sharīf. *Kitāb al-taʿrifāt*. Beirut: Maktaba Lubnān, 1985.

Kāshānī, ʿAbd al-Razzāq al-. *Iṣṭilāḥāt al-ṣūfiyya*. Edited by ʿAbd al-ʿĀli al-Shāhīn. Cairo: Dār al-Manār, 1992.

Kharrāz, Abū Saʿīd. *Kitāb al-ṣidq*. Published as *Ṭarīq ilā Allāh*. Edited by ʿAbd al-Ḥalīm Maḥmūd. Cairo: Dār al-Maʿārif, 1988.

Makkī, Abū Ṭālib. *Qūt al-qulūb*. Beirut: Dār al-Kutub al-ʿIlmiyya, 1997.

Muslim, Abū l-Ḥusayn b. al-Ḥujāj al-. *al-Musnad al-ṣaḥīḥ al-mukhtaṣar min al-sunan*. Riyadh: Dār al-Ṭayba, 1427/2006.

Qushayrī, Abū l-Qasim al-. *al-Risālat al-qushayriyya*. Edited by ʿAbd al-Ḥalīm Maḥmūd. Cairo: Dār al-Maʿārif, 1995.

———. *al-Risālat al-qushayriyya fī ʿilm al-taṣawwuf*. Edited by Maʿrūf Muṣtafā Zarīq. Beirut: al-Maktaba al-ʿAṣriyya, 2001.

Suyūṭī, Jalāl al-Dīn al. *al-Durr al-manthūr fī tafsīr bi-l-mā'thūr*. Cairo: Markaz Hajar, 2003.

Ṭabarānī, al-Ḥāfiẓ al-. *al-Muʿjam al-awsaṭ*. Edited by Muḥammad al-Ṭaḥḥān. Riyadh: Maktaba al-Maʿarif li'l-Nashr wa-l-Tawzīʿ, 1995/1316.

———. *al-Muʿjam al-kabīr*. Mosul: Maktaba l-ʿUlūm wa-l-Ḥikam, 1983.

Tādilī, Abū Yaʿqūb Yūsuf b. Yaḥyā al-. *al-Tashawwuf ilā rijāl al-taṣawwuf*, Edited by Ahmed Toufiq. Rabat: Faculté des Lettres et Sciences Humaines, 1984.

Tamīmī, Abū ʿAbdallāh Muḥammad b. Qāsim al-. *al-Mustafād fī manāqib al-ʿubbād bi madīna al-Fās wa mā yalīhā min al-bilād*. Rabat: Maṭbaʿat Ṭūb Barīs, 2002.

Tirmidhī, Muḥammad b. ʿAlī b. al-Ḥusayn Abū ʿAbdallāh al-Ḥakīm al-. *Nawādir al-uṣūl fī aḥādīth al-rasūl*. Beirut: Dār al-Jīl, 1992.

Ziriklī, Khayr al-Dīn al-. *al-Aʿlām*. 11th edition. Beirut: Dār al-ʿIlm li'l-Malāyin, 1995.

Works in English and French

ʿAmrānī, Sidi ʿAlī l-Jamal, al-. *The Meaning of Man: The Foundations of the Science of Knowledge*. Translation into English of *al-Yawāqīt al-ḥisān fī taṣrīf maʿānī l-insān* by Aisha ʿAbd ar-Rahman at-Tarjumana. Norwich: Diwan Press, 1977.

Arberry, A. J. *Arabic Poetry: A Primer for Students*. Cambridge: Cambridge University Press, 1965.

Colby, Frederick S. *Narrating Muḥammad's Night Journey: Tracing the Development of the Ibn ʿAbbās Ascension Discourse*. Albany: State University of New York Press, 2008.

Cornell, Vincent J. *Realm of the Saint: Power and Authority in Moroccan Sufism*. Austin: University of Texas Press, 1989

Darqāwī, Mulay al-ʿArabī. *Lettres sur la Voie spirituelle (du) Shaykh al-ʿArabī, al-Darqāwī*. Translated into French by M. Chabry. Paris: Librarie al-Ghazali, 2003.

Heer, Nicholas, and Kenneth Honerkamp (trans.). *Three Early Sufi Texts*. Louisville, Kentucky: Fons Vitae, 2003.

Ibn ʿAjība, Aḥmad. (*Fahrasa*) *The Autobiography of a Moroccan Soufi*. Translated from the Arabic by Jean-Louis Michon and from the French by David Streight. Louisville, Kentucky: Fons Vitae, 1999.

———. *The Basic Research—Al-Futuhat al Ilahiyya fi Sharh al Mabaahith al-Asliyya*. Translated into English by Abdalkhabir al-Munawwarah and Haj Abdassabur al-Ustadh. Capetown: Madinah Press, 1998.

———. *The Immense Ocean* (*al-Baḥr al-Madīd*). Translated from the Arabic by Mohamed Fouad Aresmouk and Michael Abdurrahman Fitzgerald. Louisville, Kentucky: Fons Vitae, 2009.

Ibn ʿAṭāʾ Allāh, Abū l-Faḍl Aḥmad ibn Muḥammad. *The Book of Wisdom*. Translated into English by Victor Danner. New York: Paulist Press, 1978.

———. *Laṭāʾif al-minan fi Manaqib Abi'l-Abbas al-Mursi wa Shaykhihi Abi'l-Hasan*. Translated into English by Nancy Roberts. Louisville, Kentucky: Fons Vitae, 2005.

Jackson, James Grey. *An Account of the Empire of Marocco*. London: W. Bulmer & Co., 1811.

Jurji, Edward Jabra. *Illumination in Islamic Mysticism*. (Translation into English of Abu'l-Mawāhib al-Shādhili's *Qawānīn Ḥikam al-Ishrāq*). Princeton: Princeton University Press, 1938.

Karamustafa, Ahmed. *Sufism: The Formative Period*. Edinburgh: Edinburgh University Press, 2007.

Kharrāz, Abū Saʿīd. *Kitāb al-ṣidq* (The Book of Truthfulness). Translated into English by A. J. Arberry. London: Oxford University Press, 1937.

Michon, Jean-Louis. *The Autobiography* (*Fahrasa*) *of a Moroccan Soufi: Ahmad ibn ʿAjiba*. Translated by Michael Streight. Louisville, Kentucky: Fons Vitae, 1999.

———. *Le Soufi Marocain Aḥmad ibn ʿAjība et son Miʿrāj. Glossaire de la mystique musulmane*. Paris: Vrin, 1973.

Murad, Abdal Hakim. *The Mantle Adorned. Imam Būsīrī's* Burda. London: Quilliam Press, 2009.

Nwyia, Paul. *Ibn ʿAṭā Allāh et la naissance de la confrérie šāḏilite*. Beirut: Dar al-Machreq, 1990.

Pickthall, Marmaduke (trans.). *The Meaning of the Glorious Koran*. London: Allen & Unwin, 1976.

Qushayri, Abu'l-Qasim. *Al-Qushayri's Epistle on Sufism*. Translated into English by Alexander D. Knysh. Reading: Garnet, 2007.

Renard, John. *Historical Dictionary of Sufism*. Lanham, Maryland: Scarecrow Press, 2005.

———. *Knowledge of God in Classical Sufism*. New York: Paulist Press, 2004.

———. *Seven Doors to Islam: Spirituality and the Religious Life of Muslims.* Berkeley: University of California Press, 1996.

Sands, Kristin Zahra. *Ṣūfī Commentaries on the Qurʾān in Classical Islam.* New York: Routledge, 2006.

Sarrāj, Abū Naṣr ʿAbdallāh b. ʿAlī al-. *The Kitāb al-lumaʿ fi 'l-taṣawwuf.* Translated into English by R. A. Nicholson. London: Brill, 1914.

Schimmel, Annemarie. *Mystical Dimensions of Islam.* Chapel Hill: University of North Carolina Press, 1975.

Smith, Margaret. *Rābiʿa the Mystic and Her Fellow Saints in Islam.* Cambridge: Cambridge University Press, 1924, 1984.

Index of Qurʾānic Verses Cited
Index of *Ḥadīth* Cited
General Index

Index of Qurʾānic Verses Cited

The numbers on the right refer to item numbers either in the main text of the *Miʿrāj* or in appendices I or II.

Index of *Ḥadīth* Cited

The numbers refer to item numbers either in the main text of the *Miʿrāj* or in appendices I or II.

(God most high says) 'I am *Allāh*. There is no god but Me. I created good and evil.' II:18

(God most high says) 'Nothing brings those who seek to approach Me nearer than accomplishing what I have made obligatory upon them. And a servant will continue to approach me by voluntary devotions until I love him, and when I love him, I am his hearing and sight.' 68

(God most high says) 'When I love him, I am he.' 68

General Index

Numbers refer to the number of the term as listed in *al-Miʿrāj*. An asterix * following an item number indicates the principle listing for that item. Listings in appendices I or II are designated by either I: or II: followed by the item number. Proper names of persons mentioned in the main text or appendices (other than Prophets) are listed in appendix III.

tajallī (illumination, epiphany, Self-revelation), 22 15, 23, 29, 36, 45, 48, 54, 56, 57, 64, 69, 70, 71, 74, 76, 79
takhliyya wa taḥliyya (emptying and beautifying), 54
talwīn (change or transformation), 67*, II:20
ṭamaᶜ (covetousness), 8
tamkīn (stability, mastery), 5, 16, 21, 34, 63*, 67, 76, II:1, 20*
al-Tanwīr fī isqāṭ al-tadbīr (Ibn ᶜAṭāᵓ Allāh), 8
al-Ṭarīqat al-Darqāwiyya al-ᶜAjībiyya, xviii
taqwā (piety or reverant fear), 17*, 48
tasdīd (firmness of purpose), 46*
taslīm (submission), 11*
taṭwī (folding up distances), II:9
taᶜūdh (formula of seeking refuge), 44
tawḥid (God's unity), 49*, 50, II:14, 19
ṭawāliᶜ (dawnings), 65*
tawājud (seeking ecstacy), 60*
tawakkul (dependence upon God), 10*, II:5
tawba (repentance), 2, 42, I :1–5, II:2
taᵓyīd (inward help), 46*
Tetouan, xv–xvii, xix
textual proof, 70
"those brought nigh" (*muqarrabūn*), 77*, II:18
traces (*athar*), 70
truthfulness (*ṣidq*), II.1
ṭumaᵓnīna (serenity), 21*, 43, II:13,
turbidity, 1, 73
ᶜubbād wa zuhhād (devotees and ascetics), 21, 64, 73, 78*
ᶜubūda (complete devotion), 30
ᶜubūdiyya (servanthood, servitude), 27, 29, 30*, 56
unity, doctrine of, 45
unlawful. *See ḥaram*

veils of obscurity. *See astār al-khumūl*
vicissitudes (*aghyār*), 25, 66, 67, 73
virtues, 1, 14, 18, 37, 38, 45, 79, I:1, 5

waḥdāniyya (unity), 51*
wajd, wijdān, wujūd (forms of ecstacy), 58, 60*, 70, 75, 76, I:3, II:2
walāya (sanctity), 28*, 40
wālī, awliyāᵓ (friend of God, saintly), 20, 28, 48, 55, 79*, II:2, 3, 9, 18
waqt (moment), 41*, 66, 73
waraᶜ (scrupulousness), 8*, 31, 42: II:5
wāridāt (intimate impressions), 44*, II:15
waswās (whisperings), 44
water, image of, 53, 57, II:1
wijdān, 60*, 70
wine (*khamra*), 71, 76, II:19
wird (litany), xvii
wisdom (divine). *See ḥikma*
womb, 48, 79
wuṣūl (arrival), 10, 13, 25, 27, 74, II:16, 20

yaqīn (certainty), 32, 33*, 34*, 42, II:12

مِعْرَاجُ التَّشَوُّفِ

إلى

حَقَائِقِ التَّصَوُّفِ

بسم الله الرحمن الرحيم

مِعْرَاجُ التَّشَوُّفِ

إِلَى

حَقَائِقِ التَّصَوُّفِ

للشيخ الإمام سيدي أحمد بن عجيبه

(١١٦١-١٢٢٤هـ)

دار فنس فيتى للنشر والترجمة

طبعة دار فنس فيتى الاولى

ترجمة وتدقيق النص العربي

محمد فؤاد أرسموك ومايكل عبدالرحمٰن فتزجرالد

طُبِعَ في ١٤٣٢هـ - ٢٠١١ م

بسم الله الرحمن الرحيم

الحمد لله الّذي حَقَّقَ الحقائِقَ وأوضَحَ الطَّرائِقَ، والصَّلاةُ والسَّلامُ على مولانا محمّدٍ سيِّدِ الخلائقِ، المخصُوصِ بتواتُرِ الْمُعْجِزَاتِ وتظاهُرِ الخَوَارِقِ، ورضي الله تعالى عن أصْحابِه الأعلاَمِ الّذينَ أظهَرَ اللهُ بِهِمْ دِينَهُ القويمَ في أقصَى الْمَغَارِبِ والْمَشَارِقِ.

وبعد: فعِلْمُ التَّصَوُّفِ هو سَيِّدُ العلُومِ ورئِيسُها ولُبابُ الشَّريعةِ وأَسَاسُهَا، وكَيْفَ لاَ، وهوَ تَفْسِيرٌ لِمَقامِ الإحْسَانِ الّذِي هو مقَامُ الشُّهودِ والْعِيَّانِ، كَمَا أنَّ عِلْمَ الكَلاَمِ تفسيرٌ لِمَقَامِ الإيمانِ، وعِلْمُ الفِقْهِ تفسِيرٌ لِمَقامِ الإسلاَمِ. وقد اِشْتَمَلَ حدِيثُ جبريلَ عليه السلام عَلَى تَفسِيرِ الْجَمِيعِ. فإذا تَقَرَّرَ أنَّهُ أفضَلُ العلُومِ، تَبَيَّنَ أنَّ الإشْتِغالَ بهِ أَفضَلُ ما يُتَقَرَّبُ بِهِ إلى اللهِ تعالى لِكَونِهِ سبَباً لِلْمَعرِفةِ الْخَاصَّةِ الّتِي هي معرفَةُ الْعِيَّانِ. وقد اِشْتَمَلَ عَلَى حَقَائِقِ غرِيبَةٍ وعِبَارَاتٍ دَقِيقَةٍ، اِصْطَلَحَ القومُ عَلَى استِعْمالِها.

فيَنْبَغِي الوُقُوف على مَعَانِيها لِمَنْ أرَادَ الْخَوْضَ فِيه والْوُقُوف عَلَى مَعَانِيهِ. وقد أرَدْتُ بِحَوْلِ الله وقُوَّتِه أنْ أجْمَعَ نُبْذَةً صَالِحَةً مِنْ حَقَائِقِ هَذَا الْفَنِّ واصْطِلاَحاتِه لَعَلَّ اللهَ يَنفَعُ من يُرِيدُ الوقُوف عَلَى هَذَا الْعِلْم. وسَمَّيتُهُ: مِعْرَاجَ التَّشَوُّفِ إلَى حَقائِقِ التَّصَوُّفِ. وباللهِ التَّوفِيق وهُوَ الْهَادِي إلَى سَوَاءِ الطَّرِيقِ. وسأذْكُرُ لِكُلِّ حَقِيقَةٍ مَا يَتَعلَّقُ بِهَا بِدَايةً وَوَسَطًا ونِهَايَةً.

١- **التَّصوُّف**: عِلمٌ يُعرَفُ بِهِ كَيفِيَةُ السُّلُوكِ إلَى حَضْرَةِ مَلِكِ الْمُلُوكِ، أَوْ تَصفِيَّةُ الْبَوَاطِنِ مِنَ الرَّذَائِلِ وتَحْلِيَّتُهَا بِأَنْوَاعِ الْفَضَائِلِ، أو غَيْبَةُ الْخَلْقِ فِي شُهُودِ الْحَقِّ، أو مع الرُّجوعِ إلَى الأَثَرِ؛ فَأَوَّلُهُ عِلمٌ ووَسَطُه عَمَلٌ وآخِرُهُ مَوهِبَةٌ. واشْتِقاقُهُ إمّا مِنَ الصَّفَاءِ، لِأَنَّ مَدارَهُ عَلَى التَّصفيَّةِ، أو مِنَ الصِّفَةِ لأنَّهُ اِتِّصافٌ بالْكَمَالاَتِ، أو مِنْ صُفَّةِ الْمَسْجِدِ النَّبَوي لأَنَّهم مُتَشَبِّهُونَ بِأَهْلِ الصُّفَّةِ فِي التَّوَجُّهِ والإنقِطَاعِ، أو مِنَ الصُّوفِ، لأجلِ لِبَاسِهِمْ الصُّوفَ تَقَلُّلاً مِنَ الدُّنيَا وزُهدًا فِيهَا اخْتَارُوا ذَلِكَ لأَنَّهُ كانَ لِبَاسَ الأنبِيَاءِ عَلَيهِم الصَّلاة والسَّلاَم. وهذا الإشتِقَاقُ أَلْيَقُ لُغَةً وأَظْهَرُ نِسْبَةً لِأنَّ لِبَاسَ الصُّوفِ حُكْمٌ ظاهِرٌ عَلَى الظَّاهِرِ ونِسْبَتُهُمْ إلَى غَيْرِهِ أمْرٌ باطِنٌ. والْحُكمُ بالظّاهِرِ أوْفَقُ وأَقْرَبُ: يُقَالُ تَصَوَّفَ إذا لَبِسَ الصُّوفَ كما يُقَالُ تَقَمَّصَ إذا لَبِس القَمِيصَ، والنِّسْبَةُ إليه صُوفِي.

قال سَهْل: « الصُّوفِيُّ مَن صَفِىَ مِنَ الكَدَرِ وامْتِلأَ مِنَ الفِكْرِ وانْقَطَعَ إلى اللهِ مِنَ البَشَرِ، واستوَى عِندَهُ الذَّهَبُ والْمَدَرُ » أَيْ لاَ رَغْبَةَ له فِي شَيءٍ دُون مَوْلاَهُ. وقال الْجُنَيد: « الصُّوفِيُّ كالأَرْضِ يُطْرَحُ عليه كُلُّ قَبِيحٍ

ولا يَخْرُجُ مِنهُ إلاَّ مَلِيحٌ »، وقال أيضاً: « الصُّوفِيُّ كالأَرضِ يَطَأُها البَرُّ والْفَاجِرُ، وكالسَّماءِ يُظِلُّ كُلَّ شَيْءٍ، وكالْمَطَرِ يَسْقِي كُلَّ شيءٍ ».

٢ - **التَّوبَةُ**: الرُّجوعُ عن كُلِّ فِعْلٍ قبيحٍ إلَى كلّ فِعْلٍ مَليحٍ، أو عَنْ كُلِّ وَصْفٍ دَنِيٍّ إلَى التَّحقُّقِ بكُلِّ وَصْفٍ سَنِيٍّ، أو عَنْ شُهُودِ الْخَلْقِ إلى الإستِغْرَاقِ فِي شُهُودِ الْحقِّ. وشُرُوطُهَا النَّدَمُ والإقْلاَعُ ونَفْيُ الإصْرَارِ، وأمَّا رَدُّ الْمَظَالِمِ ففَرْضٌ مُستَقِلٌّ تَصِحُّ بِدُونِه، كَمَا تَصِحُّ مِن ذَنْبٍ مَعَ الإصْرَارِ عَلى آخَرَ مِن غيرِ نَوعِه. فَتَوْبَةُ العامَّةِ من الذُّنوبِ، وتَوْبَةُ الْخَاصَّةِ من العُيُوبِ، وتوبَةُ خاصَّةِ الْخَاصَّة مِن كُلِّ ما يَشْغَلُ السِّرَّ عن حَضْرَةِ عَلاَّمِ الغُيوبِ. وكُلُّ الْمَقاماتِ تَفْتَقِرُ إلى التَّوبةِ، فالتَّوبةُ تَفتَقِرُ إلى توبةٍ أُخرى بِعَدَمِ نَصُوحِها، والْخَوفُ يَفْتَقِرُ إليها بِحُصُولِ الأَمْنِ والإغْتِرَارِ، والرَّجاءُ بِحُصُول القُنُوطِ والإياس، والصَّبْرُ بحصول الْجَزَعِ، والزُّهْدُ بِخَوَاطِرِ الرَّغْبَةِ، والوَرَعُ بِتَتَبُّعِ الرُّخَصِ أو بِخواطر الطَّمع، وَالتَّوَكُّلُ بخواطر التَّدْبِير والإخْتِيار والإهْتِمَام بالرِّزْقِ، والرِّضَى والتَّسْلِيمُ بالكَرَاهِيَّةِ والتَّبَرِّي عند نُزولِ الأقْدار، والْمَرَاقَبَةُ بسُوءِ الأدَبِ في الظَّاهِرِ وخَوَاطِر السُّوء في الباطِنِ، والْمُحاسَبة بتَضْييعِ الأوقاتِ في غير ما يُقَرِّبُ إلى الحقِّ، والْمَحَبَّةُ بِمَيلِ القَلبِ إلى غيرِ الْمَحْبُوبِ، وَالْمُشاهَدَةُ بالْتِفاتِ السِّرّ إلى غَيْرِ الْمَشْهُودِ أو بإشْتِغالِه بالوُقُوفِ مع شيءٍ من الْحِسِّ وعَدَمِ زيادةِ التَّرَقِّي في مَعارِيجِ الأسرار. ولذلك كان عليه الصلاة والسلام يَسْتَغْفِرُ في الْمَجْلِسِ الْوَاحِدِ سَبْعِين مرَّة أو مائة.

والتّوبة النَّصُوحُ يَجْمَعُها أربعةُ أشياء: الإسْتِغْفَارُ باللِّسانِ والإقْلاعُ بالأَبْدَانِ وعَدَمُ الإصْرَارِ بالْجَنَانِ ومُهَاجَرَةُ سَيِّءِ الخِلاَّنِ. وقال سُفيان الثَّوري : « عَلاَمَةُ التَّوبَةِ النَّصُوحِ أربعةٌ: القِلَّةُ والعِلَّةُ والذِّلَّةُ والغُرْبَة ».

٣ – **الإِنَابَةُ**: وهي أَخَصُّ من التَّوبَةِ لأنَّها رُجُوعٌ يَصْحَبُه إِنكِسَارٌ ونُهُوضٌ إلى السَّيرِ. وهي ثلاثُ مرَاتِبَ: رجوعٌ مِن الذَّنب إلى التَّوبة، ومِن الغَفْلَة إلى اليَقَظَةِ، ومِن الفَرْقِ إلى الجَمْعِ على اللهِ.

٤ - **الخَوْف**: انْزِعاجُ القَلْبِ من لُحُوقِ مكروهٍ أو فَوَاتِ مَرغُوبٍ، وثَمَرَتُه النُّهوضُ إلى الطّاعَةِ والْهُرُوبِ من الْمَعْصِيَّةِ. فإظْهَارُ الخَوفِ مع التَّقْصِيرِ دَعْوَى. فخَوفُ العامَّة من العِقابِ وفَوْتِ الثَّوَابِ. وخوفُ الخاصَّةِ من الْعِتَابِ وفَوْتِ الإقتِرَابِ. وخَوفُ خاصَّةِ الْخَاصَّةِ من الإحْتِجَابِ بعُرُوضِ سُوءِ الأَدَبِ.

٥ - **الرَّجاءُ**: سُكُونُ القلْبِ إلى إنتِظَارِ مَحبوبٍ بشَرْطِ السَّعْيِ في أَسْبَابِهِ، وإلاّ فأُمْنِيَّةٌ وغُرورٌ. فرجاء العَامَّةِ حُسْنُ الْمَآبِ بِحُصُولِ الثَّوَابِ. ورجاءُ الْخَاصَّةِ حُصولُ الرِّضْوَانِ والإقتِرَابِ، ورجاءُ خَاصَّةِ الْخَاصَّةِ التَّمْكِينُ من الشُّهودِ وزِيَّادَةُ التَّرَقِّي في أسْرَارِ الْمَلِكِ الْمَعْبُودِ. والخوف والرَّجاءُ لِلْقَلْبِ كجَنَاحَيْ الطَّيْرِ لا يَطِيرُ إلاَّ بِهِمَا ورُبَّمَا يُرَجَّحُ الرجاءُ عندَ الْعارِفِينَ والخوفُ عند الصَّالِحِينَ.

٦ - **الصَّبر**: حَبْسُ القَلْبِ على حُكمِ الرَّبِّ، فصَبْرُ العامّة حَبْسُ القَلْبِ على مَشَاقِّ الطَّاعَاتِ ورفْضُ الْمُخَالَفَاتِ. وصَبْرُ الخاصّة حَبْسُ النَّفْسِ على الرِّياضَاتِ والْمُجاهَدَاتِ وارتِكَابُ الأَهْوَالِ في سُلُوكِ طريقِ الأَحْوَالِ مع مُراقَبَةِ القلْبِ في دَوَامِ الْحُضُورِ وطَلَبُ رفْعِ السُّتُورِ. وصبر خَاصَّةِ الْخَاصَّةِ حَبْسُ الرُّوحِ والسِّرِّ في حضرَةِ الْمُشاهَدَاتِ والمعايَنَاتِ، أو دَوَامُ النَّظْرَةِ والْعُكُوفُ في الْحَضْرَةِ.

٧ - **الشُّكْر**: فَرَحُ الْقَلْبِ بِحُصُولِ النِّعْمَةِ مع صَرْفِ الْجَوَارِحِ في طَاعَةِ الْمُنْعِمِ، والإعْتِرَافُ بنِعمةِ الْمُنْعِمِ على وَجْهِ الْخُضُوعِ. ومَرجِعُهُ لثلاثٍ: شُكرٌ باللسان وهو اعْتِرَافُهُ بالنِّعْمَةِ بِنَعْتِ الإسْتِكَانَةِ، وشُكْرٌ بالبدَنِ وهو اِتِّصَافُهُ بالْخِدْمَةِ، وشكرٌ بالقَلْبِ وهو شُهُودُ الْمُنْعِمِ عند حُصولِ النِّعْمَةِ. ومرجِعُ الْكُلِّ إلى ما قال الْجُنَيد: « أن لاَ يُعْصَى اللهُ بِنِعَمِهِ ». فشُكرُ العامَّةِ الثَّنَاءُ باللِّسَانِ، وشكر الخاصَّةِ الْخِدْمَةُ بالأَرْكَانِ، وشُكْرُ خاصَّةِ الخَاصَّةِ الإِسْتِغْرَاقُ في شهُودِ الْمَنَّانِ.

٨ - **الْوَرَع**: كَفُّ النَّفسِ عنِ ارتِكابِ ما تُكْرَهُ عاقِبَتُهُ. فَوَرَعُ العامَّة تَرْكُ الْحَرَامِ والْمُتَشَابِه، ووَرَعُ الخاصَّةِ ترك كلِّ ما يُكَدِّرُ القَلْبَ ويَجِدُ منهُ كَزَازَةً وظُلمَةً. ويَجْمَعُهُ قولُهُ ﷺ: « دَعْ مَا يَرِيبُكَ إلى مَا لاَ يَرِيبُكَ ». ووَرَعُ خاصَّةِ الخاصَّةِ رَفْضُ التَّعلُّقِ بغيرِ اللهِ، وسَدُّ بابِ الطَّمعِ فِي غيرِ اللهِ، وعُكوفُ الْهَمِّ على اللهِ، وعَدَمُ الركُونِ إلى شَيءٍ سِوَاهُ. وهذا هُوَ الوَرَعُ الَّذي هو مِلاَكُ الدِّينِ كما قال الحَسَن البَصْرِي حين سُئِلَ « ما مِلاكُ

الدِّين؟ » فقال: « الوَرَعُ »، فَقِيلَ له « ومَا فَسادُ الدِّينِ؟ » فقال « الطَّمَعُ ». فالوَرَعُ الّذي يُقابِلُ الطَّمَعَ كُلَّ الْمُقَابَلَةِ هو وَرَعُ خاصَّةِ الخاصّة وجُزْءٌ منه يَعْدِلُ آلافاً مِنَ الصَّلاةِ والصِّيام. ولِذَا قال في التنوير: «ولَيْسَ يَدُلُّ على فَهْمِ العَبدِ كَثْرَةُ عِلمِهِ ولا مُداوَمَتُهُ على وِرْدِهِ وإنّما يَدُلُّ عَلى نُورِه وفَهْمِهِ غِناهُ بِربِّهِ وانْحِياشُهُ إلَيهِ بقَلبِه، والتَّحَرُّرُ من رِقِّ الطَّمَعِ، والتَّحَلِّي بِحِلْيَةِ الْوَرَعِ » يعني وَرَعَ الخاصَّةِ أو خَاصَّةِ الخاصَّةِ، واللهُ تعالى أعلم.

٩ - **الزُّهْدُ**: خُلُوُّ القلْبِ من التَّعلُّقِ بغَيْرِ الرَّبِّ، أو بُرُودَةُ الدُّنْيَا مِنَ القلبِ وعُزُوفُ النَّفْسِ عنْهَا، فزُهدُ العامّةِ تَرْكُ ما فَضَلَ عن الْحَاجَةِ في كلِّ شيءٍ، وزُهْدُ الخاصَّةِ ترْكُ ما يَشْغَلُ عن التَّقَرُّبِ إلى الله فِي كلِّ حَالٍ، وزُهْدُ خاصَّةِ الْخاصَّةِ تَرْكُ النَّظَرِ إلى ما سِوَى اللهِ في جَميعِ الأوقاتِ. وحاصِلُ الجميعِ بُرُودَةُ القَلْبِ عَنِ السِّوَى وعن الرَّغْبَةِ في غيْرِ الْحَبيبِ. وهو سَبَبُ الْمَحَبَّةِ كما قال عليه الصّلاة والسّلام: « ازْهَدْ فِي الدُّنيا يُحِبُّكَ اللهُ » الحديث. وهو سَبَبُ السَّيْرِ والْوُصُولِ، إذْ لاَ سيْرَ لِلْقلْبِ إذاَ تَعَلَّقَ بشيءٍ سِوَى الْمَحْبُوبِ.

١٠ - **التَّوَكل**: ثِقَةُ القلبِ بالله حتَّى لا يَعْتَمِدَ على شَيْءٍ سواهُ، أو التَّعَلُّقُ باللهِ والتَّعْويلُ عَليه في كلِّ شيءٍ عِلْمًا بأَنَّهُ عالِمٌ بكلِّ شَيءٍ وأنْ تَكُونَ بما في يَدِ الله أوثَقُ مِنْكَ بما في يَدِكَ. فأدْنَاهُ أنْ تَكونَ معَ اللهِ كالْمُوَكِّلِ مع الْوَكِيلِ الشَّفِيقِ الْمُلاطِفِ. ووَسَطُهُ كالطِّفْلِ مع أُمِّهِ لاَ يَرْجِعُ في جميعِ أمورِهِ إلاّ إليْهَا. وأعلاهُ أن تكونَ كالْمَيِّتِ مع الْغَاسِلِ. فالأوَّلُ للْعَامَّةِ

والثّاني للخاصّة، والثالث لِخاصَّةِ الخاصّة، فالأوّلُ قد تَخْطُرُ بِبَالِهِ تُهْمَةٌ. والثّاني لا اتِّهَامَ له، لكن يَتعلَّقُ بأُمِّهِ عِنْدَ الحاجَةِ. والثالث لاَ اِتِّهَامَ ولا تَعلُّقَ لهُ لِأنّه فَانٍ عَن نفسِه، يَنْظُرُ كلَّ ساعةٍ ما يَفْعَلُ اللهُ بِه.

١١ - **الرِّضَى والتَّسْلِيم**: الرضى تَلَقِّي الْمَهَالِكِ بِوَجْهٍ ضَاحِكٍ، أو سرُورٌ يَجِدُهُ القلْبُ عندَ حُلُولِ القَضَاءِ، أو تركُ الاِخْتيَارِ على الله فيما دَبَّرَ وأمْضَى، أو شَرْحُ الصَّدْرِ ورَفْعُ الإنْكَارِ لِمَا يَرِدُ من الْوَاحِدِ القَهَّارِ. (والتَّسْلِيمُ) تَرْكُ التدبيرِ والاِختيَارِ بالسُّكُونِ تحْتَ مجارِي الأقْدَارِ فيُرَادِفُ الرِّضَى على الْحَدِّ الأَخِيرِ، والرضى أعْظَمُ منه على الأوّلين، وقيل الرِّضَى يَكُونُ عند النُّزُولِ والتَّسْلِيمِ قَبْلَ النُّزُولِ، وهو التَّفْوِيضُ بِعَينِهِ. فبِدَايَتُهُمَا بالصَّبْرِ والْمُجاهَدَةِ، ووسَطُهُمَا بالسُّكُونِ مع خَوَاطِرِ التَّبَرُّمِ والكراهيَّةِ ونِهَايَتُهُمَا بِفَرَحٍ وسكونٍ مع عَدَمِ التَّبَرُّمِ. فالأول للعامّة، والثاني للخاصّة، والثالث لخاصّة الخاصّة. ويُغْتَفَرُ الْخَاطِرُ الأوَّلُ عند الْجَمِيعِ لِضُعْفِ الْبَشَرِيَّةِ إذ لاَ يَخْلُو منهُ بَشَرٌ.

١٢ - **الْمُرَاقَبَة**: إِدَامَةُ عِلْمِ العبد باطّلاَعِ الرَّبِّ، أوالقِيَّامُ بِحُقُوقِ الله سِرًّا وجَهْرًا خالِصًا من الأَوْهَامِ، صادِقًا في الاِحْتِرَامِ، وهي أَصْلُ كلِّ خيرٍ وبِقَدْرِهَا تكُونُ الْمُشَاهَدَةُ، فَمَن عَظُمَتْ مراقَبَتُهُ عَظُمَتْ بعدَ ذَلِكَ مُشاهَدَتُهُ، فمُراقَبَةُ أهْلِ الظَّاهِرِ حِفْظُ الْجَوَارِحِ من الْهَفَوَاتِ، ومرَاقبَةُ أهْلِ البَاطِنِ حفْظُ القُلُوبِ من الاِسْتِرْسَالِ مَعَ الْخَوَاطِرِ والْغَفَلاَتِ، ومراقبةُ أهل باطِنِ البَاطِنِ حِفظُ السِّرِّ مِنَ الْمُسَاكَنَةِ إلى غيرِ الله.

١٣ - **الْمُحَاسَبَةُ والْمُشَارَطَةُ**: عِتَابُ النَّفسِ على تَضْيِيعِ الأَنْفَاسِ والأوقَاتِ في غيرِ أنواعِ الطاعات، وتكونُ آخِرَ النَّهار كما أن (الْمُشَارَطَةَ) تكون أَوَّلَ النَّهَارِ. يقول لنَفسِه في أوّلِ نَهَارِهِ: هذا يومٌ جَدِيدٌ وهو علَيْكَ شهيدٌ، فاجتهِدِي في تَعْمِيرِ أوقاتِهِ بِمَا يُقَرِّبُكِ إلى اللهِ، وَلَو مُتِّ بالأَمْسِ لَفَاتَكِ الْخَيْرُ الّذي تفوزِينَ بِهِ فيهِ. وكذلك يَقُولُ لَهَا عنْدَ إقبَالِ اللَّيْلِ، ويُحاسِبُهَا عند إدْبَارِهِ هكذا يَدُومُ عليها مَعَهَا حتىّ تَتَمَكَّنَ مِنَ الْحَضْرَةِ، فَحِينَئِذٍ يَتَّحِدُ الوَقْتُ وهو الإستِغْرَاقُ في الشُّهُودِ، فلا يَبْقَى مَن يُحَاسِب ولاَ مَنْ يُعَاقِبُ فَتَحَصَّلَ أنَّ الْمُشَارَطَةَ أَوَّلاً والْمُحَاسَبَةَ آخِرًا والْمُراقَبَةَ دَائِمًا ما دَامَ في السَّيْرِ. فَإذَا حَصَلَ الْوُصولُ فَلاَ مُحَاسَبَةَ ولاَ مُشَارَطَة.

١٤ - **الْمَحَبَّةُ**: مَيْلٌ دَائِمٌ بِقَلْبٍ هَائِمٍ، ويَظْهَرُ هذا الْمَيْلُ أَوَّلاً على الْجَوَارِحِ الظَّاهِرَةِ بالْخِدْمَةِ، وهو مَقَامُ الأَبْرَارِ، وثانياً على الْقُلُوبِ الشَّائِقَةِ بالتَّصْفِيَةِ والتَّحْلِيَةِ وهو مَقَامُ الْمُرِيدِينَ السَّالِكِينَ، وثالثًا على الأَرْوَاحِ والأَسْرَارِ الصَّافِيَّة بالتَّمْكِينِ من شُهُودِ الْمَحْبُوبِ وهو مَقَامُ العَارِفِينَ، فبِدَايَةُ الْمَحَبَّةِ ظهورُ أَثَرِهَا بالْخِدْمَةِ وَوَسَطُهَا ظُهُورُ أثَرِهَا بالسُّكْرِ والْهُيَامِ، ونِهايَتُهَا ظُهورُهاَ بالسُّكُونِ والصَّحْوِ في مَقَامِ العِرفانِ. فَلِهَذَا اِنْقَسَمَ النّاسُ على ثلاَثِ مَرَاتِبَ: أَرْبَابُ الْخِدْمَةِ، وأَرْبَابُ الأَحْوَالِ، وأرْبَابُ الْمَقَامَاتِ، فَبِدَايَتُها سُلُوكٌ وخِدْمَةٌ، ووسَطُهَا جَذْبٌ وفَنَاءٌ، ونِهَايَتُهَا صَحْوٌ وبَقَاءٌ.

١٥ - الْمُشَاهَدَةُ وَالْمُعَايَنَةُ: الْمُشَاهَدَةُ رُؤْيَةُ الذَّاتِ اللَّطِيفَةِ فِي مَظَاهِرِ
تَجَلِّيَاتِهَا الْكَثِيفَةِ فَتَرْجِعُ إِلَى تَكْثِيفِ اللَّطِيفِ، فَإِذَا تَرَقَّقَ الْوِدَادُ
وَرَجَعَتِ الأنوارُ الكثيفةُ لَطِيفَةً فَهِيَ الْمُعَايَنَةُ فترجع إِلَى تلْطِيفِ
الْكَثِيفِ. فالْمُعَايَنَةُ أَرَقُّ مِنَ الْمُشَاهَدَةِ وأتَمُّ والْحَاصِلُ أن شُهُودَ الذَّاتِ
لاَ يُمْكِنُ إلاَّ بِواسِطَةِ تَكْثِيفِ أَسْرَارِهَا اللَّطِيفَةِ فِي مظاهِرِ التَّجَلِّيَاتِ،
إِذْ لا يُمْكِنُ إِدْرَاكُ اللَّطِيفِ ما دام لطيفاً. فَرُؤْيَةُ التَّجَلِّيَاتِ كَثِيفَةً
مُشَاهَدَةٌ، وَرَدُّهَا إِلَى أَصْلِهَا بِانْطِباقِ بَحْرِ الأَحَدِيَّةِ عليهَا مُعَايَنَةٌ. وقِيلَ
هُمَا سَوَاءٌ.

١٦ - الْمَعْرِفَة: وهي التَّمَكُّنُ مِنَ الْمُشَاهَدَةِ واتِّصَالُهَا، فهِي شُهُودٌ دَائِمٌ
بِقَلْبٍ هَائِمٍ، فَلاَ يَشْهَدُ إلاَّ مَوْلاَهُ ولاَ يُعَرِّجُ على أَحَدٍ سِوَاهُ، مع إِقَامَةِ
الْعَدْلِ وحِفْظِ مَرَاسِمِ الشَّرِيعَةِ.
فَهَذِهِ حُدُودُ المقاماتِ قد انْتَهَتْ فِي الْمَعْرِفَةِ. ثمّ نرجِعُ إِلَى حَقائِقَ أُخْرَى
يَكْثُرُ استِعْمالُهَا بِدَايَةً ونِهَايَةً، منها:

١٧ - التَّقْوَى: وهي امْتِثَالُ الأوامِرِ واجْتِنابُ الْمَنَاكِرِ فِي الظَّوَاهِرِ والسَّرَائِرِ
ومواصَلَةُ الطَّاعَاتِ والإِعْرَاضُ عن الْمُخَالَفَاتِ، فتقْوَى الْعَامَّةِ اجتِنابُ
الذُّنُوبِ، وتقْوَى الْخَاصَّةِ التَّخَلِّي من الْعُيُوبِ، وتقْوَى خَاصَّةِ الْخَاصَّةِ
الْغَيْبَةُ عن السِّوَى بِالْعُكُوفِ فِي حضْرَةِ عالِمِ الغُيُوبِ.

١٨ - **الإِسْتِقَامَة**: اِسْتِعْمَالُ العِلْمِ بأقوالِ الرَّسولِ ﷺ وأَفْعَالِهِ وأَحْوَالِهِ وأخْلاَقِهِ، من غَيْرِ تَعمُّقٍ ولاَ تَأَنُّقٍ ولاَ مَيْلٍ مع أوهَامِ الْوَسْوَاسِ أو الخُرُوجُ عن الْمَعْهُودَاتِ ومُفارقَةُ الرُّسُومِ والعَادَاتِ، أو القيَّامُ بين يَدَي الله تعالى على حَقِيقَةِ الصِّدْقِ في جميع الحَالاَتِ. وهي في الأَقوَالِ بِتَرْكِ الْغِيبَةِ، وفي الأفعال بِتَرْكِ الْبِدْعَةِ، وفي الأَحْوَالِ بعَدَمِ الخُروجِ عَن سُنَنِ الشَّرِيعَةِ. فإستِقَامَةُ العامَّةِ بِمُوافَقَةِ السُّنَّةِ، وإستقَامَةُ الخَاصَّةِ بالتَّخَلُّقِ بالأَخْلاَقِ النَّبَوِيَّةِ، وإِسْتِقَامَةُ خاصّةِ الخاصّة بالتَّخَلُّقِ بأَخْلاَقِ الرَّحْمنِ مَعَ الإستِغْرَاقِ في حَضْرَةِ الْعِيّانِ.

١٩ - **الإِخْلاَص**: إخرَاجُ الخَلْقِ عن مُعَامَلة الحَقِّ، وإِفْرَادُ الحَقِّ تعالى في الطَّاعَةِ بالْقَصْدِ، أو غَيْبَةُ القَلْبِ عن غَيْرِ الرَّبِّ، فإِخلاَصُ العامَّةِ تَصْفِيَةُ الأَعمَالِ عن مُلاَحَظَةِ الْمَخْلُوقِينَ. وإِخْلاَصُ الخَاصَّةِ تصفيَّتُهَا عن طَلَبِ الْعِوَضِ في الدَّارين، وإِخْلاَصُ خَاصَّةِ الخَاصَّةِ التَّبَرِّي مِنَ الحَوْلِ والْقُوَّةِ ومِن رؤْيَةِ الغَيْرِ في الْقَصْدِ والحَرَكَةِ حتى يَكُون الْعَمَلُ بِاللهِ ومِنَ اللهِ وإلى اللهِ غَائِباً عن ما سِوَاهُ.

٢٠ - **الصِّدْق**: إِسْقاطُ حظُوظِ النَّفْسِ في الْمُوَاجَهَةِ إلى الله تعالى تَعْوِيلاً على ثَلْجِ الْيَقِينِ، أو اسْتِوَاءُ الظَّاهِرِ والباطِنِ في الأقوالِ والأفعَالِ والأَحوَالِ، أو مُلاَزَمَةُ الْكِتْمَانِ غيْرَةً عن أَسْرَارِ الرَّحْمنِ، وحاصِلُهُ تصفيَةُ البَاطِنِ من الإِلْتِفَاتِ إلى الغيْرِ بالْكُلِّيَّةِ. والفَرقُ بَيْنَهُ وبَيْنَ الإِخْلاَصِ أَنَّ الإخلاَص ينْفِي الشِّرْكَ الجَلِيَّ والخَفِيَّ، والصِّدْقُ ينفِي النِّفاقَ والْمُدَاهَنَةَ بالْكُلِّيَّةِ.

فمِثَالُ الصِّدْقِ مع الإِخْلاَصِ كالتَّشْحِرَةِ لِلذَّهَبِ فَهُوَ ينْفِي عَنْه عوَارِضَ النِّفَاقِ ويُصَفِّيهِ من كُدُورَةِ الأَوْهَامِ وذَلِكَ أَنَّ صَاحبَ الإِخْلاَصِ لا يَخْلُو من مُدَاهَنَةِ النَّفْسِ ومُسَامَحَةِ الْهَوَى بِخَلاَصِ صَاحِبِ الصِّدْقِ فإِنَّهُ يُذْهِبُ الْمُدَاهَنَاتِ ويَرْفَعُ الْمُسَامَحَاتِ، إِذْ لاَ يَشُمُّ رَائِحَةَ الصِّدْقِ منْ دَاهَنَ نَفْسَهُ أو غَيْرَهُ فِيمَا دَقَّ أو جَلَّ. وعلامَةُ الصِّدْقِ استواءُ السِّرِّ والعَلاَنِيَّةِ فَلاَ يُبَالِي صَاحِبُ الصِّدْقِ بِكشْفِ ما يَكْرَهُ اطلاَعَ النَّاسِ عليْهِ ولاَيستَحِي مِن ظُهُورِهِ لِغَيْرِهِ اِكْتِفَاءً بعِلْمِ اللهِ بِهِ. فصِدْقُ العَامَّةِ تصفيَّةُ الأَعْمَالِ من طَلَبِ الأَعْوَاضِ، وصدْقُ الْخَاصَّةِ تصْفِيَّةُ الأَحْوَالِ من قَصْدِ غَيْرِ اللهِ، وصدق خاصة الخاصة تَصْفِيَّةُ مَشْرَبِ التَّوحيدِ من الإلْتِفَاتِ إلى ما سِوَى اللهِ، ويُقَالُ لصاحِبِ الْمَقَامِ الأَوَّلِ صادقٌ، والثّاني والثّالثِ صِدِّيقٌ. وأمّا التَّصْدِيقُ بوُجُودِ الْحَقِّ أو بِوُجُودِ الْخُصُوصِيَّةِ عندَ الأَوْلِيَّاءِ وتعظِيمِهِمْ لأَجْلِهَا فهو تَصْدِيقٌ لا صِدْقٌ خِلاَفَ ما يعتقده بعض فُقَرَاءِ زمانِنا هذا ويُقَالُ لِمَنْ عَظُمَ تصديقُهُ صدِّيقٌ أيْضًا فالصِّدِّيقُ يُطْلَقُ على من عَظُمَ صِدْقُهُ وتَصْدِيقُهُ.

٢١ - **الطُّمَأْنِينَة**: وهي سكونُ الْقَلْبِ إلى الله عَارِيًّا عن التَّقَلُّبِ والإِضْطِرَابِ ثِقَةً بِضَمَانٍ أو اِكْتِفَاءً بعلْمِهِ أو رسُوخًا في معرفَتِهِ وتَكونُ من وَرَاءِ الْحِجَابِ بتَوَاتُرِ الأَدِلَّةِ واستعمَالِ الْفِكْرَةِ أو بتَوَالِي الطَّاعَةِ ومُجَاهَدَةِ الرِّيَّاضَةِ وتكون بعد زَوَالِ الْحِجَابِ بتمْكينِ النَّظْرَةِ ورُسُوخِ الْمَعْرِفَةِ. فَقَوْمٌ اطْمَأَنُّوا بِوُجُودِ اللهِ من طريقِ الْبُرْهَانِ أو الْبَيَانِ، وقومٌ

اطْمَأَنُّوا بشُهُودِ الله بعد ظهُورِهِ من طريقِ العِيَّانِ. فالأوّل للعلماءِ، والثَّانِي للعُبَّادِ والزُّهَّادِ والصالحين، والثَّالثُ للعارفين الْمُتَّقرِبين.

٢٢ - **الشَّوْق والإشْتِيَاق**: الشَّوقُ إنزعاجُ القَلْبِ إلى لِقَاءِ الْحَبِيبِ، والاِشْتِيَّاقُ ارْتِياحُ القلبِ إلى دَوَامِ الإتِّصَالِ بِه. فالشَّوْقُ يزُولُ برُؤْيَةِ الحبيب ولقائِهِ، والاشْتِيَّاقُ لاَيَزُولُ أَبَدًا لطَلَبِ الرُّوحِ الزِّيَادَة في كَشْفِ الأَسْرَارِ والقُرْبِ إلى الأبدِ. فشَوْقُ العَامَّةِ إلى زَخَارِفِ جِنَانِهِ، وشَوْقُ الْخَاصَّةِ إلى نَيْلِ رِضْوَانِهِ، وشَوْقُ خاصّة الخاصَّةِ إلى حَضْرَةِ عِيَّانِهِ.

٢٣ - **الغَيْرَة**: كَرَاهِيَّةُ رُؤْيَةِ حَبِيبِكَ عند غَيْرِكَ فَيَهِيجَ التَّنَافُسُ في حِيَّازَتِهِ. قال الشِّبْلِي « الْغَيْرَةُ غَيْرَتَانِ: فغَيْرَةُ البَشَرِيَّةِ على النُّفُوسِ، وغَيْرَةٌ إلَهِيَّةٌ على القُلُوبِ ». ومعناه أن الطَّبعَ الْبَشَرِيَّ يَكْرَهُ أن يَرَى مَحْبُوبَهُ عند غيرِهِ كالزَّوْجَةِ مثلاً، والْحَقُّ تعالى يَكْرَهُ أن يرى قلوبَ أَوْلِيَّائِهِ مُتَعَلِّقَةً بغيره. وفي الحديث: « لا أَحَدَ أَغْيَرُ مِنَ اللهِ وَلِذَلِكَ حَرَّمَ الْفَوَاحِشَ مَا ظَهَرَ مِنْهَا وَمَا بَطَنَ ». وما في الوُجودِ إلاّ الغَيْرَةُ الإلَهِيَّةُ سَرَتْ في مظَاهِرِ تَجَلِّيَّاتِهِ. فَغَيْرَةُ النُّفُوسِ للعامّة وهي غيْرَتُهُمْ على هَتْكِ حُرمَةِ حَرِيمِهِمْ، وغيْرَةُ القلوبِ للخاصّة وهي غيرَتُهم على قلُوبِهِمْ أن تَمِيلَ لغير مَحْبوبِهم، وغيرةُ الأَرْوَاحِ والأَسْرَارِ لخاصّة الخاصّة، وهي غيرتُهم على أرواحهم أن تَلْتَفِتَ إلى شيءٍ دونَ مَحبوبِهِمْ، وغيْرَتُهُمْ على حبِيبِهِمْ أن يَمِيلَ إلى غيرِهِمْ. وعلى هذا الأمرِ العَظِيمِ حُقَّ لِلْعَبْدِ أن يَغَارَ، كما قال الشاعر:

إذا لمْ أُنافسِ في هوَاكَ ولمْ أَغِرْ عليكَ ففيمنَ ليتَ شِعرِي أُنــــافسْ
فلا تحتقِرْ نفسِي وأنتَ حبيبُها فكلُّ امْرِئٍ يَصْبُو إلى مَنْ يُجَــــانسْ

وقد يغار الحق تعالى على أوليائه فينْتَقِمُ من أعدائِهِمْ إذَا آذَوْهُمْ. ومن غيْرَتِهِ أيضًا عليْهِمْ أن لاَ يُظْهِرَهُمْ لجُمْلَةِ الخلقِ فَيَضِنُّ بهم على خَلْقِهِ حتى يَلْقَوْهُ تَحْتَ أَسْتَارِ الخُمُولِ وهمْ عرَائِسُ حضْرَتِهِ.

٢٤ - **الْفُتُوَّةُ**: وهيَ الإيثارُ علَى النَّفْسِ بما تُحِبُّ والإحسان إلى الخَلْقِ بما يُحِبُّ ولذَا قِيلَ لَمْ تَكمُلِ الْفُتُوَّةُ إلاَّ لِرسولِ الله ﷺ حيْثُ يقول في موضع لا يَذْكُرُ فيهِ أحَدٌ إلاَّ نفسَهُ: « أُمَّتي أُمَّتي ». وقيل أن لا ترَى لِنَفسِكَ فَضْلاً على غيْرِكَ. والْفَتَى من لا خَصْمَ لَهُ. ومرْجِعُهَا إلى السَّخَاءِ والتَّوَاضُعِ والشَّجَاعَةِ في مَواطِنِ الاضْطِرَابِ. فَفُتُوَّةُ العامَّة بالأموَالِ، وفُتُوَّةُ الخاصة بالنفوس، وفتوة خاصّة الخاصّة بالأرواح وبَذْلِ الْمُهَجِ في جانِبِ الْمَحْبُوبِ.

٢٥ - **الإِرَادَةُ**: وهي قَصْدُ الوُصُولِ إلى المحبوب بِنَعْتِ الْمُجاهَدَةِ أو التَّحَبُّبُ إلى الله بِما يَرضى، والخُلوُصُ في نَصيحَةِ الأمَّةِ والأنس بالْخُلوَةِ والصبر على مَقَاسَاةِ الأَهْوَالِ ومُنَازَلاَتِ الأَحْوَالِ والإيثَارُ لأمْرِهِ والحياء من نَظَرِهِ وبَذْلُ المجهود في محبوبه والتَّعَرُّضُ لكل سَبَبٍ يُوصِلُ إليه وصُحْبَةُ من يَدُلُّ عليه، والقَناعَةُ بالخُمُولِ، وعدم سُكُونِ القلبِ إلى شيءٍ دونَ الوُصُولِ وهي، أَوَّلُ منْزِلَةِ القاصِدِينَ وبَدْءُ طريقِ السَّالِكِينَ.

٢٦ - **والْمُرِيد**: من لاَ إرَادَةَ لَهُ دون مَولاَه، وهي ثلاثُ مرَاتِب: إرادَةُ التَّبَرُّكِ والْحُرْمَةِ وهي لمن ضَعُفَتْ هِمَّتُه أو كَثُرت علاَئِقُهُ، وإرادَةُ الوُصولِ إلى الحضرَةِ وهي لأَهْلِ التَّجْرِيدِ وقوَّةِ العَزْمِ، وإرادة الخِلاَفَةِ وكَمَالِ المعرفة وهي لمن ظَهَرَتْ نجَابَتُهُ وكَمُلَتْ أهلِيَّتُهُ وصُرِّحَ له بالْخِلاَفَةِ من شَيْخٍ كامِلٍ أو هَاتِفٍ صَادِقٍ.

٢٧ - **الْمُجَاهَدَة**: وَهِي فَطْمُ النَّفْس عَن الْمَأْلُوفَات، وَحَمْلُهَا عَلَى مُخَالَفَةِ هَوَاهَا فِي عُمُومِ الأَوْقَات، وَخَرْقِ عَوَائِدِهَا فِي جَمِيع الحَالاَت. قَال بَعْضُهم مَرْجِعُهَا إِلَى ثَلاثٍ: لاَ تَأْكُلُ إِلاّ عِنْد الْفَاقَة، وَلا تَنَام إِلاّ عِنْد الْغَلَبَة، وَلا تَتَكَلَّمُ إِلاّ عِنْد الْضَّرُورَة. وَنِهَايَتُهَا الْمُشَاهَدَة فَلا مُجَاهَدَة بَعْدَهَا فَلا تَجْتَمِع مُجَاهَدَة وَمُشَاهَدَة، إِذ نِهَايَةُ التَّعَبِ تَمَامُ السَّفَر، فَإِذَا حَصَلَ الْوُصُول فَمَا بَقِي إِلاّ الرَّاحَة، وَمُشَاهَدَة الْحَبِيبِ مَع حِفْظِ الأَدَب. وَهِي ثَلاثَة: مُجَاهَدَةُ الظَّاهِر وَدَوَام الطَّاعَات وَكَفُّ الْمَنْهِيَّات، وَمُجَاهَدَة الْبَوَاطِن بِنَفْي الْخَوَاطِر الرَّدِيئَة وَدَوَام الْحُضُور فِي الْحَضْرَة الْقُدْسِيَّة، وَمُجَاهَدَة السَّرَائِر بِاسْتِدَامَة الْشُّهُود وَعَدَم الالْتِفَات إِلَى غَيْر الْمَعْبُود.

٢٨ - **الْوِلاَيَة**: وَهِي حُصُول الأُنْس بَعْد الْمُكَابَدَة وَاعْتِنَاق الرُّوح بَعْد الْمُجَاهَدَة. وَحَاصِلُهَا تَحْقِيقُ الْفَنَاء فِي الذّاتِ بَعْد ذَهَابِ حِسِّ الْكَائِنَات فَيَفْنَى مَن لَم يَكُن وَيَبْقَى مَن لَم يَزَل. فَأَوَّلُهَا التَّمَكُّن مِن الْفَنَاء، وَنِهَايَتُهَا التَّحَقُّق بِالْبَقَاء وَبَقَاءِ الْبَقَاءِ وَيَبْقَى التَّرَقِّي وَالاِتِّسَاع فِيهَا أَبَدًا سَرْمَدًا إِلَى مَا لا نِهَايَةَ لَه. قَال إِبْرَاهِيم بْن أَدْهَم لِرَجُلٍ: « أَتُحِب أَن تَكُونَ

لله وَلِيًّا ؟ » قال « نعم » قَال « لا تَرْغَب فِي شَيْء مَنِ الدُّنْيَا وَالآخِرَة وَفرِّغ نَفْسَك لله عَزَّوَجَلَّ وَأَقْبِل بِوَجْهِك عَلَيْه يَرْفُق عَلَيْك وَيُوَالِيك ». وَقَال غَيْرُه: « الْوَلِي مِن كَان هَمُّه اللهُ وَشُغْلُه اللهُ وَفَنَائُه دَائِمًا فِي اللهِ». وَتُطْلَق عَلَى ثَلاث مَرَاتِب: وِلايَة عَامَّة وَهِي لأَهْل الإِيمَان وَالتَّقْوى كَمَا فِي الْآيَةِ وَهِي قَوْلُه: ﴿ أَلَآ إِنَّ أَوۡلِيَآءَ ٱللَّهِ لَا خَوۡفٌ عَلَيۡهِمۡ وَلَا هُمۡ يَحۡزَنُونَ ﴿٦٢﴾ ٱلَّذِينَ ءَامَنُواْ وَكَانُواْ يَتَّقُونَ ﴿٦٣﴾ ﴾. وَوِلايَة خَاصَّةٌ وَهِي لأَهْل الإِسْتِشْرَافِ عَلَى الْعِلْم بِالله. وَوِلايَةُ خَاصَّةِ الْخَاصَّة، وَهِي لِأَهْلِ التَّمَكُّن فِي مَعْرِفَة الله عَلَى نَعْت الْعِيَان. قِيلَ « مَن أَوْلِيَّاء الله، يَا رَسُولَ الله ؟» قَال: « الْمُتَحَابُّون فِي الله » وَفِي رِوَايَة: « الَّذِين نَظَرُوا إِلَى بَاطِنِ الدُّنْيَا حِين نَظَرَ النَّاسُ إِلَى ظَاهِرِهَا » الْحَدِيث. فَشَمَلَ الْحَدِيثُ وِلايَة الْخَاصَّة وَخَاصَّة الْخَاصَّةِ. وَاللهُ تَعَالَى أَعْلَم.

٢٩ - **الْحُرِّيَّة**: وَهِي تَصْفِيَّة الْبَاطِن مِن حُبِّ غَيْر الْحَقِّ حَتَّى لاتَبْقَى فِيهِ بَقِيَّةٌ لِغَيْرِ الله، وَهَذِه الْحُرِّيَّة الْكَسْبِيَّة وَهِي سَبَبُ الظَّفَر بِالْحُرِّيَّة الْوَهْبِيَّة، وَهِي غَيْبَة الْعَبْد فِي مَظَاهِر الرَّبِّ، فَتَنْتَفِي ظُلْمَة الْحُدُوث فِي نُورِ الْقِدَمِ، وَتَخْتَفِي قَوَالِب الْعُبُودِيَّة فِي تَجَلِّي مَظَاهِر الرُّبُوبِيَّة، فَيَبْقَى الْحَقُّ بِلا خَلْقٍ فَحِينَئِذٍ يُكْتَب لِلْعَبْد عَقْد الْحُرِّيَّة، فَتَكُون عِبَادَتُه وَعُبُودِيَّتُه شُكْرًا لا قَهْراً كَمَا قَال سَيِّدِ الْعَارِفِينَ ﷺ « أَفَلا أَكُونُ عَبْدًا شَكُوراً ». وَقَال إِمَام هَذِه الطَّائِفَة الْجُنَيْد: « عِبَادَةُ الْعَارِفِ تَاجٌ عَلَى الرُّؤُوسِ »، يَعْنِي كَمَالُ الْكَمَال.

٣٠ - **الْعُبُودِيَّة**: وَهِي الْقِيَام بِآدَاب الرُّبُوبِيَّة مَع شُهُودِ ضَعُفِ الْبَشَرِيَّة. وَقَال بَعْضُهُم هِي الْقِيَّام بِحَق الطَّاعَات بِشَرْط التَّوْقِير وَالنَّظَر إِلَى مَا مِنْك بِعَيْن التَّقْصِير أَو تَرْك الإخْتِيَّار فِيمَا يَبْدُو مِن الأَقْدَار أَو التَّبَرِّي مِن الْحَوْل وَالْقُوَّة وَالإِقْرَارِ بِمَا يُولِيكَ وَيُعْطِيك مِن الْمِنَّة. وَأَجْمَعُ الْعِبَارَات فِيهَا مَا قَال ابْن عَطَاء: « حِفْظُ الْحُدُودِ، وَالْوَفَاءُ بِالْعُهُودِ، وَالرِّضَا بِالْمَوْجُودِ، وَالصَّبْرُ عَلَى الْمَفْقُودِ ». قُلْت وَأَحْسَن مَا فِي تَفْسِير الْعُبُودِيَّةِ أَن تُقَدِّرَ أَنَّ لَك عَبْدًا اشْتَرَيْته بِمَالِكَ، فَكَمَا تُحِبُّ أَن يَكُونَ عَبْدُكَ مَعَكَ فَكُن أَنْت مَع مَوْلاكَ، فَالْعَبْدُ لا يَمْلِك مَع سَيِّدِه شَيْئاً مِن نَفْسِه وَلا مَالِه وَلا يُمْكِنُه مَع قَهْرِيَّةِ سَيِّدِه تَدْبِيرٌ وَلا إِخْتِيَّارٌ وَلا يَتَزَيَّى إِلاّ بِزِيِّ الْعَبِيدِ أَهْلِ الْخِدْمَةِ وَيَكُونُ عِنْد أَمْر سَيِّدِه وَنَهْيِهِ، وَإِذَا كَان حَاذِقًا فَاهِماً عَمَلَ مَا يُرْضِي سَيِّدَه قَبْل أَن يَأْمُرَه وَيَفْهَم عَن سَيِّدِه بِأَدْنَى إِشَارَةٍ إِلَى غَيْر ذَلِك مِن الآدَاب الْمَرْضِيَّةِ فِي الْعَبِيد الْمُؤَدَّبِينَ. وَقَال أَبُو عَلِي الدَّقَّاقْ رَضِيَ اللهُ عَنْهُ « الْعُبُودِيَّةُ أَتَمُّ مِن الْعِبَادَةِ، فَأَوَّلُ الْمَرَاتِبِ عِبَادَةٌ ثُم عُبُودِيَّةٌ ثُم عُبُودَةٌ. فَالْعِبَادَة لِلْعَوَامِّ وَالْعُبُودِيَّةُ لِلْخَوَاصِّ وَالْعُبُودَةُ لِخَوَاصِّ الْخَوَاصِّ». قُلْت وَالْعُبُودَة هِي الْحُرِّيَّة الْوَهْبِيَّةُ، وَاللهُ تَعَالَى أَعْلَم.

٣١ - **الْقَنَاعَة**: الإكْتِفَاءُ بِالْقِسْمَةِ وَعَدَمُ التَّشَوُّفِ لِلزِّيَادَةِ وَالإسْتِغْنَاءُ بِالْمَوْجُودِ وَتَرْكُ التَّشَوُّفِ إِلَى الْمَفْقُودِ. وَهِيَ الْحَيَاةُ الطَّيِّبَةُ وَالرِّزْقُ الْحَسَنُ فِيْ قَوْلِهِ تَعَالَى: ﴿ لَيَرْزُقَنَّهُمُ ٱللَّهُ رِزْقًا حَسَنًا ﴾ أَيْ وَالَّذِينَ هَاجَرُوا فِي سَبِيلِ اللهِ، ثُمَّ قُتِلَ بَعْضُهُم أَوْ مَاتَ، لَيَرْزُقَنَّ اللهُ مَنْ بَقِيَ مِنْهُمْ رِزْقًا حَسَنًا، وَهِيَ مِنْ ثَمْرَةِ الْغِنَى بِاللهِ. قَالَ وَهْب بْن منبه: « إِنَّ الْعِزَّ وَالْغِنَى

خَرَجَا يَجُولانِ فَلَقِيَا الْقَنَاعَةَ فَاسْتَقَرَّا فِيهَا ». وَمَرْجِعُهَا إِلَى سَدِّ بَابِ الطَّمَعِ وَفَتْحِ بَابِ الْوَرَعِ وَهِيَ مَطْلُوبَةٌ فِي أُمُورِ الدُّنْيَا فَقَطْ، وَأَمَّا فِي أُمُورِ الآخِرَةِ أَوْ فِي زِيَادَةِ الْعِلْمِ وَالتَّرَقِّي فِي الْمَعْرِفَةِ فَمَذْمُومَةٌ وَلِذَلِكَ قِيلَ « الْقَنَاعَةُ مِنَ اللهِ حِرْمَانٌ ».

٣٢ - **الْعَافِيَّةُ**: وَهِيَ سُكُونُ الْقَلْبِ وَخُلُوُّهُ مِنَ الإِنْزِعَاجِ وَالاضْطِرَابِ وَالتَّقَلُّبِ، ثُمَّ إِنْ كَانَ بِالسُّكُونِ إِلَى اللهِ وَالرِّضَا عَنْهُ فَهِيَ الْعَافِيَّةَ الْكَامِلَةُ، وَإِنْ كَانَ بِجَرَيَانِ الأَسْبَابِ الْمُوَافِقَةِ فَهِيَ الْعَافِيَّةُ الْعَادِيَّةُ. وَفِي الْحَدِيثِ «ما أُعْطِي أَحَدٌ بَعْدَ الْيَقِينِ خَيْراً مِنَ الْعَافِيَةِ». فَعَافِيَّةُ الْعَامَّةِ سُكُونُهُمْ إِلَى الأَسْبَابِ فَإِذَا انْخَرَمَتْ اضْطَرَبَتْ قُلُوبُهُمْ وَتَزَلْزَلَتْ لِخَرَابِهَا مِنْ نُورِ الْيَقِينِ، وَعَافِيَّةُ الْخَاصَّةِ سُكُونُهُمْ إِلَى مُسَبِّبِ الأَسْبَابِ، فَعَافِيَّتُهُمْ دَائِمَةٌ وَرُبَّمَا يَزِيدُ يَقِينُهُمْ إِذَا انْخَرَمَتِ الأَسْبَابُ كَمَا قَالَ بَعْضُهُمْ: « نَحْنُ كَالنُّجُومِ كُلَّمَا اشْتَدَّتِ الظُّلْمَةُ قَوِيَ نُورُنَا ». وَقَالَ ذُو النُّونِ رَضِيَ اللهُ عَنْهُ: « لَوْ كَانَتِ السَّمَاءُ مِنْ زُجَاجٍ وَالأَرْضُ مِنْ نُحَاسٍ وَمِصْرُكُلُّهَا عِيَالِي مَا اهْتَمَمْتُ لَهُمْ بِرِزْقٍ ». وَعَافِيَّةُ خَاصَّةِ الْخَاصَّةِ سُكُونُهُمْ إِلَى شُهُودِ الْحَقِّ غَائِبِينَ عَنِ الأَسْبَابِ وَعَدَمِهَا غَرْقَى فِي بَحْرِ التَّوْحِيدِ وَأَسْرَارِ التَّفْرِيدِ لا تَنْزِلُ الْهُمُومُ بِسَاحَتِهِمْ وَلا تُكَدِّرُ صَفَاءَ مَشْرَبِهِمْ. جَعَلَنَا اللهُ مِنْهُمْ، آمِين!

٣٣ - **الْيَقِينُ**: وَهُوَ سُكُونُ الْقَلْبِ إِلَى اللهِ بِعِلْمٍ لا يَتَغَيَّرُ وَلا يَحُولُ وَلا يَتَقَلَّبُ وَلا يَزُولُ عِنْدَ هَيَجَانِ الْمُحَرِّكَاتِ وَارْتِفَاعِ الرِّيَبِ فِي مُشَاهَدَةِ الْغَيْبِ. وَعَلامَتُهُ ثَلاثٌ: رَفْعُ الْهِمَّةِ عَنِ الْخَلْقِ عَنِ

الْحَاجَةِ، وَتَرْكُ الْمَدْحِ لَهُمْ فِي الْعَطِيَّةِ، وَالتَّنَزُّهُ عَنِ ذَمِّهِمْ عِنْدَ الْمَنَعَةِ. فَيَقِينُ الْعَامَّةِ بِتَوْحِيدِ أَفْعَالِهِ فَسَكَنُوا إِلَيْهِ فِي الْمَنْعِ وَالْعَطَاءِ. وَيَقِينُ الْخَاصَّةِ بِتَوْحِيدِ صِفَاتِهِ فَرَأَوْا الْخَلْقَ مَوْتَى لَيْسَ بِيَدِهِمْ حَرَكَةٌ وَلا سُكُونٌ، وَيَقِينُ خَاصَّةِ الْخَاصَّةِ بِتَوْحِيدِ ذَاتِهِ فَشَاهَدُوهُ فِي كُلِّ شَيْءٍ وَعَرَفُوهُ عِنْدَ كُلِّ شَيْءٍ وَلَمْ يَشْهَدُوا مَعَهُ شَيْئًا.

٣٤ - **عِلْمُ الْيَقِينِ، وَعَيْنُ الْيَقِينِ، وَحَقُّ الْيَقِينِ**: عِلْمُ الْيَقِينِ مَا كَانَ نَاشِئًا عَنِ الْبُرْهَانِ، وَعَيْنُ الْيَقِينِ مَا نَشَأَ عَنِ الْكَشْفِ وَالْبَيَانِ، وَحَقُّ الْيَقِينِ مَا نَشَأَ عَنِ الشُّهُودِ وَالْعِيَانِ. فَعِلْمُ الْيَقِينِ لِأَرْبَابِ الْعُقُولِ مِنْ أَهْلِ الإِيمَانِ، وَعَيْنُ الْيَقِينِ لِأَرْبَابِ الْوِجْدَانِ مِنْ أَهْلِ الاسْتِشْرَافِ عَلَى الْعِيَانِ، وَحَقُّ الْيَقِينِ لِأَهْلِ الرُّسُوخِ وَالتَّمْكِينِ فِي مَقَامِ الإِحْسَانِ. وَمِثَالُ ذَلِكَ كَمَنْ سَمِعَ بِمَكَّةَ، مَثَلاً، وَلَمْ يَرَهَا فَعِنْدَهُ عِلْمُ الْيَقِينِ. فَإِذَا اسْتَشْرَفَ عَلَيْهَا وَرَآهَا وَلَمْ يَدْخُلْهَا فَعِنْدَهُ عَيْنُ الْيَقِينِ. فَإِذَا دَخَلَهَا وَعَرَفَ طُرُقَهَا وَأَمَاكِنَهَا، فَهَذَا عِنْدَهُ حَقُّ الْيَقِينِ. وَكَذَلِكَ النَّاسُ فِي مَعْرِفَةِ الْحَقِّ تَعَالَى فَأَهْلُ الْحِجَابِ اسْتَدَلُّوا حَتَّى حَصَلَ لَهُمُ الْعِلْمُ الْيَقِينِيُّ بِوُجُودِ الْحَقِّ، وَأَهْلُ السَّيْرِ مِنَ الْمُرِيدِينَ الْمُسْتَشْرِفِينَ عَلَى الْفَنَاءِ فِي الذَّاتِ حَصَلَ لَهُمْ عَيْنُ الْيَقِينِ حِينَ أَشْرَقَتْ عَلَيْهِمْ أَنْوَارُ الْمَعَانِي وَغَابَتْ عَنْهُمْ ظِلَالُ الأَوَانِي، غَيْرَ أَنَّهُمْ بَاقُونَ فِي دَهْشَةِ الْفَنَاءِ، لَمْ يَتَمَكَّنُوا مِنْ دَوَامِ شُهُودِ الْحَقِّ. فَإِذَا تَمَكَّنُوا مِنْ دَوَامِ شُهُودِهِ وَرَسَخَتْ أَقْدَامُهُمْ فِي مَعْرِفَتِهِ حَصَلَ لَهُمْ حَقُّ الْيَقِينِ، وَهَذِهِ نِهَايَةُ النِّعْمَةِ وَغَايَةُ السَّعَادَةِ. جَعَلَنَا اللهُ مِنْهُمْ بِمَنِّهِ وَكَرَمِهِ، آمِين!

٣٥ - **النِّعْمَةُ**: هِيَ مُلازَمَةُ الأَفْرَاحِ، وَمُبَاعَدَةُ الأَتْرَاحِ، وَإِصَابَةُ الأَغْرَاضِ، وَنَزَاهَةُ الأَعْرَاضِ، وَهِيَ عَلَى قِسْمَيْنِ: نِعْمَةٌ ظَاهِرَةٌ كالصِّحَّة وَالْعَافِيَّةِ وَالْكِفَايَةِ مِنَ الحَلالِ، وَنِعْمَةٌ بَاطِنَةٌ كَالْإِيمَانِ وَالْهِدَايَةِ وَالْمَعْرِفَةِ. وَالنَّاسُ فِي النِّعْمَةِ الظَّاهِرَةِ عَلَى ثَلاثَةِ أَقْسَامٍ: قَوْمٌ فَرِحُوا بِالنِّعْمَةِ لِمَا لَهُمْ فِيهَا مِنَ الْمُتْعَةِ فَحُجِبُوا بِهَا عَنِ الْمُنْعِمِ، وَقَوْمٌ فَرِحُوا بِالنِّعْمَةِ لِإِقْبَالِ الْمُنْعِمِ عَلَيْهِمْ حَيْثُ ذَكَرَهُمْ بِهَا، وَقَوْمٌ فَرِحُوا بِالْمُنْعِمِ دُونَ شَيْءٍ سِوَاهُ: قَالَ اللهُ تَعَالَى ﴿ قُلِ ٱللَّهُۖ ثُمَّ ذَرْهُمْ فِي خَوْضِهِمْ يَلْعَبُونَ ٩١ ﴾. فَشُكْرُ الأَوَّلِينَ يَزِيدُ بِزِيَادَتِهَا وَيَزُولُ بِزَوَالِهَا، وَشُكْرُ الثَّالِثِ دَائِمٌ فِي السَّرَّاءِ وَالضَّرَّاءِ، وَهَذَا هُوَ شُكْرُ الْخَوَاصِّ.

٣٦ - **الفِرَاسَة**: وَهِيَ خَاطِرٌ يَهْجُمُ عَلَى الْقَلْبِ أَوْ وَارِدٌ، يَتَجَلَّى فِيهِ لا يُخْطِئُ غَالِباً إِذَا صَفَا الْقَلْبُ. وَفِي الْحَدِيثِ: « اتَّقُوا فِرَاسَةَ الْمُؤْمِنِ فَإِنَّهُ يَنْظُرُ بِنُورِ اللهِ». وَهِيَ عَلَى حَسَبِ قُوَّةِ الْقُرْبِ وَالْمَعْرِفَةِ. فَكُلَّمَا قَوِيَ الْقُرْبُ وَتَمَكَّنَتِ الْمَعْرِفَةُ صَدَقَتِ الْفِرَاسَةِ، لِأَنَّ الرُّوحَ إِذَا قَرُبَتْ مِنْ حَضْرَةِ الْحَقِّ لا يَتَجَلَّى فِيهَا غَالِباً إِلاّ الْحَقُّ. وَهِيَ ثَلاثُ مَرَاتِبَ: فِرَاسَةُ الْعَامَّةِ وَهِيَ كَشْفُ مَا فِي ضَمَائِرِ النَّاسِ وَمَا غَابَ مِنْ أَحْوَالِهِمْ، وَهِيَ فِتْنَةٌ فِي حَقِّ مَنْ لَمْ يَتَخَلَّقْ بِأَخْلاقِ الرَّحْمَنِ، وَفِرَاسَةُ الْخَاصَّةِ وَهِيَ كَشْفُ أَسْرَارِ الْمَقَامَاتِ وَالْمُنَازَلاتِ وَالإِطِّلاعُ عَلَى أَنْوَارِ الْمَلَكُوتِ، وَفِرَاسَةُ خَاصَّةِ الْخَاصَّةِ وَهِيَ كَشْفُ أَسْرَارِ الذَّاتِ وَأَنْوَارِ الصِّفَاتِ وَالْغَرَقُ فِي بَحْرِ أَسْرَارِ الْجَبَرُوتِ. وَقَالَ الْكَتّانِي « هِيَ مُكَاشَفَةُ الْحَقِّ وَمُعَايَنَةُ الْغَيْبِ ». وَقَالَ الْوَاسِطِي « هِيَ سَوَاطِعُ أَنْوَارِ الذَّاتِ وتَمْكِينُ جُمْلَةِ السَّرَائِرِ فِي

الغُيُوبِ مِنْ غَيْبٍ إِلَى غَيْبٍ حَتَّى يَشْهَدَ الأَشْيَاءَ مِنْ حَيْثُ أَشْهَدَهُ الْحَقُّ إِيَّاهَا، فَيَتَكَلَّمُ عَلَى ضَمَائِرِ الْخَلْقِ». قُلْتُ قَوْلُهُ «فَيَتَكَلَّمُ. .» لَيْسَ بِشَرْطٍ فِي فِرَاسَةِ الْخَاصَّةِ، وَاللهُ تَعَالَى أَعْلَمُ.

٣٧ - الخُلُقُ: وَهِيَ مَلَكَةٌ تَصْدُرُ عَنْهُ الأَفْعَالُ بِسُهُولَةٍ ثُمَّ إِنْ كَانَتِ الأَفْعَالُ حَسَنَةً كَالْحِلْمِ وَالْعَفْوِ وَالْجُودِ وَنَحْوِهَا سُمِّيَ خُلُقاً حَسَناً وَإِنْ كَانَتْ سَيِّئَةً كَالْغَضَبِ وَالْعَجَلَةِ وَالْبُخْلِ سُمِّيَ خُلُقاً سَيِّئاً. قَالَ وَهْبٌ: «مَا تَخَلَّقَ عَبْدٌ بِخُلُقٍ أَرْبَعِينَ صَبَاحاً إِلاَّ جَعَلَ اللهُ لَهُ ذَلِكَ طَبِيعَةً فِيهِ». فَالْخُلُقُ الْحَسَنُ يُكْتَسَبُ، وَالسَّيِّءُ يُجَاهَدُ حَتَّى يَزُولَ، وَالْخُلُقُ الْحَسَنُ يَعْدِلُ الصِّيَامَ وَالْقِيَامَ وَهُوَ ثَمَرَةُ التَّصَوُّفِ. فَمَنْ لَمْ يُحَسِّنْ خُلُقَهُ، فَتَصَوُّفُهُ أَشْجَارٌ بِلا ثِمَارٍ. وَمَرْجِعُ حُسْنِ الْخُلُقِ أَنْ لا تَغْضَبَ وَلا تَبْخَلَ وَلا تَحْقِدَ. وَبِاللهِ التَّوْفِيقُ.

٣٨ - الجُودُ وَالسَّخَاءُ وَالإِيثَارُ: فَالجُودُ أَنْ لاَيَصْعُبَ عَلَيْهِ الْبَذْلُ، فَمَنْ أَعْطَى الْبَعْضَ وَأَبْقَى الأَكْثَرَ فَصَاحِبُ سَخَاءٍ، وَمَنْ بَذَلَ الأَكْثَرَ فَصَاحِبُ جُودٍ، وَمَنْ قَاسَى الضَّرَّاءَ وَآثَرَ غَيْرَهُ فَصَاحِبُ إِيثَارٍ. فَجُودُ الْعَامَّةِ بِالأَمْوَالِ وَجُودُ الْخَاصَّةِ بِالنُّفُوسِ وجُودُ خَاصَّةِ الْخَاصَّةِ بِالأَرْوَاحِ يَبْذُلُونَهَا لِلْمَوْتِ بِالْمُجَاهَدَةِ ثُمَّ تَحْيَا الْحَيَاةَ الأَبَدِيَّةَ بِالْمُشَاهَدَةِ.

٣٩ - الفَقْرُ: وَهُوَ نَفْضُ الْيَدِ مِنَ الدُّنْيَا وَصِيَانَةُ الْقَلْبِ مِنْ إِظْهَارِ الشَّكْوَى، وَنَعَتُ الْفَقِيرِ الصَّادِقِ ثَلاثَةُ أَشْيَاءٍ: صِيَانَةُ فَقْرِهِ وَحِفْظُ سِرِّهِ

وَإِقَامَةُ دِينِهِ. وَقَالَ جَعْفَر الخُلْدِي: « خَدَمْتُ سِتَّمِائَةَ شَيْخٍ فَمَا وَجَدْتُ مَنْ شَفَى قَلْبِي مِنْ أَرْبَعِ مَسَائِلَ حَتَّى رَأَيْتُ رَسُولَ اللهِ ﷺ فِي النَّوْمِ فَقَالَ لِي: سَلْ عَنْ مَسَائِلِكَ. فَقُلْتُ: يَا رَسُولَ اللهِ، مَا الْعَقْلُ ؟ فَقَالَ أَدْنَاهُ تُرْكُ الدُّنْيَا وَأَعْلاهُ تَرْكُ التَّفَكُّرِ فِي ذَاتِ اللهِ. فَقُلْتُ وَمَا التَّوْحِيدُ ؟ فَقَالَ كُلُّ مَا أَتَى بِهِ الْوَهْمُ أَوْ جَلاَّهُ الْفَهْمُ فَرَبُّنَا جَلّ وَعَزّ مُخَالِفٌ لِذَلِكَ. فَقُلْتُ وَمَا التَّصَوُّفُ ؟ فَقَالَ: تَرْكَ الدَّعَاوِي وَكِتْمَانُ الْمَعَانِي. فَقُلْتُ وَمَا الْفَقْرُ ؟ فَقَالَ: هُوَ سِرٌّ مِنْ أَسْرَارِ اللهِ يُودِعُهُ فِيمَنْ يَشَاءُ مِنْ عِبَادِهِ. فَمَنْ كَتَمَهُ فَهُوَ مِنْ أَهْلِهِ وَزَادَهُ اللهُ مِنْهُ، وَمَنْ بَاحَ بِهِ نَفَاهُ اللهُ عَنْهُ ». قُلْتُ جَوَابُ كُلِّ إِنْسَانٍ عَلَى قَدْرِ مَقَامِهِ كَمَا قَالَ عليه الصلاة والسلام: « خَاطِبُوا النَّاسَ بِقَدْرِ مَا يَفْهَمُونَ ». فَقَوْلُهُ عليه الصلاة والسلام فِي الْعَقْلِ «أَعْلاهُ تَرَكَ التَّفَكُّرِ فِي ذَاتِ اللهِ»، أَمَّا التَّفَكُّرُ فِي كُنْهِ الرُّبُوبِيَّةِ فَمَنْهِيٌّ عَنْهُ، إِذْ لا يُدْرَكُ، وَأَمَّا التَّفَكُّرُ فِي أَسْرَارِ الرُّبُوبِيَّةِ وَأَنْوَارِ صِفَاتِهَا فَلا عِبَادَةَ أَعْظَمُ مِنْهَا. وَقَوْلُهُ أَيْضا عَلَيْهِ الصَّلاةُ وَالسَّلامُ فِي التَّوْحِيدِ « كُلُّ مَا أَتَى بِهِ الْوَهْمُ . . .إلخ » الْوَهْمُ لا يُدْرِكُ أَسْرَارَ التَّوْحِيدِ لأَنَّهَا خَارِجَةٌ عَنِ الْوَهْمِ وَدَرْكِ الْعَقْلِ، فَظَهَرَ مَعْنَى قَوْلِهِ عليه الصلاة والسلام « كُلُّ مَا أَتَى بِهِ الْوَهْمُ. . . إلخ »، وَقَوْلُهُ عليه الصلاة والسلام فِي شَأْنِ الْفَقْرِ «مَنْ كَتَمَهُ فَهُوَ مِنْ أَهْلِهِ» أَيْ فَيَكُونُ مِنَ السَّابِقِينَ وَيَزِيدُهُ تَعَالَى مِنْ أَسْرَارِهِ وَأَنْوَارِهِ وَهِيَ حَلاوَةُ الْمُعَامَلَةِ وَالْمَعْرِفَةِ. يُحْكَى عَنْ أَبِي عَلِي الدقّاق أَنَّهُ جَلَسَ يَوْماً مَعَ بَعْضِ أَصْحَابِهِ فَكَانَتْ مِنْهُ غَفْلَةٌ حَتَّى شَكَى ضِيقَ حَالِهِ، فَلَمَّا تَفَرَّقَ أَصْحَابُهُ نَامَ بَعْضُهُمْ فَهَتَفَ بِهِ هَاتِفٌ وَقَالَ « بِاللهِ أَبْلِغْ أَبَا عَبْدِ اللهِ الدقّاق مَا أَقُولُ لَكَ » ثُمَّ أَنْشَدَ:

قُـلْ لِلرُّوَيجِلِ مِنْ ذَوِي الأَقْدَارِ — الْفَقْرُ أَفْضَلُ شِيمَةِ الأَحْـــرَارِ
يَـــا مَنْ شَكَا لِلْخَلْقِ فِعْلَةَ رَبِّهِ — هَلاَّ شَكَوْتَ تَحَمُّـــــلَ الأَوْزَارِ
إِنّ الّذِي أُلْبِسْتَ مِنْ حُلَلِ التُّقَى — لَوْ شَاءَ رَبُّكَ كُنْتَ عَنْهَا عَـــارِ

٤٠ - **الذِّكْر**: وَهُوَ إِذَا أُطْلِقَ يَنْصَرِفُ لِذِكْرِ اللِّسَانِ، وَهُوَ رُكْنٌ قَوِيٌّ فِي طَرِيقِ الْوُصُولِ، وَهُوَ مَنْشُورُ الْوِلايَةِ، فَمَنْ أُلْهِمَ الذِّكْرَ فَقَدْ أُعْطِيَ الْمَنْشُورَ، وَمَنْ سُلِبَ الذِّكْرَ فَقَدْ عُزِلَ. فَذِكْرُ الْعَامَّةِ بِاللِّسَانِ وَذِكْرُ الْخَاصَّةِ بِالْجَنَانِ وَذِكْرُ خَاصَّةِ الْخَاصَّةِ بِالرُّوحِ وَالسِّرِّ وَهُوَ الشُّهُودُ وَالْعِيَّانُ، فَيَذْكُرُ اللهَ عِنْدَ كُلِّ شَيْءٍ وَعَلَى كُلِّ شَيْءٍ، أَيْ يَعْرِفُ اللهُ فِيهِ وَهُنَا يَخْرَسُ اللِّسَانُ وَيَبْقَى كَالْمَبْهُوتِ فِي مَحَلِّ الْعِيَّانِ، وَيُعَدُّ ذِكْرُ اللِّسَانِ فِي هَذَا الْمَقَامِ ضُعْفاً وَبِطَالَةً، كَمَا قَالَ الْقَائِلُ:

مَـــا إِنْ ذَكَرْتُكَ الاَّ هَمَّ يَلْعَنُنِي — سِرِّي وَقَلْبِي وَرُوحِي عِنْدَ ذِكْـرَاكَ
حَتَّى كَـأَنّ رَقِيبًا مِنْكَ يَهْتِفُ بِي — إِيَّاكَ وَيْـحَـكَ وَالتِّذْكَارَ إِيَّـــاكَ
أَمَا تَرَى الْحَقَّ قَدْ لاحَتْ شَوَاهِدُهُ — وَوَاصَلَ الْكُلَّ مِنْ مَعْنَاهُ مَعْنَـــاكَ

وَقَالَ الْوَاسِطِيُّ مُشِيرًا لِهَذَا الْمَقَامِ: «الذَّاكِرُونَ فِي ذِكْرِهِ أَشَدُّ غَفْلَةً مِنَ النَّاسِينَ لِذِكْرِهِ لِأَنَّ ذِكْرَهُ سِوَاهُ».

٤١ - **الوَقْت**: قَدْ يُطْلِقُونَهُ عَلَى مَا يَكُونُ الْعَبْدُ عَلَيْهِ فِي الْحَالِ مِنْ قَبْضٍ أَوْ بَسْطٍ أَوْ حُزْنٍ أَوْ سُرُورٍ. قَالَ أَبُو عَلِي الدقّاق: «الْوَقْتُ مَا أَنْتَ بِهِ

فِي الْحَالِ، فَإِنْ كُنْتَ بِالدُّنْيَا فوقتُكَ الدُّنْيَا، وَإِن كُنْتَ بِالْعُقْبَى فوقتُكَ الْعُقْبَى». يُرِيدُ أَنَّ الْوَقْتَ مَا كَانَ الْغَالِبُ عَلَى الإنْسَانِ وَقَدْ يَعْنُونَ بِهِ الزَّمَانَ الّذي بَيْنَ الْمَاضِي وَالْمُسْتَقْبَلِ يَقُولُونَ: «الصُّوفِيُّ ابْنُ وَقْتِهِ» يُرِيدُونَ أَنَّهُ مُشْتَغِلٌ بِمَا هُوَ أَوْلَى بِهِ فِي الْوَقْتِ لا يُدَبِّرُ فِي مُسْتَقْبَلٍ وَلا مَاضٍ، بَلْ يَهُمُّهُ ما هوَ فِيهِ. وَكُلُّ وَقْتٍ لَهُ آدَابٌ تُطْلَبُ فِيهِ فَمَنْ أَخَلَّ بِآدَابِهِ مَقتَهُ، وَلِذَلِكَ قِيلَ الْوَقْتُ كَالسَّيْفِ فَمَنْ لايَنَهُ سَلِمَ وَمَنْ خَاشَنَهُ قُصِمَ وَمُلاينَتُهُ الْقِيَّامُ بِآدَابِهِ، فَوَقْتُ الْقَهْرِيَّةِ آدَابُهُ الرِّضَى وَالتَّسْلِيمُ تَحْتَ مَجَارِي الأَقْدَارِ، وَوَقْتُ النِّعْمَةِ آدَابُهُ الشُّكْرُ، وَوَقْتُ الطَّاعَةِ آدَابُهُ شُهُودُ الْمِنَّةِ مِنَ اللهِ، وَوَقْتُ الْمَعْصِيَّةِ آدَابُهُ التَّوْبَةُ وَالإِنَابَةُ.

٤٢ - **الْحَال والْمَقَام**: الْحَالُ مَعْنَى يَرِدُ عَلَى الْقَلْبِ مِنْ غَيْرِ تَعَمُّلٍ وَلا اجْتِلابٍ وَلا تَسَبُّبٍ وَلا اكْتِسَابٍ مِنْ بَسْطٍ أَوْ قَبْضٍ أَوْ شَوْقٍ أَوْ انْزِعَاجٍ أَوْ هَيْبَةٍ أَوْ اهْتِيَاجٍ، وَيَظْهَرُ أَثَرُهُ عَلَى الْجَوَارِحِ قَبْلَ التَّمَكُّنِ مِنْ شَطْحٍ وَرَقْصٍ وَسَيْرٍ وَهُيَامٍ، وَهُوَ أَثَرُ الْمَحَبَّةِ لِانَّهَا تُحَرِّكُ السَّاكِنَ أَوَّلاً ثُمَّ تَسْكُنُ وَتَطْمَئِنُّ، وَلِذَا قِيلَ فِيهَا: أَوَّلُهَا جُنُونٌ وَوَسَطُهَا فُنُونٌ وَآخِرُهَا سُكُونٌ، وَقَدْ يُكْتَسَبُ الْحَالُ بِنَوْعِ تَعَمُّلٍ كَحُضُورِ حِلَقِ الذِّكْرِ وَاسْتِعْمَالِ السَّمَاعِ وَقَدْ يُطْلَبُ اكْتِسَابُهُ بِخَرْقِ عَوَائِدِ النَّفْسِ حِينَ تَعْتَرِيهَا بُرُودَةٌ وَفُتُورٌ وَفَرْقٌ وَكَسَلٌ فَيَنْبَغِي أَنْ يَتَحَرَّكَ فِي تَسْخِينِهَا بِمَا يَثْقُلُ عَلَيْهَا مِنْ خَرْقِ الْعَوَائِدِ. وَقَدْ يُطْلَقُ الْحَالُ عَلَى الْمَقَامِ فَيُقَالُ فُلانٌ صَارَ عِنْدَهُ الشُّهُودُ مَثَلاً حَالاً وَمِنْهُ قَوْلُ الْمَجْذُوبِ:

حَقَّقْتُ مَا وَجَدْتُ غَيْرَهُ ... وَأَمْسَيْتُ فِي الْحَالِ هَانِي

وَأَمَّا الْمَقَامُ فَهُوَ مَا يَتَحَقَّقُهُ الْعَبْدُ بِمُنَازَلَةٍ وَاجْتِهَادٍ مِنَ الأَدَبِ وَمَا يَتَمَكَّنُ فِيهِ مِنْ مَقَامَاتِ الْيَقِينِ بِتَكَسُّبٍ وَتَطَلُّبٍ، فَمَقَامُ كُلِّ وَاحِدٍ مَوْضِعُ إِقَامَتِهِ فَالْمَقَامَاتُ تَكُونُ أَوَّلاً أَحْوَالاً حَيْثُ لا يَتَمَكَّنُ الْمُرِيدُ مِنْهَا لأَنَّهَا تَتَحَوَّلُ ثُمَّ تَصِيرُ مَقَامَاتٍ بَعْدَ التَّمْكِينِ كَالتَّوْبَةِ مَثَلاً تَحْصُلُ ثُمَّ تَنْقُصُ حَتَّى تَصِيرَ مَقَامًا وَهِيَ التَّوْبَةُ النَّصُوحُ وَهَكَذَا بَقِيَّةُ الْمَقَامَاتِ، وَشَرْطُهُ أَنْ لا يَرْتَقِي مَقَامًا حَتَّى يسْتَوْفِي أَحْكَامَهُ فَمَنْ لا تَوْبَةَ لَهُ لا يَصِحُّ لَهُ إِنَابَةٌ، وَمَنْ لا إِنَابَةَ لَهُ لا تَصِحُّ لَهُ اسْتِقَامَةٌ، وَمَنْ لا وَرَعَ لَهُ لا تَصِحُّ لَهُ زُهْدٌ، وَهَكَذَا. وَقَدْ يَتَحَقَّقُ الْمَقَامُ الأَوَّلِ بِالثَّانِي إِذَا تَرَقَّى عَنْهُ قَبْلَ إِحْكَامِهِ إِنْ كَانَ لَهُ شَيْخٌ كَامِلٌ وَقَد يَطْوِي عَنْهُ الْمَقَامَاتِ وَيَدُسُّهُ إِلَى الْفَنَاءِ إِنْ رَآهُ أَهْلاً بِتَوَقُّدِ قَرِيحَتِهِ وَرِقَّةِ فِطْنَتِهِ فَالأَحْوَالُ مَوَاهِبُ، وَالْمَقَامَاتُ مَكَاسِبُ، هَذَا مَعْنَى الْمَقَامِ بِفَتْحِ الْمِيمِ. وَأَمَّا الْمُقَامُ بِالضَّمِّ فَمَعْنَاهُ الإِقَامَةُ وَلا يَكْمُلُ لأَحَدٍ مُنَازَلَةُ مَقَامٍ إِلاَّ بِشُهُودِ إِقَامَةِ الْحَقِّ تَعَالَى فِيهِ. وَفِي الْحِكَمِ « مِنْ عَلامَاتِ النُّجْحِ فِي النِّهَايَاتِ، الرُّجُوعُ إِلَى اللهِ تَعَالَى فِي الْبِدَايَاتِ». وَقَالَ أَيْضاً « مَنْ كَانَتْ بِاللهِ بِدَايَتُهُ كَانَتْ إِلَيْهِ نِهَايَتُهُ ».

٤٣ - **القَبْضُ والبَسْطُ**: هُمَا حَالَتَانِ بَعْدَ التَّرَقِّي مِنْ حَالِ الْخَوْفِ وَالرَّجَاءِ، فَالْقَبْضُ لِلْعَارِفِ بِمَنْزِلَةِ الْخَوْفِ لِلطَّالِبِ وَالْبَسْطُ لِلْعَارِفِ بِمَنْزِلَةِ الرَّجَاءِ لِلْمُرِيدِ. وَالْفَرْقُ بَيْنَ الْقَبْضِ وَالْخَوْفِ وَبَيْنَ الرَّجَاءِ وَالْبَسْطِ أَنّ الْخَوْفَ مُتَعَلَّقُهُ مُسْتَقِلٌّ، إِمَّا فَوَاتُ مَحْبُوبٍ أَوْ هُجُومُ مَحْذُورٍ، بِخِلافِ الْقَبْضِ فَإِنَّهُ مَعْنَى يَحْصُلُ فِي الْقَلْبِ إِمَّا بِسَبَبٍ أَوْ لا. وَكَذَلِكَ الرَّجَاءُ يَكُونُ لِإِنْتِظَارِ مَحْبُوبٍ فِي الْمُسْتَقْبَلِ، وَالْبَسْطُ شَيْءٌ مَوْهُوبٌ يَحْصُلُ فِي الْوَقْتِ. فَحَقِيقَةُ

الْقَبْضِ انْكِمَاشٌ وَضِيقٌ يَحْصُلُ فِي الْقَلْبِ يُوجِبُ السُّكُونَ وَالْهُدُوءَ، وَالْبَسْطُ انْطِلَاقٌ وَانْشِرَاحٌ لِلْقَلْبِ يُوجِبُ التَّحَرُّكَ وَالِانْبِسَاطَ وَلِكُلِّ وَاحِدٍ آدَابٌ مَذْكُورَةٌ فِي الْمُطَوَّلَاتِ .

٤٤ - الْخَوَاطِرُ وَالْوَارِدَاتُ: الْخَوَاطِرُ خِطَابَاتٌ تَرِدُ عَلَى الْقُلُوبِ تَكُونُ بِإِلْقَاءِ مَلَكٍ أَوْ شَيْطَانٍ أَوْ حَدِيثِ نَفْسٍ، فَإِنْ كَانَ مِنَ الْمَلَكِ فَإِلْهَامٌ أَوْ مِنَ الشَّيْطَانِ فَوَسْوَاسٌ أَوْ مِنَ النَّفْسِ فَهَوَاجِسُ، فَمَا وَافَقَ الْحَقَّ وَدَعَا إِلَى اتِّبَاعِهِ فَمِنَ الْمَلَكِ، وَمَا وَافَقَ الْبَاطِلَ أَوْ دَعَا إِلَى مَعْصِيَّةٍ غَالِبًا فَمِنَ الشَّيْطَانِ، وَقَدْ يَدْعُو إِلَى الطَّاعَةِ حَيْثُ يَتَرَتَّبُ عَلَيْهَا مَعْصِيَّةٌ كَالرِّيَاءِ وَحُبِّ الْمَدْحِ. وَمَا دَعَا إِلَى اتِّبَاعِ الشَّهْوَةِ وَالدَّعَةِ، أَيِ الرَّاحَةِ، فَمِنَ النَّفْسِ. قَالَ أَبُو عَلِي الدقاق « مَنْ أَكَلَ الْحَرَامَ لَمْ يُفَرِّقْ بَيْنَ الْإِلْهَامِ وَالْوَسْوَاسِ، وَكَذَلِكَ مَنْ كَانَ قُوتُهُ مَعْلُومًا ». وَفَرَّقَ الْجُنَيْدُ بَيْنَ هَوَاجِسِ النَّفْسِ وَوَسْوَاسِ الشَّيْطَانِ بِأَنَّ مَا دَعَتْ إِلَيْهِ النَّفْسُ لَا تَنْتَقِلُ عَنْهُ، بَلْ تُعَاوِدُهُ مَرَّةً بَعْدَ مَرَّةٍ إِلَّا بَعْدَ مُجَاهَدَةٍ كَبِيرَةٍ، وَوَسْوَاسُ الشَّيْطَانِ يَنْتَقِلُ عَنْهَا فَإِذَا خَالَفْتَهُ فِي مَعْصِيَّةٍ انْتَقَلَ لِأُخْرَى، وَرُبَّمَا ذَهَبَ بِالتَّعَوُّذِ وَنَحْوِهِ. وَلِذَلِكَ كَانَتِ النَّفْسُ أَخْبَثَ مِنْ سَبْعِينَ شَيْطَانًا. وَأَمَّا الْوَارِدَاتُ فَهِيَ مَا يَرِدُ عَلَى الْقُلُوبِ مِنَ التَّجَلِّيَاتِ الْقَوِيَّةِ أَوِ الْخَوَاطِرِ الْمَحْمُودَةِ بِمَا لَا يَكُونُ لِلْعَبْدِ فِيهِ تَكَسُّبٌ. وَالْفَرْقُ بَيْنَ الْخَوَاطِرِ وَالْوَارِدَاتِ أَنَّ الْوَارِدَاتِ أَعَمُّ مِنَ الْخَوَاطِرِ لِأَنَّ الْخَوَاطِرَ تَخْتَصُّ بِنَوْعٍ أَوْ مَا يَتَضَمَّنُ مَعْنَاهُ وَالْوَارِدَاتُ تَكُونُ وَارِدَ سُرُورٍ وَوَارِدَ حُزْنٍ وَوَارِدَ قَبْضٍ وَوَارِدَ بَسْطٍ وَوَارِدَ شَوْقٍ وَوَارِدَ خَوْفٍ إِلَى غَيْرِ ذَلِكَ مِنَ الْمَعَانِي، وَقَدْ يَخْتَطِفُهُ عَنْ شَاهِدِ حِسِّهِ،

وَهُوَ قَرِيبٌ مِنَ الحَالِ، وَقَدْ يَأْتِي الْوَارِدُ بِكَشْفِ غَيْبٍ فَيَجِبُ تَصْدِيقُهُ إِنْ صَفَا الْقَلْبُ مِنْ كُدورَةِ الْخَوَاطِرِ، وَاللهُ تَعَالَى أَعْلَمُ.

٤٥ - **النَّفْسُ والرُّوحُ والسِّرُّ**: النَّفْسُ عِنْدَ الْقَوْمِ عِبارَةٌ عَمَّا يُذَمُّ مِن أَفْعَالِ الْعَبْدِ وَأَخْلاقِهِ، فَالأَوَّلُ ما كَانَ مِنْ كَسْبِ الْعَبْدِ كَمَعَاصِيهِ وَمُخَالَفَتِهِ، وَالثَّانِي مَا كَانَ مِنْ جِبِلَّتِهِ وَطَبِيعَتِهِ كَالْكِبْرِ وَالْحَسَدِ وَالْغَضَبِ وَسُوءِ الْخُلُقِ وَقِلَّةِ الاحْتِمَالِ وَغَيْرِ ذَلِكَ مِنَ الأَخْلاقِ الذَّمِيمَةِ يُنْسَبُ لِلنَّفْسِ أَدَباً مَعَ الْحَقِّ. وَالرُّوحُ عِبارَةٌ عَنْ مَحَلِّ التَّجَلِّيَاتِ الإِلَهِيَّةِ وَكَشْفِ الأَنْوَارِ الْمَلَكُوتِيَّةِ. وَالسِّرُّ عِبارَةٌ عَنْ مَحَلِّ تَجَلِّيَاتِ الأَسْرَارِ الْجَبَرُوتِيَّةِ. فَالنَّفْسُ لِلْعَوَامِّ، وَالرُّوحُ لِلْخَوَاصِّ، والسِّرُّ لِخَوَاصِّ الْخَوَاصِّ، النَّفْسُ لِأَهْلِ عَالَمِ الْمُلْكِ، وَالرُّوحُ لِأَهْلِ عَالَمِ الْمَلَكُوتِ، وَالسِّرُّ لِأَهْلِ عَالَمِ الْجَبَرُوتِ، وَسَيَأْتِي حَقَائِقُهَا. وَهَلِ النَّفْسُ وَالرُّوحُ وَالسِّرُّ مُتَعَدِّدَاتٌ فِي نَفْسِهَا أَوْ مُتَّحِدَةٌ وَإِنَّمَا تَخْتَلِفُ التَّسْمِيَةُ بِاخْتِلافِ التَّصْفِيَةِ ؟ قَالَ بَعْضُهُمْ: النَّفْسُ لَطِيفَةٌ مُودَعَةٌ فِي هَذَا الْقَالَبِ هِيَ مَحَلُّ الأَخْلاقِ الْمَعْلُولَةِ كَمَا أَنَّ الرُّوحَ لَطِيفَةٌ مُودَعَةٌ فِي هَذَا الْقَالَبِ هِيَ مَحَلُّ الأَخْلاقِ الْمَحْمُودَةِ. وَمَحَلُّهُمَا وَاحِدٌ وَهُوَ الإِنْسَانُ، فَالنَّفْسُ وَالرُّوحُ مِنَ الأَجْسَادِ اللَّطِيفَةِ كَالْمَلائِكَةِ وَالشَّيَاطِينِ وَهُمَا سَاكِنَانِ فِي الإِنْسَانِ. فَكَمَا أَنَّ الْبَصَرَ مَحَلُّ الرُّؤْيَةِ وَالأُذُنَ مَحَلُّ السَّمْعِ وَالأَنْفَ مَحَلُّ الشَّمِّ مِنْ ذَاتٍ وَاحِدَةٍ، فَكَذَلِكَ مَحَلُّ الأَوْصَافِ الذَّمِيمَةِ النَّفْسُ، وَمَحَلُّ الأَوْصَافِ الْحَمِيدَةِ الرُّوحُ. وَأَمَّا السِّرُّ فَهُوَ لَطِيفَةٌ مُودَعَةٌ فِي الْقَلْبِ كَالرُّوحِ إِلاَّ أَنَّهُ أَشْرَفُ مِنَ الرُّوحِ لِكَمَالِ أَوْصَافِهِ. وَقَالَ السَّاحِلِي: « النَّفْسُ وَالْقَلْبُ وَالرُّوحُ وَالسِّرُّ وَالْبَاطِنُ أَسْمَاءٌ لِمُسَمًّى وَاحِدٍ

وَهُوَ اللَّطِيفَةُ الرَّبَّانِيَّةُ الّتِي كَانَ الإِنْسَانُ بِهَا إِنْسَانًا، وَتَخْتَلِفُ أَسْمَاؤُهَا بِاخْتِلافِ أَوْصَافِهَا. فَإِنْ مَالَتْ لِجِهَةِ النَّقْصِ سُمِّيَتْ نَفْسًا وَإِنْ تَخَلَّصَتْ مِنْ مَقَامِ الإِسْلامِ إِلَى مَقَامِ الإِيمَانِ سُمِّيَتْ قَلْبًا وَإِنْ خَلُصَتْ مِنْهُ إِلَى مَقَامِ الإِحْسَانِ وَلَكِنْ بَقِيَ فِيهَا أَثَرُ النَّقْصِ كَأَثَرِ الجِرَاحَاتِ بَعْدَ الْبُرْءِ سُمِّيَتْ رُوحاً وَإِنْ ذَهَبَتْ تِلْكَ الآثَارُ وَصَفَتْ سُمِّيَتْ سِرًّا وَإِنْ أَشْكَلَ الأَمْرُ سُمِّيَتْ بِالْبَاطِنِ. وَالإِخْتِلافُ فِي الرُّوحِ شَهِيرٌ. قَالَ بَعْضُهُمْ هِيَ الْحَيَاةُ، وَقَالَ بَعْضُهُمْ أَعْيَانٌ مُودعَةٌ فِي هَذِهِ الْقَوَالِبِ أَجْرَى اللهُ الْعَادَةَ بِخَلْقِ الْحَيَاةِ فِي الْقَالَبِ مَا دَامَتِ الْحَيَاةُ فِيهِ فَالإِنْسَانُ حَيٌّ بِالْحَيَاةِ، وَلَكِنَّ الأَرْوَاحَ مُودَعة فِي الْقَوَالِبِ وَلَهَا تَرَقٍّ فِي حَالِ النَّوْمِ، وَمُفَارَقَةٌ وَرُجُوعٌ. وَهِيَ الَّتِي وَقَعَ بِهَا النَّفْخُ. وَأَمَّا النَّفْسُ فَهِيَ مَخْلُوقَةٌ فِي الْجَنِينِ قَبْلَ نَفْخِ الرُّوحِ، بِهَا يَقَعُ التَّحَرُّكُ، وَهِيَ مُلازِمَةٌ لِلْبَدَنِ لا تُفَارِقُهُ إِلاّ بِالْمَوْتِ فَتَخْرُجُ الرُّوحُ أَوّلاً ثُمَّ تَنْقَطِعُ النَّفْسُ فَتُقْطَعُ الْحَيَاةُ. فَالإِنْسَانُ رُوحٌ وَنَفسٌ وَجَسَدٌ، وَالْحَشْرُ لِلْجُمْلَةِ، وَكَذلِكَ الْعِقَابُ وَالثَّوَاب. وَالأَرْوَاحُ مَخْلُوقَةٌ قَبْلَ الأَبْدَانِ سَارِيَةٌ فِيهَا سَرَيَانَ النَّارِ فِي الْفَحْمِ وَالْمَاء فِي الْعُودِ الرَّطْبِ ». قُلْتُ هَذِهِ الأَعْيَانُ الْمُودَعَةُ فِي الْقَوَالِبِ هِيَ اللَّطِيفَةُ الرّبّانِيّةُ اللاّهُوتِيّةُ وَهِيَ الَّتِي تَتَطَوّرُ وَتَخْتَلِفُ أَسْمَاؤُهَا بِاخْتِلافِ تَطَوُّرِهَا كَمَا قَالَ الساحِلِي، وَاللهُ أَعْلَم، وَكَوْنُ الأَرْوَاحِ حَادِثَةٌ يَجْرِي عَلَى مَذْهَبِ أَهْلِ الْفَرْقِ، وَأَمَّا أَهْلُ الْجَمْعِ فَلا حَادِثَ عِنْدَهُمْ لِفَنَاءِ الْكَائِنَاتِ عَنْ نَظَرِهِمْ، قَالَ الْجُنَيْدُ « إِذَا اقْتَرَنَ الْحَادِثُ بِالْقَدِيمِ تَلاشَى الْحَادِثُ وَبَقِي الْقَدِيمُ ». وَسَأَلْتُ بَعْضَ إِخْوَانِنَا الْعَارِفِينَ هَلِ الأَرْوَاحُ حَادِثَةٌ أَوْ قَدِيمَةٌ ؟ قَالَ

« الرِّجَالُ الأشْبَاحُ عِنْدَهُمْ قَدِيمَةٌ »، يُشِيرُ إِلَى مَقَامِ الْفنَاءِ كَمَا تَقَدَّمَ، لَكِنَّهُ سِرٌّ مَكْتُوم.

٤٦ - **النَّصر والتَّأْيِيدُ والعِصْمَة والرُّشْدُ والتَّسْدِيد**: النَّصْرُ تَقْوِيَّةُ الْجَوَارِحِ عَلَى فِعْلِ الْخَيْرِ، وَالتَّأْيِيدُ تقْوِيَّةُ الْبَصِيرَةِ مِنْ دَاخِلٍ، فَالْبَاعِثُ الْبَاطِنِيُّ تَأْيِيدٌ، وَالْبَطْشُ وَمُسَاعَدَةُ الأسْبَابِ مِنْ خَارِجٍ نَصْرٌ، وَهُوَ جَامِعٌ لِلْهِدَايَةِ الَّتِي مَرْجِعُهَا لِلْبَصِيرَةِ الْعِلْمِيَّةِ الْكَاشِفَةِ لِمَا عَلَيْهِ الشَّيْءُ بِحَقِيقَتِهِ وَالرُّشْدُ الَّذِي مَرْجِعُهُ إِلَى الإِرَادَةِ الْبَاعِثَةِ إِلَى جِهَةِ السَّعَادَةِ، وَالتَّسْدِيدُ الَّذي مَرْجِعُهُ إِلَى الْقُدْرَةِ عَلَى تَوْجِيهِ الْحَرَكَاتِ إِلَى نَحْوِ الْمَطْلُوبِ وَتَيْسِيرِهَا عَلَيْهِ مِنَ التَّأْيِيدِ، وَيَقْتَرِب مِن التَّأْيِيدِ الْجَامِعِ لِمَا ذُكِرَ الْعِصْمَةُ وَهِيَ عِبَارَةٌ عَنْ وُجُودٍ إِلَهِي يُسَبِّحُ فِي الْبَطْنِ يَقْوَى بِهِ الإِنْسَانُ عَلَى تَحَرِّي الْخَيْرِ وَتَجَنُّبِ الشَّرِّ حَتَّى يَصِيرَ كَمَانِعٍ فِي بَاطِنِهِ غَيْرِ مَحْسُوسٍ. قَالَ الْغَزَالِي: فَهَذِهِ سِتُّ حَقائِق: الْهِدَايَةُ، وَالرُّشْدُ، وَالْعِصْمَةُ، وَالتَّسْدِيدُ، النَّصْرُ، وَالتَّأْيِيدُ. وَقَدْ عَلِمْتُ كُلَّهَا مِنْ كَلامِ الْغَزَالِي رَضِيَ اللهُ عَنْهُ، وَالتَّحْقِيقُ أَنّ الْهِدَايَةَ هِيَ تَصْوِيبُ الْعَبْدِ إِلَى طَرِيقٍ تُوصِلُهُ إِلَى الْحَقِّ وَقَدْ تُطْلَقُ عَلَى بَيَانِهَا فَقَطْ (وَالرُّشْدُ) هُوَ تَوْجِيهُ الْقَلْبِ إِلَى طَرِيقِ السَّعَادَةِ (وَالتَّسْدِيدُ) هُوَ الْقُدْرَةُ عَلَى سُلُوكِ طَرِيقِ الْخَيْرِ وَتَجَنُّبِ الشَّرِّ (وَالْعِصْمَةُ) هُوَ وُجُودٌ إِلَهِيٌّ إِلَى آخِرِ مَا تَقَدَّمَ

٤٧ - **الْحِكْمَة**: وَهِي إِتْقَان الشَّيْء وَإِبْدَاعُهُ، فَفِي الْعِلْم تَحْقِيقُه وَالْعَمَل بِه وَفِي الْقَوْل إِيجَازُه وَتَكْثِيرُ مَعَانِيه وَفِي الْعَمَل إِتْقَانُه وَإِكْمَالُه، وَيُقَالُ

نَزَلَتِ الْحِكْمَةُ عَلَى ثَلَاثِ فِرَقٍ: عَلَى أَلْسِنَةِ الْعَرَبِ وَأَيْدِي الصِّينِ وَعُقُولِ الْيُونَانِ وَاللهُ أَعْلَم

٤٨ - الْعَقْل: وَهُوَ نُورٌ يُمَيَّزُ بِهِ بَيْنَ النَّافِعِ وَالضَّارِّ، وَيَحْجِزُ صَاحِبَهُ عَنِ ارْتِكَابِ الْأَوْزَارِ أَوْ نُورٌ رُوحَانِيٌّ تُدْرِكُ بِهِ النَّفْسُ الْعُلُومَ الضَّرُورِيَّةَ وَالنَّظَرِيَّةَ أَوْ قُوَّةٌ مُهَيَّئَةٌ لِقَبُولِ الْعِلْمِ، سُمِّيَ عَقْلاً لِأَنَّهُ يَعْقِلُ صَاحِبَهُ عَمَّا لَا يَنْبَغِي، وَهُوَ عَلَى قِسْمَيْنِ: عَقْلٌ أَكْبَرُ وَعَقْلٌ أَصْغَرُ، أَمَّا الْعَقْلُ الْأَكْبَرُ فَهُوَ أَوَّلُ نُورٍ أَظْهَرَهُ اللهُ لِلْوُجُودِ وَيُقَالُ لَهُ الرُّوحُ الْأَعْظَمُ، وَيُسَمَّى أَيْضًا بِالْقَبْضَةِ الْمُحَمَّدِيَّةِ وَمِنْ نُورِهِ يَمْتَدُّ الْعَقْلُ الْأَصْغَرُ كَامْتِدَادِ الْقَمَرِ مِنْ نُورِ الشَّمْسِ فَلَا يَزَالُ نُورُهُ يَنْمُو بِالطَّاعَةِ وَالرِّيَاضَةِ وَالتَّطْهِيرِ مِنَ الْهَوَى حَتَّى يَدْخُلَ الْعَبْدُ مَقَامَ الْإِحْسَانِ وَتُشْرِقَ عَلَيْهِ شَمْسُ الْعِرْفَانِ فَيَنْطَوِي نُورُهُ فِي نُورِ الْعَقْلِ الْأَكْبَرِ كَانْطِوَاءِ نُورِ الْقَمَرِ عِنْدَ طُلُوعِ الشَّمْسِ فَيَرَى مِنَ الْأَسْرَارِ وَالْغُيُوبِ مَا لَمْ يَكُنْ يَرَهُ قَبْلُ، لِأَنَّ الْعَقْلَ الْأَصْغَرَ نُورُهُ ضَعِيفٌ لَايُدْرِكُ إِلا افْتِقَارَ الصَّنْعَةِ إِلَى صَانِعِهَا وَلَا يَدْرِى مَا وَرَاءَ ذَلِكَ بِخِلافِ الْعَقْلِ الْأَكْبَرِ فَإِنَّهُ يُدْرِكُ الصَّانِعَ الْقَدِيمَ قَبْلَ التَّجَلِّي وَبَعْدَهُ لِصَفَاءِ نُورِهِ وَشِدَّةَ شُعَاعِهِ. وَفِي بَعْضِ الْأَخْبَارِ: «أَوَّلُ مَا خَلَقَ اللهُ الْعَقْلَ. فَقَالَ لَهُ أَقْبِلْ فَأَقْبَلَ، ثُمَّ قَالَ أَدْبِرْ فَأَدْبَرَ ثُمَّ قَالَ لَهُ اقْعُدْ فَقَعَدَ ثُمَّ قَالَ لَهُ قُمْ فَقَامَ فَقَالَ: وَعِزَّتِي وَجَلَالِي مَا خَلَقْتُ خَلْقاً وَلَا شَيْئًا أَعَزَّ عَلَيَّ مِنْكَ. بِكَ آخُذُ وَبِكَ أُعْطِي». وَفِي بَعْضِ الرِّوَايَاتِ: «بِكَ أُعْبَدُ وَبِكَ أُعْصَى» أَوْ كَمَا قَالَ ﷺ، وَالْحَدِيثُ مُتَكَلَّمٌ فِيهِ. فَالْعَقْلُ الْأَكْبَرُ لَا يَنَالُهُ إِلا الْمَحْبُوبُونَ الَّذِينَ اخْتَرَاهُمُ اللهُ لِمَعْرِفَتِهِ الْخَاصَّةِ، وَأَمَّا الْعَقْلُ

الأَصْغَرُ فَيُعْطِيهِ لِلْخَاصِّ وَالْعَامِّ وَهُوَ عَلَى قِسْمَيْنِ: عَقْلٌ مَوْهُوبٌ وَعَقْلٌ مَكْسُوبٌ، فَالْمَوْهُوبُ هُوَ الَّذِي جَعَلَ اللهُ فِيهِ غَرِيزَةً وَالْمَكْسُوبُ هُوَ الَّذِي يُكْتَسَبُ بِالتَّجَارِيبِ وَالرِّيَاضَاتِ وَارْتِكَابِ الْمِحَنِ. قَالَ بَعْضُهُمْ: وَعَلامَةُ الْعَقْلِ ثَلاثٌ: تَقْوَى اللهِ عَزَّوَجَلَّ، وَصِدْقُ الْحَدِيثِ، وَتَرْكُ مَا لا يَعْنِي. وَقَالَ عَلَيْهِ الصَّلَاةُ وَالسَّلَامُ: «أَلا وَإِنَّ مِنْ علامَاتِ الْعَقْلِ التَّجَافِي عَنْ دَارِ الْغُرُورِ وَالإِنَابَةُ إِلَى دَارِ الْخُلُودِ وَالتَّزَوُّدُ لِسُكْنَى الْقُبُورِ وَالتَّأَهُّبُ لِيَوْمِ النُّشُورِ». وَقَالَ بَعْضُ الْحُكَمَاءِ: خَيْرُ مَا أُعْطِيَ الإِنْسَانُ عَقْلٌ يَزْجُرُهُ، فَإِنْ لَمْ يَكُنْ فَحَيَاءٌ يَمْنَعُهُ فَإِنْ لَمْ يَكُنْ فَمَالٌ يَسْتُرُهُ، فَإِنْ لَمْ يَكُنْ فَصَاعِقَةٌ تُحْرِقُهُ تَسْتَرِيحُ مِنْهُ الْبِلادُ وَالْعِبادُ. وَهَلِ الأَرْوَاحُ قَبْلَ الأَشْبَاحِ كَانَ لَهَا عَقْلٌ وَالتَّحْقِيقُ أَنَّهَا كَانَتْ لَهَا عُقُولٌ مُقْتَبَسَةٌ مِنَ الْعَقْلِ الأَكْبَرِ فَلِذَلِكَ أَقَرَّتْ بِالرُّبُوبِيَّةِ بَلْ كَانَتْ عَلامَةً دَارِكَةً لِلأَشْيَاءِ كَمَا قَالَ ابْنُ الْبَنَّا. وَالْمَعْرِفَةُ وَالإِدْرَاكُ إِنَّمَا يَكُونَانِ بِالْعَقْلِ فَلَمَّا بَرَزَتْ لِعَالَمِ الأَشْبَاحِ أَزَالَ اللهُ مِنْهَا ذَلِكَ الْعَقْلَ الَّذِي هُوَ مِنَ الْعَقْلِ الأَكْبَرِ، وَأَنْبَتَ فِيهَا الْعَقْلُ الأَصْغَرُ عِنْدَ اجْتِنَانِ الْوَلَدِ فِي الْبَطْنِ فَمَا زَالَ يَنْمُو إِلَى الْحُلُمِ. وَقِيلَ إِلَى أَرْبَعِينَ سَنَة. فَإِذَا اتَّصَلَ الْعَبْدُ بِالطَّبِيبِ عَالَجَهُ حَتَّى يُوصِلَهُ إِلَى الْعَقْلِ الأَكْبَرِ فَيَكُونُ صَاحِبُهُ مِنَ الأَوْلِيَاءِ الْكِبَارِ، وَبِاللهِ التَّوْفِيق.

٤٩ - **التَّوْحِيد**: وَهُوَ عَلَى قِسْمَيْنِ: تَوْحِيدُ الْبُرْهَانِ وَهُوَ إِفْرَادُ الْحَقِّ بِالأَفْعَالِ وَالصِّفَاتِ وَالذَّاتِ مِنْ طَرِيقِ الْبُرْهَانِ، وَتَوْحِيدُ الْعِيَانِ وَهُوَ إِفْرَادُ الْحَقِّ بِالْوُجُودِ فِي الأَزَلِ وَالأَبَدِ. وَقَالَ الْجُنَيْد رَضِيَ اللهُ عَنْهُ: «هُوَ مَعْنًى تَضْمَحِلُّ فِيهِ الرُّسُومُ وَتَنْدَرِجُ فِيهِ الْعُلُومُ وَيَكُونُ

اللّٰهُ كَمَا لَمْ يَزَلْ، وَأُصُولُهُ خَمْسَةُ أَشْيَاءٍ: رَفْعُ الْحَدَثِ وَإِفْرَادُ الْقِدَمِ وَهُجْرَانُ الإِخْوَانِ وَمُفَارَقَةُ الأَوْطَانِ وَنِسْيَانُ مَا عُلِمَ وَمَا جُهِلَ». قُلْتُ: وَالْمَعْنَى الَّذِي تَضْمَحِلُّ فِيهِ الرُّسُومُ هُوَ ظُهُورُ أَسْرَارِ الذَّاتِ فَإِذَا وَقَعَ الْكَشْفُ عَنْهَا بِغَيْبَةِ حِسّ الْكَائِنَاتِ الَّتِي هِيَ أَوَانِي لِتِلْكَ الْمَعَانِي انْفَرَدَ الْحَقُّ بِالْوُجُودِ وَيَكُونُ فِيمَا لَمْ يَزَلْ كَمَا كَانَ فِي الأَزَلِ: كَانَ اللّٰهُ وَلا شَيْءَ مَعَهُ وَهُوَ الآنَ كَمَا كَانَ. فَيَرْتَفِعُ الْحَدَثُ وَيَنْفَرِدُ وَيَهْجُرُ صَاحِبُ هَذَا الذَّوْقِ جَمِيعَ الإِخْوَانِ إِلاّ مَنْ يَسْتَعِينُ بِهِمْ عَلَى رَبِّهِ وَيُفَارِقُ الاوطَانَ فِي طَلَبِ الْحَقِّ لأَنَّ الْهِجْرَةُ سُنَّةٌ وَيَنْسَى مَا عَلِمَ وَمَا جَهِلَ، أَيْ يَغِيب عَنْهُ فِي جَنْبِ الْكَنْزِ الَّذِي ظَفِرَ بِهِ. وَسُئِلَ أَيْضاً رَضِيَ اللهُ عَنْهُ عَنِ التَّوْحِيدِ فَقَالَ: « لَوْنُ الْمَاءِ لَوْنُ إِنَائِهِ » وَمَعْنَى كَلامِهِ رَضِيَ اللهُ عَنْهُ أَنَّ الذَّاتَ الْعَلِيَّةَ كَانَتْ لَطِيفَةً خَفِيَّةً نُورَانِيَّةً فَلَمَّا تَجَلَّتْ بِالرُّسُومِ وَالأَشْكَالِ تَلَوَّنَتْ بِتَلَوُّنِهَا فَافْهَمْ وَسَلِّمْ إِنْ لَمْ تَذُقْ وَمَقَامَاتُ التَّوْحِيدِ غَيْرُ مُتَنَاهِيَةٍ، لِأَنَّهَا تَتَزَايَدُ بِتَزَايُدِ الْكَشْفِ وَالتَّرَقِّي. فَفَوْقَ التَّوْحِيدِ التَّفْرِيد.

٥٠ - **التَّفْرِيدُ**: فَإِنَّهُ أَرَقُّ مِنَ التَّوْحِيدِ وَأَعْلَى، لِأَنّ التَّوْحِيدَ يَصْدُقُ عَلَى تَوْحِيدِ أَهْلِ الْعِلْمِ وَالتَّفْرِيدُ خَاصٌّ بِأَهْلِ الذّوْقِ. وَفَوْقَ التَّفْرِيدِ:

٥١ - **الأَحَدِيَّةُ، والإِيجَادُ، والفَرْدَانِيَّةُ، الوَحْدَانِيَّةُ، والإِنْفِرَادُ**: وَهَكَذَا رُتْبَتُهُم فِي الْقُوَّةِ، فَالأَحدِيّةُ مُبَالَغَةٌ فِي الْوَحْدَةِ، وَالإِيجَادُ مَصْدَرُ أَوْحَدَ الشَّيْءَ إِذَا صَارَ وَاحِدًا وَالْفَرْدَانِيَّةُ وَالْوَحْدَانِيَّةُ وَالانفِرَادُ مَعْنَاهَا: إِفْرَادُ الْحَقِّ بِالْوُجُودِ وَلا يَكُونُ إِلا بَعْدَ انْطِبَاقِ بَحْرِ الأَحَدِيَّةِ عَلَى الْكُلِّ بِحَيْثُ

لَمْ يَبْقَ وُجُودٌ لِغَيْرِهِ قَطُّ وَهُوَ يَذُوقُ ذَلِكَ ذَوْقاً وَيَغْرَقُ فِيهِ غَرَقاً، وَيُقَالُ لِأَهْلِ هَذَا الْمَقَامِ الأَفْرَادُ وَالآحَادُ وَهُمْ أَكْمَلُ مِنَ الْقُطْبِ فِي الْعِلْمِ بِاللهِ كَمَا قَالَ الْحَاتِمِي وَخَارِجُونَ عَنْ دَائِرَةِ تَصَرُّفِهِ، وَاللهُ تَعَالَى أَعْلَمُ.

٥٢ - **حَقِيقَةُ الذَّاتِ العَلِيَّة**: هِيَ ذَاتٌ كُلِّيَّةٌ أَزَلِيَّةٌ لَطِيفَةٌ خَفِيَّةٌ، مُتَجَلِّيَّةٌ بِالرُّسُومِ وَالأَشْكَالِ مُتَّصِفَةٌ بِصِفَاتِ الْكَمَالِ، وَاحِدَةٌ فِي الأَزَلِ وَفِيمَا لا يَزَالُ هَذَا رَسْمُهَا بِالْخَوَاصِّ وَأَمَّا كُنْهُ الْحَقِيقَةِ فَلا يُحِيطُ بِهَا إِلاّ هُوَ تَعَالَى.

٥٣ - **العَمَا**: وَهُوَ عِبَارَةٌ عَنْ صِفَةِ الذَّاتِ الْعَلِيَّةِ فِي الأَزَلِ قَبْلَ التَّجَلِّي وَحَقِيقَتُهُ فَضَاءٌ لَطِيفٌ خَفِيٌّ صَافِي لايُدْرَكُ. لا حَدَّ لِفَوْقِيَّتِهِ وَلا لِتَحْتِيَّتِهِ وَلا لِجَوَانِبِهِ الأَرْبَعِ، وَلا نِهَايَةَ لأَوَّلِيَّتِهِ وَلا لآخِرِيَّتِهِ، خَالٍ عَنِ الرُّسُومِ وَالأَشْكَالِ مُتَّصِفٌ بِأَوْصَافِ الْكَمَالِ مِنَ الْقُدْرَةِ وَالإِرَادَةِ وَالْعِلْمِ وَالْحَيَاةِ وَالسَّمْعِ وَالْبَصَرِ وَالْكَلامِ، وَيَجْمَعُهُ قَوْلُ ابْنِ الْفَارِضِ فِي خَمرِيَّتِهِ:

يَقُولُونَ لِي صِفْهَا فَأَنْتَ بِوَصْفِهَا ... خَبِيرٌ أَجَلْ عِنْدِي بِأَوْصَافِهَا عِلْمُ
صَفَاءٌ وَلا مَاءٌ وَلُطْفٌ وَلا هَوَى ... وَنُورٌ وَلا نَارٌ وَرُوحٌ وَلاَ جِسْمُ
تَقَدَّمَ كُلَّ الْكَائِنَاتِ حَدِيثُهَا قَدِيماً ... وَلاَ شَكْلٌ هُنَاكَ وَلاَ رَسْمُ

ثُمَّ تَجَلَّتْ بِالرُّسُومِ وَالأَشْكَالِ بِحَيْثُ صَارَ اللَّطِيفُ كَثِيفًا وَالْخَفِيُّ ظَاهِرًا وَالْغَيْبُ شَهَادَةً، فَمَا كَانَ فِي الأَزَلِ هُوَ عَيْنُ مَا تَجَلَّى بِهِ فِي الأَبَدِ: كَانَ اللهُ وَلا شَيْءَ مَعَهُ وَهُوَ الآنَ عَلَى مَا عَلَيْهِ كَانَ. وَفِي حَدِيثِ التِّرْمِذِي عَنْ ابِي

رزين الْعُقيلي قُلْتُ « يَا رَسُولَ اللهِ أَيْنَ كَانَ رَبُّنَا قَبْلَ أَنْ يَخْلُقَ خَلْقَهُ ؟ » قَالَ: « كَانَ فِي عَمَا، مَا فَوْقَهُ هَوَاءٌ وَمَا تَحْتَهُ هَوَاءٌ » أَيْ كَانَ فِي خَفَاءٍ وَلَطَافَةٍ لَيْسَ فَوْقَهُ هَوَاءٌ وَلا تَحْتَهُ هَوَاءٌ، بَلْ عَظَمَةُ ذَاتِهِ أَحَاطَتْ بِكُلِّ فَوْقٍ وَبِكُلِّ تَحْتٍ وَبِكُلِّ هَوَاءٍ. وَقِيلَ لِسَيِّدِنَا عَلِي كَرَّمَ اللهُ وَجْهَهُ « يَا ابْنَ عَمِّ رَسُولِ اللهِ، أَيْنَ كَانَ رَبُّنَا أَوْ هَلْ لَهُ مَكَانٌ ؟» فَتَغَيَّرَ وَجْهُهُ وَسَكَتَ سَاعَةً ثُمَّ قَالَ « قَوْلُكُمْ أَيْنَ اللهُ سُؤَالٌ عَنْ مَكَانٍ، وَكَانَ اللهُ وَلا مَكَان ثُمَّ خَلَقَ الزَّمَانَ وَالْمَكَانَ وَهُوَ الآنَ كَمَا كَانَ دُونَ زَمَانٍ وَلا مَكَانٍ » أَيْ كان اللهُ وَلاَ شَيْءَ مَعَهُ وَهُوَ الآنَ لا شَيْءَ مَعَهُ، فَافْهَمْ.

٥٤ - **الفَناءُ والبَقاءُ**: إِذَا أُطْلِقَ الْفَنَاءُ إِنَّمَا يَنْصَرِفُ لِلْفَنَاءِ فِي الذَّاتِ وَحَقِيقَتُهُ مَحْوُ الرُّسُومِ وَالأَشْكَالِ بِشُهُودِ الْكَبِيرِ الْمُتَعَالِ أَوْ اسْتِهْلاكُ الْحِسِّ فِي ظُهُورِ الْمَعْنَى. وَقَالَ أَبُو الْمَوَاهِبِ: « (الفناء) مَحْوٌ وَاضمِحْلالٌ، وَذَهَابٌ عَنْكَ وَزَوَالٌ »، وَقَالَ أَبُو سَعِيد بْنُ الأَعْرَابِي « هُوَ أَنْ تَبْدُوَ الْعَظَمَةُ وَالإِجْلالُ عَلَى الْعَبْدِ فَتُنْسِيَهُ الدُّنْيَا وَالآخِرَةَ وَالأَحْوَالَ وَالدَّرَجَاتِ وَالْمَقَامَاتِ وَالأَذْكَارَ، يُفْنِيهِ عَنْ كُلِّ شَيْءٍ وَعَنْ عَقْلِهُ وَعَنْ نَفْسِهِ، وَفَنَائِهِ عَنِ الأَشْيَاءِ وَعَنْ فَنَائِهِ عَنِ الْفِنَاءِ لأَنَّهُ يَغْرَقُ فِي التَّعْظِيمِ » أَيْ تَتَجَلَّى لَهُ عَظَمَةُ الذَّاتِ فَتُفْنِيهِ عَنْ رُؤْيَةِ الأَشْيَاءِ وَمِنْ جُمْلَتِهَا نَفْسُهُ، فَيَصِيرُ عَيْنَ الْعَيْنِ وَيَغْرَقُ فِي بَحْرِ الأَحَدِيَّةِ. وَقَدْ يُطْلَقُ الْفَنَاءُ عَلَى الْفَنَاءِ فِي الأَفْعَالِ فَلا يَرَى فَاعِلاً إِلاّ الله. وَعَلَى الْفَنَاءِ فِي الصِّفَاتِ، فَلا قَدِيرٌ وَلا سَمِيعٌ وَلا بَصِيرٌ إِلاَّ الله، يَعْنِي أَنَّهُ يَرَى الْخَلْقَ مَوْتَى لا قُدْرَةَ لَهُمْ وَلا سَمْعَ وَلا بَصَرَ إِلاَّ بِاللهِ، وَبَعْدَ هَذَا يَقَعُ الْفَنَاءُ فِي الذّاتِ وَفِي ذَلِكَ يَقُولُ الشَّاعِرُ:

فَيَفْنَى ثُـمَّ يَفْنَى ثُـمَّ يَفْنَى فَـكَانَ فَنَاؤُهُ عَيْنُ الْبَقَـاءِ

وَأَمَّا الْبَقَاءُ فَهُوَ الرُّجُوعُ إِلَى شُهُودِ الأثَرِ بَعْدَ الْغَيْبَةِ عَنْهُ أَوْ شُهُودُ الْحِسِّ بَعْدَ الْغَيْبَةِ عَنْهُ بِشُهُودِ الْمَعْنَى لَكِنَّهُ يَرَاهُ قَائِماً بِاللهِ وَنُوراً مِنْ أَنْوَارِ تَجَلِّيَّاتِهِ إِذْ لَوْ لا الْحِسُّ مَا ظَهَرَتِ الْمَعْنَى وَلَوْ لا الْوَاسِطَةُ مَا عُرِفَ الْمَوْسُوطُ، فَالْحَقُّ تَعَالَى تَجَلَّى بَيْنَ الضِّدَّينِ: بَيْنَ الْحِسِّ وَالْمَعْنَى، وَبَيْنَ الْقُدْرَةِ وَالْحِكْمَةِ، وَبَيْنَ الْفَرْقِ وَالْجَمْعِ. فَالغَيْبَةُ عَنْ أَحَدِ الضِّدَّينِ فَنَاءٌ، وَرُؤْيَتُهُمَا مَعًا بَقَاءٌ، فَالْغَيْبَةُ عَنِ الْحِسِّ وَعَنِ الْحِكْمَةِ وَعَنِ الْفَرْقِ فَنَاءٌ، وَمُلاحَظَتُهُما مَعًا بَقَاءٌ، فَالْبَقَاءُ اِتِّسَاعٌ فِي الْفَنَاءِ بِحَيْثُ لا يَحْجُبُهُ جَمْعُهُ عَنْ فَرْقِهِ وَلا فَنَاؤُهُ عَنْ بَقَائِهِ وَلا شُهُودُ الْقُدْرَةِ عَنِ الْحِكْمَةِ بَلْ يُعْطِى كُلَّ ذِي حَقٍّ حَقَّهُ وَيُوَفِّي كُلَّ ذِي قِسْطٍ قِسْطَهُ . وَقَدْ يُطْلَقُ الْفَنَاءُ عَلَى التَّخَلِّي وَالتَّحَلِّي فَيُقَالُ فَنِيَ عَنْ أَوْصَافِهِ الْمَذْمُومَةِ وَبَقِيَ بِالأَوْصَافِ الْمَحْمُوْدَةِ، وَاللهُ تَعَالَى أَعْلَمُ.

٥٥ - **الْقُدرَةُ والحكْمَةُ**: الْقُدْرَةُ عِبَارَةٌ عَنْ إِظْهَارِ الأَشْيَاءِ عَلَى وِفْقِ الإِرَادَةِ، وَالْحِكْمَةُ عِبَارَةٌ عَنْ تَسَتُّرِهَا بِوُجُودِ الأَسْبَابِ وَالْعِلَلِ، فَالَقُدْرَةُ تُبْرِزُ وَالْحِكْمَةُ تَسْتُرُ وَالْقُدْرَةُ لا تَنْفَكُّ عَنِ الْحِكْمَةِ إِلاّ نَادِرًا فِي مُعْجِزَةٍ أَوْ كَرَامَةٍ أَوْ شَعْوَذَةٍ. وَقَدْ تُطْلَقُ الْقُدْرَةُ عَلَى الذّاتِ بَعْدَ تَجَلِّيهَا مِنْ إِطْلاقِ الصِّفَةِ عَلَى الْمَوْصُوفِ، وَالْحِكْمَةُ مَا يَسْتُرُهَا مِنَ الْحِسِّ وَأَوْصَافِ الْبَشَرِيَّةِ وَأَحْكَامِ الْعُبُودِيَّةِ. فَظُهورُهُ تَعَالَى بِمُقْتَضَى اسْمِهِ الظَّاهِرِ يُسَمَّى قُدْرَةً وَبُطُونُهُ فِي ظُهُورِهِ بِمُقْتَضَى اِسْمِهِ الْبَاطِنِ يُسَمَّى حِكْمَةً، فَتَجَلِّيهِ تَعَالَى

مِنْ عَالَمِ الْغَيْبِ إِلَى عَالَمِ الشَّهَادَةِ قُدْرَةٌ، وَخَفَاؤُهُ فِي ظُهُورِهِ حِكْمَةٌ. وَإِلَيْهِ يُشِيرُ قَوْلُ الْحِكَمِ «سُبْحَانَ مَنْ سَتَرَ سِرَّ الْخُصُوصِيَّةِ بِظُهُورِ الْبَشَرِيةِ، وَظَهَرَ بِعَظَمَةِ الرُّبُوبِيَّةِ فِي إِظْهَارِ الْعُبُودِيَّةِ.»

٥٦ - الْفَرْقُ وَالْجَمْعُ: الْفَرْقُ عِبَارَةٌ عَنْ شُهُودِ حِسِّ الْكَائِنَاتِ وَالْقِيَامِ بِأَحْكَامِهِ وَأَدَابِهِ مِنَ الْعِبَادَةِ وَالْعُبُودِيَّةِ، وَالْجَمْعُ عِبَارَةٌ عَنْ شُهُودِ الْمَعْنَى الْقَائِمِ بِالْأَشْيَاءِ مُتَّصِلاً بِالْبَحْرِ الْمُحِيطِ الْجَبَرُوتِي. أَوْ تَقُولُ الْفَرْقُ شُهُودُ الْقَوَالِبِ وَالْجَمْعُ شُهُودُ الْمَظَاهِرِ، فَالْقَوَالِبُ مَحَلُّ الشَّرَائِعِ وَالْمَظَاهِرُ عَيْنُ الْحَقَائِقِ. وَقَالَ أَبُو عَلِي الدَّقَاق: « الْفَرْقُ مَا نُسِبَ إِلَيْكَ، وَالْجَمْعُ مَا سُلِبَ عَنْكَ ». فَالْفَرْقُ بِلَا جَمْعٍ فُسُوقٌ وَجُمُودٌ وَجَهْلٌ بِاللهِ تَعَالَى، وَالْجَمْعُ بِلَا فَرْقٍ زَنْدَقَةٌ وَكُفْرٌ إِنْ لَمْ يَكُنْ سُكْرٌ، لِأَنَّهُ يُؤَدِّي إِلَى إِبْطَالِ الشَّرَائِعِ الَّتِي جَاءَتْ بِهَا الرُّسُلُ عَلَيْهِمُ الصَّلَاةُ وَالسَّلَامُ وَإِلَى إِبْطَالِ الْحِكْمَة. وَالْقُدْرَةُ لَا تَنْفَكُّ عَنِ الْحِكْمَةِ، فَالْوَاجِبُ أَنْ يَكُونَ الْعَبْدُ مَجْمُوعاً فِي فَرْقِهِ مَفْرُوقاً فِي جَمْعِهِ، الْجَمْعُ فِي الْبَاطِنِ مَوْجُودٌ وَالْفَرْقُ عَلَى الظَّاهِرِ مَشْهُودٌ.

٥٧ - الْحِسُّ وَالْمَعْنَى: الْحِسُّ عِبَارَةٌ عَنْ تَكْثِيفِ الْأَشْيَاءِ ظَاهِراً، وَالْمَعْنَى عِبَارَةٌ عَنْ تَلْطِيفِهَا بَاطِناً، فَحِسُّ الْكَائِنَاتِ أَوَانٍ حَامِلَةٌ لِلْمَعَانِي. قَالَ الشُّشْتَرِي رضي الله عنه:

| لَا تَنْظُرْ إِلَى الْأَوَانِي | وَخُضْ بَحْرَ الْمَعَانِي | لَعَلَّكَ تَـــــرَانِي |

فَمِثَالُ الْكَوْنِ كَالثَّلْجَةِ ظَاهِرُهَا ثَلْجٌ. وَبَاطِنُهَا مَاءٌ، كَذَلِكَ الْكَوْنُ ظَاهِرُهُ حِسٌّ وَبَاطِنُهُ مَعْنًى. وَالْمَعْنَى هِيَ أَسْرَارُ الذّاتِ اللَّطِيفَةِ الْقَائِمَةِ بِالأَشْيَاءِ فَقَدْ سَرَتِ الْمَعَانِي فِي الأَوَانِي سَرَيَانَ الْمَاءِ فِي الثَّلْجَةِ. وَفِي ذَلِكَ يَقُولُ قُطْبُ الأَقْطَابِ الشَّيْخُ الْجِيلانِي رَضِيَ اللهُ عَنْهُ:

وَمَا الْكَوْنُ فِي التِّمْثَالِ إِلاّ كَثَلْجَةٍ ... وَأَنْتَ لَهَا الْمَاءُ الّذِي هُوَ نَابِعُ
فَمَا الثَّلْجُ فِي تَحْقِيقِنَا غَيْرُ مَائِهِ ... وَغَيْرَان فِي حُكْمٍ دَعَتْهُ الشَّرَائِعُ

فَلا قِيَامَ لِلْحِسِّ إِلا بِالْمَعْنَى وَلا ظُهُورَ لِلْمَعْنَى إِلا بِالْحِسِّ فَالْمَعْنَى رَقِيقَةٌ لَطِيفَةٌ وَلا تُدْرَكُ إِلاّ بِتَحَسُّسِهَا فِي قَوَالِبِ الْكَائِنَاتِ، فَظُهُورُ الْمَعْنَى بِلا حِسٍّ مُحَالٌ، وَشُهُودُ الْحِسِّ بِلا مَعْنَى جَهْلٌ وَظُلْمَةٌ، وَلِذَلِكَ قَالَ فِي الْحِكَمِ: « الْكَوْنِ كُلُّهُ ظُلْمَةٌ وَإِنَّمَا أَنَارَهُ ظُهُورُ الْحَقِّ فِيهِ »... إلخ، فَلا يُرَى الْحَقُّ تَعَالَى إِلاّ بِوَاسِطَةِ التَّجَلِّيَاتِ فِي هَذِهِ الدَّارِ وَفِي تِلْكَ الدَّارِ وَفِي ذَلِكَ يَقُولُ بَعْضُهُمْ:

وَلَيْسَتْ تُنَالُ الذَّاتُ مِنْ غَيْرِ مَظْهَرٍ ... وَلَوْ هُتِكَ الإِنْسَانُ مِنْ شِدَّةِ الْحِرْصِ

٥٨ - **الْمُلْكُ وَالْمَلَكُوتُ وَالْجَبَرُوتُ**: الْمُلْكُ مَا ظَهَرَ مِنْ حِسِّ الْكَائِنَاتِ، وَالْمَلَكُوتِ مَا بَطَنَ فِيهَا مِنْ أَسْرَارِ الْمَعَانِي، وَالْجَبَرُوتُ الْبَحْرُ الْمُحِيطُ الّذِي تَدَفَّقَ مِنْهُ الْحِسُّ وَالْمَعْنَى، وَالْحَاصِلُ أَنّ الْقَبْضَةَ الّتِي ظَهَرَتْ أَوّلاً مِنْ فَضَاءِ الْعَمَاءِ حِسُّهَا الظَّاهِرُ مُلْكٌ، وَمَعْنَاهَا الْبَاطِنُ مَلَكُوتٌ، وَالْبَحْرُ اللَّطِيفُ الْمُحِيطُ الّذِي تَدَفَّقَتْ مِنْهُ جَبَرُوتٌ. فَأَسْرَارُ الْمَعَانِي رِيَّاضُ

الْعَارِفِينَ لِأَنَّهَا مَحَلُّ نُزْهَةِ أَرْوَاحِهِمْ وَلَا شَكَّ أَنَّ الْمَعَانِي لَطِيفَةٌ لَا تَظْهَرُ بَهْجَتُهَا إِلَّا فِي الْحِسِّ الَّذِي هُوَ الْمُلْكُ، وَالْحِسُّ مِنْ حَيْثُ هُوَ مُضَافٌ إِلَى نَبِيِّنَا ﷺ لِأَنَّهُ مَا ظَهَرَ إِلَّا لَهُ وَمَا إِنْشَقَّتْ أَسْرَارُ الذَّاتِ إِلَّا مِنْ نُورِهِ. فَلِذَلِكَ قَالَ الْقُطْبُ بن مَشِيش ﵁: ﴿ فَرِيَاضُ الْمَلَكُوتِ بِزَهْرِ جَمَالِهِ مُونِقَةٌ ﴾ أَيْ مُحَسَّنَة مُعْجَبَةٌ، فَقَدْ ذَكَرَ الْمُلْكَ بِالْالْتِزَامِ لِأَنَّ جَمَالَ زَهْرِ الْمَعَانِي لَا يَظْهَرُ إِلَّا فِي حِسِّ الْكَائِنَاتِ وَهُوَ الْمُلْكُ. وَقَوْلُهُ ﴿ وَحِيَاضُ الْجَبَرُوتِ بِفَيْضِ أَنْوَارِهِ مُتَدَفِّقَةٌ ﴾ الْأَصْلُ أَنْ يَقُولَ وَبَحْرُ الْجَبَرُوتِ بِفَيْضِ نُورِهِ مُتَدَفِّقٌ يُشِيرُ إِلَى ظُهُورِ الْقَبْضَةِ الْمُحَمَّدِيَّةِ مِنْ بَحْرِ نُورِهِ اللَّطِيفِ، وَإِنَّمَا عَبَّرَ بِالْحِيَاضِ لِيُنَاسِبَ الرِّيَاضَ وَإِنَّمَا جَمَعَ نُورَ الْقَبْضَةِ لِتَفَرُّعِهِ إِلَى أَنْوَارٍ كَثِيرَةٍ كَمَا جَمَعَ الْعَالَمِينَ مَعَ أَنَّ الْعَالَمَ وَاحِدٌ لِتَعَدُّدِ أَنْوَاعِهِ، وَاللهُ تَعَالَى أَعْلَم. فَحَقِيقَةُ الْمُلْكِ مَا يُدْرَكُ بِالْحِسِّ وَالْوَهْمِ وَحَقِيقَةُ الْمَلَكُوتِ مَا يُدْرَكُ بِالْعِلْمِ وَالذَّوْقِ، وَحَقِيقَةُ الْجَبَرُوتِ مَا يُدْرَكُ بِالْكَشْفِ وَالْوِجْدَانِ. فَالْوُجُودُ وَاحِدٌ وَإِنَّمَا تَخْتَلِفُ النِّسْبَةُ بِاعْتِبَارِ الرُّؤْيَةِ وَالتَّرْقِيَّةِ فَمَنْ وَقَفَ مَعَ حِسِّ الْكَائِنَاتِ وَحُجِبَ بِهَا عَنِ الْمَعْنَى سُمِّيَ فِي حَقِّهِ مُلْكاً، وَمَنْ نَفَذَ إِلَى شُهُودِ الْمَعَانِي سُمِّيَ فِي حَقِّهِ مَلَكُوتاً، وَمَنْ نَظَرَ إِلَى أَصْلِ الْقَبْضَةِ الَّذِي بَرَزَتْ مِنْهُ سَمَّاهُ جَبَرُوتًا. فَإِنْ ضَمَّ الْفُرُوعَ إِلَى الْأُصُولِ وَتَلَطَّفَتِ الْأَوَانِي حَتَّى صَارَتْ كُلُّهَا مَعَانِي، وَانْطَبَقَ بَحْرُ الْأَحَدِيَّةِ عَلَى الْكُلِّ صَارَ الْجَمِيعُ جَبَرُوتًا. فَكُلُّ مَقَامٍ يَحْجُبُ عَنْ مَا قَبْلَهُ. فَالْمَلَكُوتُ يَحْجُبُ عَنْ شُهُودِ الْمُلْكِ وَالْجَبَرُوتُ يَحْجُبُ عَنِ الْمَلَكُوتِ إِلَّا بِالتَّنَزُّلِ فِي حَالِ السُّلُوكِ، وَاللهُ تَعَالَى أَعْلَمُ.

٥٩ - النَّاسُوت واللاَّهُوتُ والرَّحَمُوت: النَّاسُوتُ عِبَارَةٌ عَنْ حِسِّ الأَوَانِي، وَاللاَهُوتُ عِبَارَةٌ عَنْ أَسْرَارِ الْمَعَانِي، وَمَرْجِعُ الأَوَّلِ لِلْمُلْكِ وَالثَّانِي لِلْمَلَكُوتِ، وَالرَّحَمُوتُ عِبَارَةٌ عَنْ سَرَيَانِ اللُّطْفِ وَالرَّحْمَةِ فِي جَمِيعِ الأَشْيَاءِ، جَلالِهَا وَجَمَالِهَا، مَنْ ظَنَّ انْفِكَاكَ لُطْفِهِ عَنْ قَدَرِهِ، فَذَلِكَ لِقُصُورِ نَظَرِهِ.

٦٠ - التَّوَاجُد والوَجْدُ والوِجْدَان والوُجُود: التَّوَاجُدِ تَكَلُّفُ الْوَجْدِ وَاسْتِعْمَالُهُ كَاسْتِعْمَالِ الرَّقْصِ وَالشَّطْحِ وَالْقِيَامِ وَغَيْرِ ذَلِكَ وَهُوَ غَيْرُ مُسَلَّمٍ إِلاَّ لِلْفُقَرَاءِ الْمُتَجَرِّدِينَ، فَلا بَأْسَ بِتَكَلُّف الْوَجْدِ وَاسْتِعْمَالِهِ كَمَا يُطْلَبُ الْحَالُ دَوَاء لِلنُّفُوسِ. وَهُوَ مَقَامُ الضُّعَفَاءِ وَقَدْ تَسْتَعْمِلُهُ الأَقْوِيَاءُ مُسَاعَفَةً أَوْ حَلاوَةً. قِيلَ لِأَبِي مُحَمَّدٍ الْجُرَيرِي: مَا حَالُكَ فِي السَّمَاعِ ؟ فَقَالَ: « إِذَا حَضَرَ هُنَاكَ مُحْتَشِم أَمْسَكْتُ وَجْدِي وَإِذَا خَلَوْتَ أَرْسَلْتُ وَجْدِي فَتَوَاجَدْتُ ». وَأَمَّا الْجُنَيْد فَكَانَ أَوّلا يَتَوَاجَدُ ثُمَّ سَكَنَ فَقِيلَ لَهُ « يَا سَيِّدِي، أَمَا لَكَ فِي السَّمَاعِ شَيْءٌ » ؟ فَقَالَ: ﴿وَتَرَى الْجِبَالَ تَحْسَبُهَا جَامِدَةً وَهِيَ تَمُرُّ مَرَّ السَّحَابِ﴾. قُلْتُ: وَقَدْ حَضَرْتُ سَمَاعا مَعَ شَيْخِنَا الْبُوزِيدي رَضِيَ اللهُ عَنْهُ فَكَانَ يَتَمَايَل يَمِينًا وَشِمَالاً، وَحَدَّثَنِي مَنْ حَضَرَ سَمَاعاً مَعَ شَيْخِهِ مَوْلاي الْعَرْبِي الدّرقاوِي فَقَالَ: مَا زَالَ قَائِما يَرْقُص حَتّى كَمُلَ السَّمَاعُ. وَلا يُنْكِرُ السَّمَاعَ إِلاّ جَامِدٌ جَاهِلٌ خَالٍ مِنْ أَسْرَارِ الْحَقِيقَةِ. وَأَمّا الْوَجْدُ فَهُوَ الّذِي يَرِدُ عَلَى الْقَلْبِ وَيُصَادِفُهُ بِلا تَأَمُّلٍ وَلا تَكَلّفٍ إِمّا شَوْقٌ مُقْلِقٌ أَوْ خَوْفٌ مُزْعِجٌ أَوْ هُوَ بَعْدَ التَّوَاجُدِ. وَيُقَالُ التّوَاجُدُ ثَمَرَاتُ الْمُنَازَلَةِ فِي أَسْرَارِ الْحَقَائِقِ كَمَا أَنّ حَلاوَةَ الطّاعَاتِ ثَمَرَاتُ الْمُنَازَلَةِ فِي

الطَّاعَةِ الظَّاهِرَةِ، فَكُلَّمَا اشْتَدّ التّحَقُّقُ بِأَسْرَارِ الْحَقَائِقِ وَالتّوْحِيدِ قَوِيَ الْوَجْدُ كَمَا أَنّهُ كُلَّمَا اشْتَدَّ الدَّوَامُ عَلَى الطّاعَةِ قَوِيَتْ حَلاوَتُها. وَأَمّا الْوِجْدَانِ فَهُوَ دَوَامُ حَلاوَةِ الشُّهُودِ وَاتِّصَالُهَا مَعَ غَلَبَةِ السُّكْرِ وَالدَّهَشِ، فَإِنْ اسْتَمَرَّ مَعَ ذَلِكَ حَتّى زَالَتِ الدّهْشَةُ وَالْحَيْرَةُ وَصَفَتِ الْفِكْرَةُ وَالنَّظْرَةُ فَهُوَ الْوُجودُ، وَإِلَيْهِ يُشِيرُ قَوْلُ الْجُنَيْدِ رَضِيَ اللهُ عَنْهُ:

وُجُودِي أَنْ أَغِيبَ عَنِ الْوُجُـــودِ　　　بِمَا يَبْدُو عَلَيَّ مِنَ الشُّهُـــــودِ

وَقَالَ أَبُو عَلِي الدّقّاق رَضِيَ اللهُ عَنْهُ: « التّوَاجُدُ يُوجِبُ اسْتِيعَابَ الْعَبْدِ، وَالْوَجْدُ يُوجِبُ اسْتِغْرَاقَ الْعَبْدِ، وَالْوُجودُ يُوجِبُ اسْتِهْلاكَ الْعَبْدِ، فَهُوَ كَمَنْ شَهِدَ الْبَحْرَ ثُمّ رَكِبَ ثُمّ غَرِقَ ». وَقَالَ الْقُشَيْرِي: « وَتَرْتِيبُ هَذَا الأَمْرِ قُصُودٌ ثُمّ وُرُودٌ ثُمّ شُهُودٌ ثُمّ وُجُودٌ ثُمّ خُمُودٌ ». فَالقصُود لِلْمُتَوَاجِدِينَ الْقَاصِدِينَ، الْوُجْدُ وَالْوِرْدُ لِلوَاجِدِينَ الشَّارِبِينَ، الْخَمْرَةُ وَالشُّهُودُ لأَهْلِ الْوِجْدَانِ السُّكَارَى، وَالْوُجودُ وَالْخُمُودُ لِأَهْلِ الصَّحْوِ. وَاللهُ تَعَالَى أَعْلَمُ.

٦١ - **الذَّوْقُ والشُّرْبُ والسُّكْرُ والصَّحْو:** الذَّوْقُ يَكُونُ بَعْدَ الْعِلْمِ بِالْحَقِيقَةِ، وَهُوَ عِبارَةٌ عَنْ بُرُوقِ أَنْوَارِ الذّاتِ الْقَدِيمَةِ عَلَى الْعَقْلِ فَيَغِيبُ عَنْ رُؤْيَةِ الْحُدُوثِ فِي أَنْوَارِ الْقِدَمِ لَكِنَّهُ لا يَدُومُ ذَلِكَ بَلْ يَلْمَعُ تَارَةً وَيَخْفَى أُخْرَى، فَصَاحِبُهُ يَدْخُلُ وَيَخْرُجُ فَإِذَا لَمَعَ غَابَ عَنْ حِسّهِ وَإِذَا خَفِيَ رَجَعَ إِلَى حِسّهِ وَرُؤْيَةِ نَفْسِهِ، فَهَذَا يُسَمَّى عِنْدَهُمْ ذَوْقاً. فَإِنْ دَامَ لَهُ ذَلِكَ النُّورُ سَاعَةً أَوْ سَاعَتَيْنِ فَهُوَ الشُّرْبُ، وَإِنْ اتَّصَلَ وَدَامَ فَهُوَ السّكْرُ. وَمَرْجِعُهُ إِلَى فَنَاءِ الرُّسُومِ فِي شُهُودِ الْحَيِّ الْقَيُّومِ وَالْغَيْبَةُ عَنِ الأَثَرِ فِي شُهُودِ الْمُؤَثِّرِ،

وَيُسَمَّى أَيْضاً الْفَنَاءُ. فَإِنْ رَجَعَ إِلَى شُهُودِ الأَثَرِ وَقِيَّامِهَا بِاللهِ وَأَنَّهَا نُورٌ مِنْ أَنْوَارِ اللهِ فَهُوَ الصَّحْوُ، وَيُسَمَّى أَيْضاً بِالرَّيِّ وَالْبَقَاءِ لإِبْقَاءِ الأَشْيَاءِ بِاللهِ بَعْدَ فَنَائِهَا، وَيُسَمَّى أَيْضاً فَنَاءُ الْفَنَاءِ لأَنَّهُ عَلِمَ أَنَّهُ لَمْ يَكُنْ ثَمَّ شَيْءٌ يُفْنِيهِ غَيْرُ الْوَهْمِ وَالْجَهْلِ وَهُمَا لا حَقِيقَةَ لَهُمَا. قَالَ الْقُشَيْرِي: «وَاعْلَمْ أَنَّ الصَّحْوَ عَلَى قَدْرِ السُّكْرِ فَكُلُّ مَنْ كَانَ سُكْرُهُ بِحَقٍّ كَانَ صَحْوُهُ بِحَقٍّ وَمَنْ كَانَ سُكْرُهُ بِحَظٍّ مَشُوبًا كَانَ صَحْوُهُ بِحَظٍّ مَصْحُوبًا، وَمَنْ كَانَ مُحِقًّا فِي حَالِهِ كَانَ مَحْفُوظاً فِي سُكْرِهِ». ثُمَّ قَالَ «فَمَنْ قَوِيَ حُبُّهُ تَسَرْمَدَ شُرْبُهُ. وَلله دَرُّ الْقَائِلِ:

شَرِبْتُ الْحُبَّ كَأْساً بَعْدَ كَأْسٍ ... فَمَا نَفَذَ الشَّرَابُ وَلا رَوِيتُ

٦٢ - **الْمَحْوُ والإِثْبَاتُ**: الْمَحْوُ الْغَيْبَةُ عَنِ الْكَائِنَاتِ فَنَاءٌ، وَالإِثْبَاتُ إِثْبَاتُهَا بَقَاءٌ، وَيُطْلَقُ عَلَى مَحْوِ الأَوْصَافِ الذَّمِيمَةِ، وَإِثْبَاتِ الأَوْصَافِ الْحَمِيدَةِ وَهِيَ ثَلاثٌ: مَحْوُ الزَّلَّةِ عَنِ الظَّوَاهِرِ وَمَحْوُ الْغَفْلَةِ عَنِ الضَّمَائِرِ وَمَحْوُ الْعِلَّةِ عَنِ السَّرَائِرِ، فَفِي مَحْوِ الزَّلَّةِ إِثْبَاتُ التَّوْبَةِ وَفِي مَحْوِ الْغَفْلَةِ إِثْبَاتُ الْيَقَظَةِ وَفِي مَحْوِ الْعِلَّةِ إِثْبَاتُ الصَّفَاءِ.

٦٣ - **السِّتْرِ والتَّجَلي**: السِّتْرُ عِنْدَهُمْ عِبَارَةٌ عَنْ غَيْبَةِ الْعَبْدِ عَنْ رَبِّهِ تَرْوِيحًا وَتَنَزُّلاً وَشُغْلاً بِشَأْنٍ مِنَ الشُّؤُونِ، وَالتَّجَلِّي عِبَارَةٌ عَنْ كَشْفِ الْعَبْدِ بِعَظَمَةِ رَبِّهِ وَهَذَا قَبْلَ الرُّسُوخِ، وَأَمَّا بَعْدَ الرُّسُوخِ فَلا غَيْبَةَ لَهُ. فَالْعَوَامُّ فِي غِطَاءِ السِّتْرِ عَلَى الدَّوَامِ وَالْخَوَاصُّ بَيْنَ كَشْفٍ وَغِطَاءٍ وَخَوَاصُّ الْخَوَاصِّ فِي دَوَامِ التَّجَلِّي فَالسِّتْرُ لِلْعَوَامِّ عُقُوبَةٌ وَلِلْخَوَاصِّ رَحْمَةٌ إِذْ لَوْلا

أَنّهُمْ يُسْتَرُ عَنْهُمْ فِي بَعْضِ الأَحْيَانِ لَتَلاَشَوْا عِنْدَ سُلْطَانِ الْحَقِيقَةِ وَلَكِنّهُ كَمَا يَظْهَرُ لَهُمْ يُسْتَرُ عَنْهُمْ فَالْخَوَاصّ بَيْنَ عَيْشٍ وَطَيْشٍ إِذَا تَجَلَّى لَهُمْ طَاشُوا وَإِذَا سُتِرَ عَنْهُمْ رُدُّوا إِلَيْهِمْ فَعَاشُوا.

٦٤ - **الْمُحَاضَرَةُ والْمُكاشَفَةُ والْمُسامَرَةُ**: الْمُحَاضَرَةُ حُضُورُ الْقَلْبِ مَعَ الرّبِّ وَيَكُونُ مِنْ وَرَاءِ الْحِجَابِ، إِمّا بِتَوَاتُرِ الْبُرْهَانِ أَوْ بِفِكْرَةِ الإعْتِبَارِ أَوْ بِاسْتِيلاءِ سُلْطَانِ الذِّكْرِ عَلَى الْقَلْبِ، ثُمّ بَعْدَهُ الْمُكَاشَفَةُ وَهِيَ حُضُورُ الْقَلْبِ مَعَ الرّبِّ بِنَعْتِ الْبَيَانِ غَيْرُ مُفْتَقِرٍ فِي هَذِهِ الْحَالَةِ إِلَى تَأَمُّلِ الدَّلِيلِ وَتَطَلُّبِ السَّبِيلِ وَيَكُونُ أَيْضاً مَعَ الْحِجَابِ بِنَعْتِ الْقُرْبِ فِي مَقَامِ الْمُرَاقَبَةِ وَهُوَ لِلْعُبَّادِ وَالزُّهّادِ وَنِهَايَةُ الأَسْرَارِ، وَأَمّا مُكَاشَفَةُ ضَمَائِرِ النّاسِ فَلَيْسَتْ بِمَقْصُودَةٍ عِنْدَهُمْ قَدْ يُعْطَاهَا مَنْ لَمْ يَبْلُغْ لِهَذَا الْمَقَامِ، وَبَعْدَ الْمُحَاضَرَةِ وَالْمُكَاشَفَةِ الْمُسامَرَةُ وَهِيَ: ظُهُورُ أَسْرَارِ الذّاتِ فَيَغِيبُ الْعَبْدُ عَنْ وُجُودِهِ وَيَغْرَقُ فِي بَحْرِ الأَحَدِيَّةِ سَاعَةً أَوْ سَاعَتَيْنِ ثُمَّ يَرْجِعُ إِلَى شَاهِدِهِ وَحِسِّهِ كَمَنْ يَسْتَمِرُّ فِي عَوْمِهِ تَحْتَ الْمَاءِ سَاعَةَ أَوْ سَاعَتَيْنِ ثُمَّ يَخْرُجُ، وَهِيَ مِنْ بِدَايَةِ الْوِجْدَانِ وَلَمَعَانِ أَنْوَارِ الْمُشَاهَدَةِ، ثُمّ بَعْدَهَا الْمُشَاهَدَةُ وَهِيَ: دَوَامُ شُهُودِ الْحَقِّ بِلا تَعَبٍ أَوْ وُجُودِ الْحَقِّ بِلا تُهْمَةٍ. وَقَالَ الْجُنَيْد رضي الله عنه: « الْمُشَاهَدَةُ وُجُودُ الْحَقِّ مَعَ فُقْدَانِكَ ». وَقَدْ تَقَدّمَ تَفْسِيرُهَا وَإِنّمَا أُعِيدَتْ هُنَا لِتَرَتُّبِهَا عَلَى مَا قَبْلَهَا. قَالَ الْقُشَيْرِي: « فَصَاحِبُ الْمُحَاضَرَةِ مَرْبُوطٌ بِآيَاتِهِ، وَصَاحِبُ الْمُكَاشَفَةِ مَبْسُوطٌ بِصِفَاتِهِ، وَصَاحِبُ الْمُشَاهَدَةِ مُلْقىً بِذَاتِهِ ». قُلْتُ: وَصَاحِبُ الْمُسْامَرَةِ تَارَةً بِتَارَةٍ، ثُمّ قَالَ الْقُشَيْرِي: « صَاحِبُ الْمُحَاضَرَةِ يَهْدِيهِ عَقْلُهُ، وَصَاحِبُ الْمُكَاشَفَةِ يُدْنِيهِ عِلْمُهِ، وَصَاحِبُ

الْمُشَاهَدَةِ تَمْحُوهُ مَعْرِفَتُهُ »، وَأَجْمَعُ مَا قِيلَ فِي الْمُشَاهَدَةِ أَنَّهُ تَوَالى أَنْوَارِ التَّجَلِّي عَلَى الْقَلْبِ مِنْ غَيْرِ أَنْ يَتَخَلَّلَهَا سِتْرٌ وَانْقِطَاعٌ كَمَا لَوْ قُدِّرَ اتِّصَالُ الْبُرُوقِ فِي اللَّيْلَةِ الظَّلْمَاءِ فَإِنَّهَا تَصِيرُ فِي ضَوْءِ النَّهَارِ، وَكَذَلِكَ الْقَلْبُ إِذَا دَامَ لَهُ دَوَامُ التَّجَلِّي فَلَا لَيْلَ وَأَنْشَدُوا:

وَظَلامُهُ فِي النَّاسِ سَــــارِ	لَيْلِي بِوَجْهِكَ مُشْـــــرِقٌ
وَنَحْنُ فِي ضَوْءِ النَّهَـــارِ	النَّاسُ فِي سَدَفِ الـــظَّلام

وَالسَّدَفُ بِالسِّينِ الظُّلْمَةُ كَمَا فِي الْقَامُوسِ. وَقَالَ النُّورِي: « إِذَا طَلَعَ الصَّبَاحُ اسْتُغْنِيَ عَنِ الْمِصْبَاحِ »، وَقَوْلُ الشَّاعِرِ « لَيْلِ بِوَجْهِكَ » إلخ: أَيْ لَيْلُ وُجُودِي مُشْرِقٌ بِوُجُودِ ذَاتِكَ فَقَدْ ذَهَبَتْ ظُلْمَةُ وُجُودِي فِي نَهَارِ وَجُودِكَ.

٦٥ - اللَّوائِحُ واللَّوامِعُ والطَّوالِعُ: وَهِي أَلْفَاظٌ مُتَقَارِبَةٌ، وَهِي لِأَهْلِ الْبِدَايَاتِ حِينَ تَبْرُقُ عَلَيْهِمْ أَنْوَارُ الشُّهُودِ ثُمَّ تُسْتَرُ فَتَكُونُ أَوَّلاً لَوَائِحَ ثُمَّ لَوَامِعَ ثُمَّ طَوَالِعَ، فَاللَّوامِعُ أَظْهَرُ مِنَ اللَّوائِحِ، والطَّوالِعُ أَظْهَرُ مِنَ اللَّوامِعِ، فَقَدْ تَبْقَى اللَّوامِعُ سَاعَتَيْنِ أَوْ ثَلاثٍ بِخِلافِ اللَّوائِحِ فَإِنَّهَا أَخَفُّ لِزَوَالِهَا بِسُرْعَةٍ كَمَا قَالَ الشَّاعِرُ:

كَانَ تَسْلِيمُهُ عَلَيَّ وَدَاعَــــا	افْتَرَقْنَا حَـــــوْلاً فَلَمَّا اجْتَمَعْنَا

وَقَالَ آخَرُ:

يَا ذَا الَّذِي زَارَ وَمَـــا زَارَا　　كَأَنَّــهُ مُقْتَبِسٌ نَــــارَا
مَرَّ بِبَابِ الدَّارِ مُسْتَعْجِـــلاً　　مَــا ضَرَّهُ لَوْ دَخَلَ الــــدَّارَا

وَأَمَّا الطَّوَالِعُ فَإِنَّهَا أَبْقَى وَقْتًا وَأَقْوَى سُلْطَانا وَأَذْهَبُ لِلظُّلْمَةِ وَأَنْفَى لِلتُّهْمَةِ، لَكِنَّهَا عَلَى خَطَرِ الأُفُولِ لَمْ يَتَمَكَّنْ صَاحِبُهَا مِنْ طُلُوعِ شَمْسِ عِرْفَانِهِ فَأَوْقَاتُ حُصُولِهَا وَشِيكَةُ الارْتِحَالِ وَأَحْوَالُ أُفُولِهَا طَوِيلَةُ الأَذْيَالِ، لَكِنْ إِذَا غَرَبَتْ أَنْوَارُهَا بَقِيَتْ آثَارُهَا فَصَاحِبُهَا إِذَا غَرَبَتْ أَنْوَارُهَا يَعِيشُ فِي بَرَكَاتِ آثَارِهَا إِلَى أَنْ تَعُودَ ثَانِيًا هَكَذَا حَتَّى تَطْلَعَ شَمْسُ نَهَارِهِ بِتَمَكُّنِهِ فَلا مَغِيبَ لَهَا حِينَئِذٍ كَمَا قَالَ الْقَائِلُ:

طَلَعَتْ شَمْسُ مَنْ أُحِبُّ بِلَيْلٍ　　وَاسْتَنَارَتْ فَمَا تَلاهَا غُــرُوبُ
إِنَّ شَمْسَ النَّهَــارِ تَغْرُبُ لَيْلاً　　وَشُمُوسُ الْقُلُوبِ لَيْسَتْ تَغِيبُ

٦٦ - **البَوَادِهُ والْهُجُوم**: الْبَوَادِهُ مَا يَفْجَأُ الْقَلْبَ مِنْ نَاحِيَةِ الْغَيْبِ عَلَى سَبِيلِ البَغْتَةِ. إِمَّا مُوجِبُ فَرَحٍ أَوْ تَرَحٍ، وَالْهُجُومُ مَا يَرِدُ عَلَى الْقَلْبِ بِقُوَّةِ الْوَقْتِ مِنْ غَيْرِ تَصَنُّعٍ وَلا تَكَسُّبٍ، وَتَخْتَلِفُ أَحْوَالُهُمْ عَلَى حَسَبِ ضُعْفِهِمْ وَقُوَّتِهِمْ، فَمِنْهُمْ مَنْ تُغَيِّرُهُ الْبَوَادِهُ، وَتَتَصَرَّفُ فِيهِ الْهَوَاجِمُ، وَمِنْهُمْ مَنْ يَكُونُ فَوْقَ مَا يَفْجَأُهُ حَالاً وَقُوَّةً، لا تُغَيِّرُهُ الْهَوَاجِمُ وَلا تَتَصَرَّفُ فِيهِ الْبَوَادِهُ وَلا تُزْعِجُهُ الْهُمُومُ وَلا تُحَرِّكُهُ الْمَخَاوِفُ. أُوْلَئِكَ سَادَاتُ الْوَقْتِ كَمَا قِيلَ:

لا تَهْتَدِي نُوَبُ الزَّمَانِ إِلَيْهِــم　　وَلَهُــمْ على الْخَطْبِ الْجَلِيلِ لِجَامُ

وَهَؤُلاءِ هُمْ أَهْلُ الرُّسُوخِ وَالتَّمْكِينِ جَعلَنَا اللهُ مِنْهُمْ. آمِين !

٦٧ - **التَّلْوِينُ والتَّمْكِينُ**: التَّلْوِينُ هُوَ الانْتِقالُ مِنْ حَالٍ إِلَى حَالٍ وَمِنْ مَقَامٍ إِلَى مَقَامٍ، وَقَدْ يَسْقُطُ وَيَقُومُ، فَإِذَا وَصلَ إِلَى صَرِيحِ الْعِرْفَانِ وَتَمَكَّنَ مِنَ الشُّهُودِ، فَصَاحِبُ تَمْكِينٍ. صَاحِبُ التَّلْوِينِ أَبَدًا فِي الزِّيَادَةِ وَصَاحِبُ التَّمْكِينِ وَصلَ وَتَمَكَّنَ، فَانْتِهَاءُ سَيْرِهِمْ الظَّفَرُ بِنُفُوسِهِمْ، فَإِنْ ظَفِرُوا بِهَا فَقَدْ وَصَلُوا فَانْخَنَسَتْ أَوْصَافُ الْبَشَرِيَّةِ وَاسْتَوْلَى عَلَيْهَا سُلْطَانُ الْحَقِيقَةِ، فَإِذَا دَامَ ذَلِكَ لِلْعَبْدِ فَهُوَ صَاحِبُ تَمْكِينٍ. وَقَدْ يَكُونُ التَّلْوِين بَعْدَ التَّمْكِينِ وَمَعْنَاهُ النُّزُولُ فِي الْمَقَامَاتِ كَنُزُولِ الشَّمْسِ فِي بُرُوجِهَا، فَيَتَلَوَّنُ الْعَارِفُ مَعَ الْمَقَادِيرِ وَيَدُورُ مَعَهَا حَيْثُ دَارَتْ وَيَتَلَوَّنُ بِتَلَوُّنِ الْوَقْتِ، فَيَكُونُ بَيْنَ قَبْضٍ وَبَسْطٍ وَقُوَّةٍ وَضُعْفٍ وَمَنْعٍ وَعَطَاءٍ وَسُرُورٍ وَحُزْنٍ وَغَيْرِ ذَلِكَ مِنْ تَقَلُّبَاتِ الأَحْوَالِ، غَيْرَ أَنَّهُ مَالِكٌ غَيْرُ مَمْلُوكٍ، لا يَتَغَيَّرُ بِتَغَيُّرِ الأَحْوَالِ وَلا يَتَأَثَّرُ بِالزَّلازِلِ وَالأَهْوَالِ. وَاللهُ تَعَالَى أَعْلَم.

٦٨ - **القُرْبُ والبُعْدُ**: الْقُرْبُ كِنَايَةٌ عَنْ قُرْبِ الْعَبْدِ مِنْ رَبِّهِ بِطَاعَتِهِ وَتَوْفِيقِهِ وَهُوَ عَلَى ثَلاثِ مَرَاتِبَ: قُرْبٌ بِالطَّاعَةِ وَتَرْكُ الْمُخَالَفَةِ، وَقُرْبٌ بِالرِّيَّاضَةِ وَالْمُجَاهَدَةِ، وَقُرْبٌ بِالْوُصُولِ وَالْمُشَاهَدَةِ، فَقُرْبُ الطَّالِبِينَ بِالطَّاعَةِ وَقُرْبُ الْمُرِيدِينَ بِالْمُجَاهَدَةِ وَقُرْبُ الْوَاصِلِينَ بِالْمُشَاهَدَةِ. فَأَوَّلُ الْبُعْدِ الْبُعْدُ عَنِ التَّوْفِيقِ، ثُمَّ البُعدُ عَنْ سُلُوكِ الطَّرِيقِ، ثُمَّ البُعْدُ عَنِ التَّحْقِيقِ. وَفِي الْحَدِيثِ الْقُدْسِيِّ عَنِ اللهِ عَزَّ وَجَلَّ يَقُولُ: « مَا تَقَرَّبَ إِلَيَّ الْمُتَقَرِّبُونَ بِمِثْلِ أَدَاءِ مَا افْتَرَضْتُهُ عَلَيْهِمْ، وَلا يَزَالُ الْعَبْدُ يَتَقَرَّبُ إِلَيَّ

بِالنَّوَافِلِ حَتَّى أُحِبَّهُ، فَإِذَا أَحْبَبْتُهُ كُنْتُ لَهُ سَمْعًا وَبَصَرًا. . .». الحَدِيث. وَفِي حَدِيثٍ آخَرَ « فَإِذَا أَحْبَبْتُهُ، كُنْتُهُ». فَقُرْبُ الْعَبْدِ مِنْ رَبِّهِ انْحِيَاشُهُ إِلَيْهِ بِقَلْبِهِ وَقُرْبُ الحَقِّ مِنْ عَبْدِهِ تَغْيِيبُهُ عَنْ وُجُودِهِ الْوَهْمِي وَكَشْفُ الحِجَابِ عَنْ عَيْنِ بَصِيرَتِهِ حَتَّى يَرَى الحَقَّ أَقْرَبَ إِلَيْهِ مِنْ كُلِّ شَيْءٍ، ثُمَّ يَغِيبُ الْقُرْبُ فِي الْقُرْبِ فَيَتَّحِدُ الْقَرِيبُ وَالْمُقَرَّبُ وَالْمُحِبُّ وَالْحَبِيبُ، كَمَا قَالَ الْقَائِلُ:

| أَنَـــــا مَـــــنْ أَهْوَى | وَمَـــــنْ أَهْوَى أَنَـــــا |

وَكَمَا قَالَ الشُّشْتَرِي:

أَنَا الْمُحِبُّ وَالْحَبِيبُ، مَا ثَمَّ ثَانِي

٦٩ - الشَّرِيعَة والطَّرِيقة والحَقِيقَة: الشَّرِيعَةُ تَكْلِيفُ الظَّوَاهِرِ، وَالطَّرِيقَةُ تَصْفِيَةُ الضَّمَائِرِ، وَالحَقِيقَةُ شُهُودُ الحَقِّ فِي تَجَلِّيَاتِ الْمَظَاهِرِ، فَالشَّرِيعَةُ أَنْ تَعْبُدَهُ، وَالطَّرِيقَةُ أَنْ تَقْصِدَهُ، وَالحَقِيقَةُ أَنْ تَشْهَدَهُ. فَلَمَّا تَجَلَّى الحَقُّ بَيْنَ الضِّدَّيْنِ فَتَجَلَّى بِمَظَاهِرِ عَظَمَةِ الرُّبُوبِيَّةِ فِي قَوَالِبِ الْعُبُودِيَّةِ، ظَهَرَتِ الشَّرِيعَةُ وَالحَقِيقَةُ. فَشُهُودُ الْعَظَمَةِ مِنْ حَيْثُ هِيَ حَقِيقَةٌ، وَالْقِيَامُ بِآدَابِ الْقَوَالِبِ عِبَادَةٌ وَعُبُودِيَّةٌ شَرِيعَةٌ. وَأَمَّا الطَّرِيقَةُ فَهِيَ إِصْلَاحُ الضَّمَائِرِ لِتَتَهَيَّأَ لِإِشْرَاقِ أَنْوَارِ الحَقَائِقِ عَلَيْهَا، فَالشَّرِيعَةُ لِإِصْلَاحِ الظَّوَاهِرِ، وَالطَّرِيقَةُ لِإِصْلَاحِ الضَّمَائِرِ، وَالحَقِيقَةُ لِتَزْيِينِ السَّرَائِرِ. وَيُقَالُ: الشَّرِيعَةُ عَيْنُ الحَقِيقَةِ مِنْ حَيْثُ إِنَّهَا وَجَبَتْ بِأَمْرِهِ، وَالحَقِيقَةُ عَيْنُ الشَّرِيعَةِ مِنْ حَيْثُ إِنَّهَا مُكَلَّفٌ بِهَا مِنْ قِبَلِ الشَّرِيعَةِ. وَقَدْ تُطْلَقُ عِنْدَهُمْ « الشَّرِيعَة »

عَلَى كُلِّ مَا يُتَوَصَّلُ بِهِ إِلَى شَيْءٍ أَوْ يَكُونُ سَبَبًا فِي إِدْرَاكِهِ، فَالأَسْبَابُ كُلُّهَا شَرَائِعُ، وَالْمَقَاصِدِ كُلُّهَا حقائِقُ. فَالحِسُّ شَرِيعَةُ الْمَعْنَى إِذْ بِهِ قُبِضَتْ، وَالْمُجَاهَدَةُ شَرِيعَةُ الْمُشَاهَدَةِ، وَالذُّلُّ شَرِيعَةُ الْعِزِّ، وَالْفَقْرُ شَرِيعَةُ الْغِنَى، وَهَكَذَا. وَالحَرْثُ وَالْغَرْسُ شَرِيعَةُ جَنْيِ الثِّمَارِ، وَلِذَلِكَ يَقُولُونَ: مَنْ غَرَسَ الشَّرَائِعَ أَثْمَرَتْ لَهُ الحَقَائِقَ وَمَنْ غَرَسَ الحَقَائِقَ أَثْمَرَتْ لَهُ الشَّرَائِعَ، أَيْ أَخْرَجَتْهُ إِلَى الرُّجُوعِ إِلَى الشَّرَائِعِ وَفِي ذَلِكَ يَقُولُ الشاعِر:

ثِمَـــارُ مَـــا قَدْ غرَسْتَ تَجْنَى وَهَـــذِهِ عَادَةُ الزَّمَـــانِ

٧٠ - **الذَّاتُ والصِّفَات**: اِعْلَمْ أَنَّ الحَقّ جَلّ جَلالُهُ ذَاتٌ وَصِفَاتٌ فِي الأَزَلِ وَفِي الأَبَدِ، أَعْنِي قَبْلَ التَّجَلِّي وَبَعْدَهُ، إِذْ صِفَاتُهُ قَدِيمَةٌ بِقِدَمِ ذَاتِهِ وَالصِّفَةُ لا تُفَارِقُ الْمَوْصُوفَ فَحَيْثُ تَجَلَّتِ الذّاتُ فَالصِّفَاتُ لازِمَةٌ لَهَا كَامِنَةٌ فِيهَا وَحَيْثُ ظَهَرَتِ الصِّفَاتُ فَالذَّاتُ لازِمَةٌ لَهَا، فَالذَّاتُ ظَاهِرَةٌ وَالصِّفَاتُ بَاطِنَةٌ، وَالْمُرَادُ بِالصِّفَاتِ صِفَاتُ الْمَعَانِي وَسَائِرِ أَوْصَافِ الْكَمَالِ. فَكُلُّ مَا وَقَعَ بِهِ التّجَلِّي وَالظُّهورُ فَهُوَ بَيْنَ ذَاتٍ وَصِفَاتٍ، الذَّات لا تُفَارِقُ الصِّفَاتَ، وَالصِّفَاتُ لا تُفَارِقُ الذَّاتَ وَهَذَا التّلازُمُ الّذِي بَيْنَهُمَا فِي الْوُجُودِ هُوَ الّذِي قَصَدَ مَنْ قَالَ: الذَّاتُ عَيْنُ الصِّفَاتِ، أَيْ مَظْهَرُهُما وَاحِدٌ، كَمَا قَالُوا: الحِسُّ عَيْنُ الْمَعْنَى اِتّحَدَ مَظْهَرُهُما. قَالَ بَعْضُ الْمَشَارِقَةِ فِي بَعْضِ أَزْجَالِهِ:

يَا وَارِدَ الْعَيْنِ إِنْ حَقَّقْتَ زَالَ الشَّكُّ الذَّاتُ عَيْنُ الصِّفَاتِ مَا فِي الْمَعَانِي شَكُّ

وَلا يَصُدَّنَّكَ عَنْ شُهُودِ الذَّاتِ رِدَاءُ الحِسِّ الْمَنْشُورِ عَلَى وَجْهِ الْمَعَانِي،

فَإِنَّ هَذَا الأَمْرَ مِنْ مَدَارِكِ الأَذْوَاقِ وَالْوِجْدَانِ لا مِنْ طَرِيقِ دَلِيلِ الْعَقْلِ وَالْبُرْهَانِ وَللهِ دَرُّ ابْنِ الْفَارِضِ حَيْثُ يَقُولُ:

فَثَمَّ وَرَاءَ النَّقْلِ عِلْمٌ يَدِقُّ   عَنْ مَدَارِكِ غَايَاتِ الْعُقُولِ السَّلِيمَةِ

وَاعْلَمْ أَنَّ الذَّاتَ لا تَتَجَلَّى إِلاَّ فِي مَظَاهِرِ أَثَرِ الصِّفَاتِ، إِذْ لَوْ تَجَلَّتْ بِلا وَاسِطَةٍ لاِضْمَحلتِ الْمُكَوِّنَاتُ وَتَلاشَتْ. وَلِذَلِكَ يَقُولُونَ تَجَلِّي الذَّاتِ جَلالِي وَتَجَلِّي الصِّفَاتِ جَمَالِي، لِأَنَّ تَجَلِّي الذَّاتِ بِلا وَاسِطَةٍ يَمْحَقُ وَيُحْرِقُ كَمَا فِي الْحَدِيْثِ. وَتَجَلِّي الصِّفَاتِ يَكُونُ بِالأَثَرِ فَيُكُونُ مَعَهُ الشُّهُودُ وَالْمَعْرِفَة،فَهُوَ جَمَالِي، ثُمَّ تَوَسَّعُوا فَأَطْلَقُوا عَلَى كُلِّ مَا هُوَ جَلالِي ذَاتٌ، وَعَلَى كُلِّ مَا هُوَ جَمَالِي صِفَاتٌ عَلَى سَبِيلِ التَّشْبِيهِ فَقَالُوا: الْفَقْرُ ذَاتٌ وَالْغِنَى صِفَاتٌ، الذُّلُّ ذَاتٌ وَالْعِزُّ صِفَاتٌ، الصَّمْتُ ذَاتٌ وَالْكَلامُ صِفَاتٌ، وَهَكَذَا، وَهَذَا الاصْطِلاحُ ذَكَرَهُ شَيْخُ شُيُوخِنَا سِيدِي عَلِي الْجَمَل الْعِمْرَانِي رَضِيَ اللهُ عَنْهُ فِي كِتَابِهِ وَلا أَدْرِي هَلْ سُبِقَ بِهِ أَمْ لا.

٧١ - **الأَنْوَارُ والأَسْرَارُ**: الأَنْوَارُ عِبَارَةٌ عَنْ مَا ظَهَرَ مِنْ كَثَائِفِ التَّجَلِّيَّاتِ، وَالأَسْرَارُ عِبَارَةٌ عَنْ مَا بَطَنَ فِيهَا مِنَ الْمَعَانِي اللَّطِيفَةِ، فَالأَسْرَارُ أَرَقُّ مِنَ الأَنْوَارِ، فَالأَسْرَارُ لِلذَّاتِ وَالأَنْوَارُ لِلصِّفَاتِ لأَنَّهَا أَثَرُهَا، فَالذَّات بَعْدَ التَّجَلِّي بَيْنَ أَنْوَارٍ ظَاهِرَةٍ وَأَسْرَارٍ بَاطِنَةٍ، وَأَمَّا فِي حَالَةِ الْكَنْزِيَّةِ فَمَا كَانَ إِلاّ الأَسْرَارُ. فَالْجَبَرُوتُ كُلُّهُ أَسْرَارٌ وَالْمَلَكُوتُ أَنْوَارٌ وَالْمُلْكُ أَغْيَارٌ وَأَكْدَارٌ. فَالْوُجُودُ وَاحِدٌ، فَمَنْ نَظَرَ إِلَى بَاطِنِهِ لَمْ يَرَ إِلاّ الأَسْرَارَ وَمَنْ نَظَرَ إِلَى ظَاهِرِهِ بِعَيْنِ الْجَمْعِ لَمْ يَرَ إِلاّ الأَنْوَارَ، وَمَنْ نَظَرَهُ بِعَيْنِ الْفَرْقِ لَمْ يَرَ إِلا

الأغْيَارَ. جَمْعُ غَيرٍ بِالسُّكونِ، وَمَنْ شَغَلَهُ عَنِ التَّوَجُّهِ إِلَى اللهِ بَتَشْغِيبِهِ وَأَهْوَالِهِ كَانَ حَقُّهُ أَكْدَارٌ. وَإِنَّمَا سُمِّيَتْ تَجَلِّيَاتُ الْحَقِّ أَنْوَاراً عَلَى وَجْهِ التَّشْبِيهِ لأَنَّ مِنْ شَأْنِ النُّورِ أَنَّ يَكْشِفَ الظُّلْمَةَ وَيُذْهِبَهَا، وَكَذَلِكَ تَجَلِّي الْحَقِّ يَكْشِفُ عَنْ ظُلْمَةِ الْجَهْلِ وَيَظْهَرُ الْعِلْمُ بِهِ وَلِذَلِكَ قَالُوا: الْعِلْمُ نُورٌ وَالْجَهْلُ ظُلْمَةٌ عَلَى وَجْهِ الاسْتِعَارَةِ. وَأَمَّا السِّرُّ فَهُوَ الأَمْرُ الْخَفِيُّ الَّذِي لا يُدْرَكُ. فَلِذَلِكَ قَالُوا فِي حَقِّ الْخَمْرَةِ الأَزَلِيَّةِ وَالْمَعَانِي الْقَدِيمَةِ أَسْرَاراً وَسَمَّوا الأَرْوَاحَ بَعْدَ التَّصْفِيَةِ أَسْرَاراً لِأَنَّهَا لَمَّا تَصَفَّتْ رَجَعَتْ لِأَصْلِهَا وَهِيَ قِطْعَةٌ مِنَ السِّرِّ الْجَبَرُوتِي الْقَدِيمِ فَإِذَا اسْتَوْلَتْ عَلَى الأَشْبَاحِ رَجَعَ الْجَمِيعُ قَدِيمًا، وَاللهُ أَعْلَم.

٧٢ - وأمّا **الضَّمَائِرُ والسَّرَائِر**: فَقِيلَ مَعْنَاهَا وَاحِدٌ، وَقِيلَ السَّرَائِرُ أَرَقُّ وَأَصْفَى كَمَا أَنَّ الرُّوحَ أَرَقُّ مِنَ الْقَلْبِ، لأَنَّ الضَّمَائِرَ كُلُّ مَا خَفِيَ فِي الْبَاطِنِ خَيْرًا أَوْ شَرًّا وَالسَّرَائِرَ مَا كُمِنَ فِيهِ مِنَ الْمَحَاسِنِ. وَالتَّحْقِيقُ أَنَّهُمَا شَيْءٌ وَاحِدٌ عِبَارَةٌ عَماَّ كَمُنَ فِي الْبَاطِنِ مِنَ الْعَقَائِدِ وَالنِّيَّاتِ بِدَلِيلِ الآيَةِ: ﴿ يَوۡمَ تُبۡلَى ٱلسَّرَآئِرُ ﴾. وَاللهُ تَعَالَى أَعْلَمْ.

٧٣ - **النَّفَس** (بِالتَّحْرِيكِ): قَالَ الْقُشَيْرِي « يَعْنُونَ بِهِ تَرْوِيحَ الْقُلُوبِ بِلَطَائِفِ الْغُيُوبِ، فَصَاحِبُ الأنْفَاسِ أَرْفَعُ مِنَ صَاحِبِ الأَحْوَالِ وَمِنْ صَاحِبِ الْوَقْتِ، فَكَأَنَّ صَاحِبَ الْوَقْتِ مُبْتَدِئٌ، وَصَاحِبُ الأَنْفَاسِ مُنْتَهِى، وَصَاحِبُ الاحوالِ بَيْنَهُمَا. فَالأَوقاتُ لأَصْحَابِ الْقُلُوبِ، وَالأَحْوَالُ لأَصْحَابِ الأَرْوَاحِ، وَالأَنْفَاسُ لِأَهْلِ السَّرَائِرِ ». قُلْتُ: النَّفَس

أَدَقُّ مِنَ الْوَقْتِ، فَحِفْظُ الأَوْقَاتِ مِنَ التَّضْيِيعِ لِلْعُبَّادِ وَالزُّهَّادِ، وَحِفْظُ الأَنْفَاسِ لِلْعَارِفِينَ الْوَاصِلِينَ، وَاسْتِعْمَالُ الأَحْوَالِ لِلْمُرِيدِينَ، وَالْمُرَادُ بِحِفْظِ الْوَقْتِ حُضُورُ الْقَلْبِ فِيهِ، وَبِحِفْظِ النَّفَسِ حُضُورُ السِّرِّ فِي مُشَاهَدَةِ الْحَقِّ، يُقَالُ فُلَانٌ طَابَتْ أَنْفَاسُهُ إِذَا صَفَا مَشْرَبُهُ مِنْ عَيْنِ التَّوْحِيدِ مِنْ كُدُورَةِ الأَغْيَارِ. فَقَوْلُهُ فِي حَدِّ النَّفَسِ « تَرْوِيحُ الْقُلُوبِ » أَيْ خُرُوجُهَا مِنْ تَعَبِ الْعُسَّةِ وَدَوَامِ الْمُرَاقَبَةِ إِلَى رَاحَةِ الْمُشَاهَدَةِ بِمَا يَبْدُو لَهَا مِنْ لَطَائِفِ أَسْرَارِ التَّوْحِيدِ وَفَضَاءِ الشُّهُودِ. ثُمَّ قَالَ الْقُشَيْرِي: « وَقَالُوا أَفْضَلُ الْعِبَادَةِ حِفْظُ الأَنْفَاسِ » أَيْ دَوَامُ الْفِكْرَةِ وَالنَّظْرَةِ كَمَا قَالَ الشَّاعِرُ:

مِنْ أَحْسَنِ الْمَذَاهِبِ سُكْرٌ عَلَى الدَّوَامِ   وَأَكْمَلُ الرَّغَائِبِ وُصْلٌ بِلا انْصِرَامِ

قَالَ أَبُو عَلِي الدقاق: « الْعَارِفُ لَا يَسْلَمُ لَهُ النَّفَسُ » أَيْ تَضْيِيعُهُ « إِذْ لَا مُسَامَحَةَ تَجْرِي مَعَهُ، وَالْمُحِبُّ لَا بُدَّ لَهُ مِنَ التَّنَفُّسِ، إِذْ لَوْلَا ذَلِكَ لَتَلَاشَا لِعَدَمِ طَاقَتِهِ ». فَالْعَارِفُ لَمَّا اتَّسَعَتْ مَعْرِفَتُهُ سَهُلَ عَلَيْهِ حِفْظُ أَنْفَاسِهِ لِسُهُولَةِ حُضُورِهِ وَتَمَكُّنِ شُهُودِهِ، بِخِلَافِ الْمُحِبِّ فَلِضِيقِ حَالِهِ لَا يَسْتَطِيعُ دَوَامَ حُضُورِهِ فِي خِدْمَتِهِ، وَعَلَى تَقْدِيرِ سُهُولَتِهَا عَلَيْهِ لِفَنَائِهِ فِيهَا قَدْ تَخْتَلُّ بَشَرِيَّتُهُ. وَلِذَلِكَ قَالَ ﷺ « رَوِّحُوا قُلُوبَكُمْ بِشَيْءٍ مِنَ الْمُبَاحِ » أَوْ كَمَا قَالَ ﷺ لِحَنْظلة والصديق: « لَوْ تَدُومُونَ كَمَا تَكُونُونَ عِنْدِي لَصَافَحَتْكُمُ الْمَلَائِكَةُ وَلَكِنْ سَاعَةً بِسَاعَةٍ ».

٧٤ - الْفِكْرَةُ وَالنَّظْرَةُ: الْفِكْرَةُ جَوَلَانُ الْقَلْبِ فِي تَجَلِّيَاتِ الرَّبِّ. وَقَالَ فِي الْحِكَمِ هِيَ « سَيْرُ الْقَلْبِ فِي مَيَادِينِ الْأَغْيَارِ». وَهَذِهِ فِكْرَةُ الطَّالِبِينَ، وَفِكْرَةُ السَّائِرِينَ سَيْرُ الْقَلْبِ فِي مَيَادِينِ الْأَنْوَارِ، وَفِكْرَةُ الْوَاصِلِينَ سَيْرُ الرُّوحِ فِي مَيَادِينِ الْأَسْرَارِ، وَتَرْجِعُ إِلَى فِكْرَتَيْنِ: فِكْرَةُ تَصْدِيقٍ وَإِيمَانٍ، وَهِيَ لِأَهْلِ الْأَعْتِبَارِ مِنْ عَامَّةِ أَهْلِ الْيَمِينِ، وَفِكْرَةُ شُهُودٍ وَعِيَانٍ وَهِيَ لِأَهْلِ الْإِسْتِبْصَارِ مِنْ نُجَبَاءِ الْمُرِيدِينَ وَخَاصَّةِ الْعَارِفِينَ الْمُتَمَكِّنِينَ. وَهِيَ سِرَاجُ الْقَلْبِ فَإِذَا ذَهَبَتْ فَلَا إِضَاءَةَ لَهُ. وَهِيَ سَبَبُ الْغِنَى الْأَكْبَرِ وَبِهَا يَتَحَقَّقُ السَّيْرُ وَيَحْصُلُ الْوُصُولُ، فَمَنْ لَا فِكْرَةَ لَهُ لَا سَيْرَ لَهُ وَمَنْ لَا سَيْرَ لَهُ لَا وُصُولَ لَهُ. وَكَانَ شَيْخُنَا البُوزِيدِي ﵁ يَقُولُ « الْفَقِيرُ بِلَا فِكْرَةٍ كَالْخَيَّاطِ بِلَا إِبْرَةٍ ». وَأَمَّا النَّظْرَةُ فَهِيَ أَرَقُّ مِنَ الْفِكْرَةِ وَأَرْفَعُ لِأَنَّهَا مَبْدَأُ الشُّهُودِ فَالْجَوَلَانُ فِي الْأَكْوَانِ وَهَدْمِهَا وَتَلْطِيفِهَا فِكْرَةٌ، وَالنَّظْرَةُ فِي نَفْسِهِ أَوْ غَيْرِهِ مِنَ التَّجَلِّيَاتِ، وَغَيْبَتُهُ عَنْهَا بِشُهُودِ الْحَقِّ نَظْرَةٌ، فَإِنْ تَمَكَّنَ مِنَ الشُّهُودِ وَدَامَ فِيهِ سُمِّيَ الْعُكُوفُ فِي الْحَضْرَةِ. وَلِذَلِكَ يُقَالُ: أَوَّلُ الْمَقَامَاتِ ذِكْرٌ ثُمَّ فِكْرَةٌ ثُمَّ نَظْرَةٌ ثُمَّ عُكُوفٌ فِي الْحَضْرَةِ، وَاللهُ تَعَالَى أَعْلَمُ.

٧٥ - الشَّاهِدُ: قَالَ الْقُشَيْرِي: « قَدْ يَجْرِي فِي كَلَامِهِمْ فُلَانٌ بِشَاهِدِ الْعِلْمِ وَفُلَانٌ بِشَاهِدِ الْوَجْدِ وَفُلَانٌ بِشَاهِدِ الْحَالِ وَيُرِيدُونَ بِلَفْظِ الشَّاهِدِ مَا يَكُونُ حَاضِرَ قَلْبِ الْإِنْسَانِ وَمَا هُوَ غَالِبُ ذِكْرِهِ كَأَنَّهُ يَرَاهُ وَيُبْصِرُهُ وَإِنْ كَانَ غَائِبًا عَنْهُ وَكُلُّ مَا يَسْتَوْلِي عَلَى قَلْبِ الْإِنْسَانِ ذِكْرُهُ فَهُوَ شَاهِدُهُ فَإِنْ كَانَ الْغَالِبُ عَلَيْهِ ذِكْرُ الْعِلْمِ فَهُوَ بِشَاهِدِ الْعِلْمِ وَإِنْ كَانَ الْغَالِبُ عَلَيْهِ

الْوَجْدُ فَهُوَ بِشَاهِدِ الْوَجْدِ وَمَعْنَى الشَّاهِدُ الْحَاضِرُ فَكُلُّ مَاهُوَ حَاضِرُ قَلْبِكَ فَهُوَ بِشاهِدِكِ ».

٧٦ - **الْخَمْرَةُ والكأْسُ والشَّرَابُ:** أَمَّا الْخَمْرَةُ فَقَدْ يُطْلِقُونَهَا عَلَى الذّاتِ الْعَلِيَّةِ قَبلَ التَّجَلِّي وَعَلَى الأسْرَارِ الْقَائِمَةِ بِالأشْيَاءِ بَعْدَ التَّجَلِّي فَيَقُولُونَ الْخَمْرَةُ: الأزَلِيَّةُ تَجَلَّتْ بِكَذَا وَمِنْ نَعتِهَا كَذَا وَقَامَتْ بِهَا الأشْيَاءُ تَسَتُّرًا عَلَى سِرِّ الرُّبُوبِيَّةِ. وَعَلَيْهَا غَنَّى ابْن الْفَارِضِ فِي خَمْرِيَّتِهِ، وَإِنَّمَا سَمَّوْهَا خَمْرَةً لِأَنَّهَا إِذَا تَجَلَّتْ لِلْقُلُوبِ غَابَتْ عَنْ حِسِّهَا كَمَا تَغِيبُ بِالْخَمْرَةِ الْحِسِّيَّةِ. وَقَدْ يُطْلِقُونَهَا عَلَى نَفْسِ السُّكْرِ وَالْوَجْدِ وَالْوُجْدَانِ، يَقُولُونَ « كُنَّا فِي خَمْرَةٍ عَظِيمَةٍ » أَيْ فِي غَيْبَةٍ عَنِ الإِحْسَاسِ كَبِيرَةٍ وَعَلَى هَذَا غَنَّى الشُّشْتَرِي حَيْثُ قَالَ:

خَمْـــرُهَا دُونَ خَمْـــرِى   خَمْـــرَتِي أَزَلِيَّـــةٌ

أَيْ سُكْرُ خَمْرَةِ الدَّوَالِي دُونَ خَمْرَتِي. وَأَمَّا الْكَأْسُ الّذِي تُشْرَبُ مِنْهُ هَذِهِ الْخَمْرَةُ فَهُوَ كِنَايَةٌ عَنْ سُطوعِ أَنْوَارِ التَّجَلِّي عَلَى الْقُلُوبِ عِنْدَ هَيَجَانِ الْمَحَبَّةِ، فَتَدْخُلُ عَلَيْهَا حَلاوَةُ الْوَجْدِ حَتَّى تَغِيبَ، وَذَلِكَ عِنْدَ سَمَاعِ أَوْ ذِكْرٍ أَوْ مُذَاكَرَةٍ، وَقِيلَ الْكَأْسُ هُوَ قَلْبُ الشَّيْخِ، فَقُلُوبُ الشُّيُوخِ الْعَارِفِينَ كُؤُوسٌ لِهَذِهِ الْخَمْرَةِ يَسْقُونَهَا لِمَنْ صَحِبَهُمْ وَأَحَبَّهُمْ. وَالشُّرْبُ حُضُورُ الْقَلْبِ وَاسْتِعْمَالُ الْفِكْرَةِ وَالنَّظْرَةِ حَتَّى تَغِيبَ عَن وُجُودِكَ فِي وُجُودِهِ، هُوَ السُّكْرُ. فَالشُّرْبُ وَالسُّكْرُ مُتَّصِلانِ فِي زَمَنٍ وَاحِدٍ فِي هَذِهِ

الْخَمْرَةِ بِخِلافِ خَمْرَةِ الدُّنْيَا. وَقَالَ الْقُطْب ابْنُ مشيش: «الْمَحَبَّةُ آخِذَةٌ مِنَ اللهِ قَلْبَ مَنْ أَحَبَّ بِمَا يَكْشِفُ لَهُ مِنْ نُورِ جَمَالِهِ وَقُدْسِ كَمَالِ جَلالِهِ. وَشَرَابُ الْمَحَبَّةِ مَزْجُ الأَوْصَافِ بِالأَوْصَافِ وَالأَخْلاقِ بِالأَخْلاقِ وَالأَنْوَارِ بِالأَنْوَارِ وَالأَسْمَاءِ بِالأَسْمَاءِ وَالنُّعُوتِ بِالنُّعُوتِ وَالأَفْعَالِ بِالأَفْعَالِ، وَيَتَّسِعُ النَّظَرُ لِمَنْ شَاءَ اللهُ عَزَّ وَجَلَّ، وَالشَّرَابُ يَسْقِي الْقُلُوبَ وَالأَوْصَالَ وَالْعُرُوقَ مِنْ هَذَا الشُّرْبِ، وَيَكُونُ الشُّرْبُ بِالتَّدْرِيبِ بَعْدَ التَّدْرِيبِ وَالتَّهْذِيبِ. فَيُسْقَى كُلٌّ عَلَى قَدْرِهِ. فَمِنْهُمْ مَنْ يُسْقَى بِغَيْرِ وَاسِطَةٍ، وَاللهُ تَعَالَى يَتَوَلَّى ذَلِكَ مِنْهُ». قُلْتُ: وَهَذَا نَادِرٌ، «وَمِنْهُمْ مَنْ يُسْقَى مِنْ جِهَةِ الْوَسَائِطِ كَالْمَلائِكَةِ وَالْعُلَمَاءِ وَالأَكَابِرِ مِنَ الْمُقَرَّبِينَ». ثُمّ قَالَ: «وَالْكَأْسُ مِغْرَفَةُ الْحَقِّ يَغْرِفُ بِهَا مِنْ ذَلِكَ الشَّرَابِ الطَّهُورِ الْمَحْضِ الصَّافِي لِمَنْ شَاءَ مِنْ عِبَادِهِ الْمَخْصُوصِينَ»... إِلَى آخِرِ كَلامِهِ، وَقَدْ فَسَّرْنَاهُ فِي شَرْحِ الْخَمْرِيَّةِ.

٧٧ - **الْمُرِيدُ والفَقِيرُ والْمَلامَتِي والْمُقَرَّبُ**: أَمّا الْمُرِيدُ فَهُوَ الّذِي تَعَلَّقَتْ إِرَادَتُهُ بِمَعْرِفَةِ الْحَقِّ وَدَخَلَ تَحْتَ تَرْبِيَةِ الْمَشَايِخِ وَقَدْ تَقَدَّمَ، وَأَمَّا الْفَقِيرُ فَهُوَ الَّذِي افْتَقَرَ مِمَّا سِوَى اللهِ وَرَفَضَ كُلَّ مَا يَشْغَلُهُ عَنِ اللهِ، وَلِذَلِكَ قَالُوا «الْفَقِيرُ لا يَمْلِكُ وَلا يُمْلَكُ» أَيْ لا يَمْلِكُ شَيْئًا وَلا يَمْلِكُهُ شَيْءٌ. فَهُوَ أَنْهَضُ مِنَ الْمُرِيدِ وَأَخَصُّ لِأَنّ الْمُرِيد قَدْ يَكُونُ مِنْ أَهْلِ الأَسْبَابِ، وَقِيلَ الْفَقِيرُ هُوَ الَّذِي لا تُقِلّهُ الأَرْضُ وَلا تُظِلُّهُ السَّمَاءُ أَيْ لا يَحْصُرُهُ الْكَوْنُ لِرَفْعِ هِمَّتِهِ وَنُفُوذِ بَصِيرَتِهِ. وَقَالَ بَعْضُهُمْ شُرُوطُ الْفَقِيرِ أَرْبَعَةٌ: رَفْعُ الْهِمَّةِ، وَحُسْنُ الْخِدْمَةِ، وَتَعْظِيمُ الْحُرْمَةِ، وَنُفُوذُ الْعَزِيمَةِ.

وَأَمَّا الْمَلامِتِي فَقَالُوا هُوَ الّذِي لا يُظْهِرُ خَيْرًا وَلا يُضْمِرُ شَرًّا، أَيْ هُوَ الّذِي يُخْفِي وِلايَتَهُ وَيُظْهِرُ مِنَ الأَحْوَالِ مَا يَنفِّرُ النَّاس عَنْهُ. وَالْمُقَرَّبُ هُوَ الْمُحقَّقُ بِالْفَنَاءِ وَالْبَقَاءِ، قَالَ بَعْضُهُمْ: الْفَقْرُ وَالْمَلامَةُ وَالتّقْرِيب أَنْوَاعٌ مِنَ التَّصَرُّفِ وَمَرَاتِبُ فِيهِ فَإِنَّ الصُّوفِيَّ هُوَ الْعَامِلُ فِي تَصْفِيَّةِ وَقْتِهِ مِمَّا سِوَى الْحَقِّ، فَإِذَا سَقَطَ مَا سِوَى الْحَقِّ مِنْ يَدِهِ فَهُوَ الْفَقِيرُ، وَإِنْ كَانَ لا يُبَالِي بِالنّاسِ فَلا يُظْهِرُ خَيْرًا وَلا يُضْمِرُ شَرًّا فَهُوَ الْمَلامِتِي، وَالْمُقَرَّبُ مَنْ كَمُلَتْ أَحْوَالُهُ فَكَانَ بِرَبِّهِ لِرَبِّهِ، وَلَيْس لَهُ عَنْ سِوَى الْحَقِّ أَخْبَارٌ وَلا مَعَ غَيْرِ اللهِ قَرَارٌ.

٧٨ - **الْعُبَّادُ والزُّهَّادُ والعَارِفُونَ**: هَذِهِ أَلْفَاظٌ مَعَانِيهَا مُتَقَارِبَةٌ يَجْمَعُهَا مَعْنَى التَّصَوُّفِ فِي الْجُمْلَةِ الّذِي هُوَ قَصْدُ التَّوَجُّهِ إِلَى اللهِ تَعَالَى، إِلاَّ أَنَّ مَنْ غَلَبَ عَلَيْهِ الْعَمَلُ كَانَ عَابِدًا، وَمَنْ غَلَبَ عَلَيْهِ التَّرْكُ كَانَ زَاهِدًا، وَمَنْ وَصَلَ إِلَى شُهُودِ الْحَقِّ وَرَسَخَ فِيهِ كَانَ عَارِفًا. فَالْعُبَّادُ وَالزُّهَّادُ شَغَلَهُمْ بِخِدْمَتِهِ إِذْ لَمْ يَصْلُحُوا لصرِيحِ مَعْرِفَتِهِ، وَالْعَارِفُونَ شَغَلَهُمْ بِمَحَبَّتِهِ ﴿كُلًّا نُّمِدُّ هَٰٓؤُلَآءِ وَهَٰٓؤُلَآءِ مِنْ عَطَآءِ رَبِّكَ ۚ وَمَا كَانَ عَطَآءُ رَبِّكَ مَحْظُورًا ﴿٢٠﴾﴾.

٧٩ - **الصَّالِحُون والأَوْلِيَاءُ والبُدَلاَءُ والنُّقَبَاءُ والنُّجَبَاءُ والأَوْتَادُ والقُطْبُ**: أَمّا الصَّالِحُونَ فَهُمْ مَنْ صَلُحَتْ أَعْمَالُهُمْ الظَّاهِرَةُ وَاسْتَقَامَتْ أَحْوَالُهُمْ البَاطِنَةُ. أَمّا الأَوْلِيَاءُ فَهُمْ أَهْلُ الْعِلْمِ بِاللهِ عَلَى نَعْتِ الْعِيَانِ مِن الْوَلِي وَهُوَ الْقُرْبُ. وَقِيلَ: مَنْ تَوَالَتْ طَاعَتُهُمْ وَتَحَقَّقَ قُرْبُهُمْ وَاتَّصَلَ مَدَدُهُمْ. وَأَمّا الْبُدَلاءُ فَهُمُ الّذينَ اسْتَبْدَلُوا الْمَسَاوِئَ بِالْمَحَاسِنِ وَاسْتَبْدَلُوا صِفَاتِهِمْ

بِصِفَاةِ مَحْبُوبِهِمْ. وَأَمّا النُّقَبَاءُ فَهُمُ الّذينَ نَقَّبُوا الْكَوْنَ وَخَرَجُوا إِلَى فَضَاءِ شُهُودِ الْمُكَوِّنِ. وَأَمّا النُّجَباءُ فَهُمْ السَّابِقُونَ إِلَى اللهِ لِنجَابَتِهِمْ وَهُمْ أَهْلُ الْجِدِّ وَالْقَرِيحَةِ مِنَ الْمُرِيدِينَ. وَأَمّا الأَوْتَاد فَهُمْ الرّاسِخُونَ فِي مَعْرِفَةِ اللهِ، وَهُمْ أَرْبَعَةٌ كَأَنّهُمْ أَوْتَادٌ لِأَرْكَانِ الْكَوْنِ الأَرْبَعَةِ. وَأَمّا الْقُطْبُ فَهُوَ الْقَائِمُ بِحَقِّ الْكَوْنِ وَالْمُكَوِّنِ، وَهُوَ وَاحِدٌ وَقَدْ يُطْلَقُ عَلَى مَنْ تَحَقَّقَ بِمَقَامٍ، وَعَلَى هَذَا يَتَعَدَّدُ فِي الزّمَانِ الْوَاحِدِ أَقْطَابٌ فِي الْمَقَامَاتِ وَالأَحْوَالِ وَالْعُلُومِ، يُقَالُ فُلانٌ قُطْبٌ فِي الْعُلُومِ أَوْ قُطْبٌ فِي الأَحْوَالِ أَوْ قُطْبٌ فِي الْمَقَامَاتِ إِذَا غَلَبَ عَلَيْهِ شَيْءٌ مِنْهَا، فَإِذَا أُرِيدَ الْمَقَامُ الّذي لاَ يَتَّصِفُ بِهِ إِلاَّ وَاحِدٌ عُبِّرَ عَنْهُ بِالْغَوْثِ، وَهُوَ الّذي يَصِلُ مِنْهُ الْمَدَدُ الرُّوحَانِي إِلَى دَوَائِرِ الأَوْلِياءِ مِنْ نَجِيبٍ وَنَقِيبٍ وَأَوْتَادٍ وَأَبْدَالٍ، وَلَهُ الإِمَامَةُ وَالإِرْثُ وَالْخِلاَفَةُ الْبَاطِنَةُ، وَهُوَ رُوحُ الْكَوْنِ الّذي عَلَيْهِ مَدَارُهُ كَمَا يُشِيرُ إِلَى ذَلِكَ كَوْنُهُ بِمَنْزِلَةِ إِنْسَانِ الْعَيْنِ مِنَ الْعَيْنِ، وَلا يَعْرِفُ ذَلِكَ إِلاَّ مَنْ لَهُ قِسْطٌ وَنَصِيبٌ مِنْ سِرِّ الْبَقَاءِ بِاللهِ، وَأَمّا تَسْمِيَّتُهُ بِالْغَوْثِ فَمِنْ حَيْثُ إِغَاثَتِهِ الْعَوَالِمَ بِمَادَّتِهِ وَرُتْبَتِهِ الْخَاصَّةِ. وَلَهُ عَلامَاتٌ يُعَرَفُ بِهَا. قَالَ الْقُطْبُ الشّهِيرُ أَبُو الْحَسَنِ الشّاذِلِي رضي الله عنه «لِلْقُطْبِ خَمْسَ عَشْرَةَ عَلامَةٍ فَمَنْ ادّعَاهَا أَوْ شَيْئاً مِنْهَا فَلْيَبْرُزْ بِمَدَدِ الرَّحْمَةِ وَالْعِصْمَةِ وَالْخِلافَةِ وَالنِّيَّابَةِ وَمَدَدِ حَمَلَةِ الْعَرْشِ الْعَظِيمِ وَيُكْشَفُ لَهُ عَنْ حَقِيقَةِ الذَّاتِ، وَإِحَاطَةِ الصِّفَاتِ، وَيُكْرَمُ بِالْحُكْمِ وَالْفَصْلِ بَيْنَ الْوُجُودَيْنِ، وَانْفِصَال الأَوّلِ عَنِ الأَوّلِ، وَمَا انْفَصَلَ عَنْهُ إِلَى مُنْتَهَاهُ وَمَا ثَبَتَ فِيهِ، وَحُكْمُ مَا قَبْلَ وَحُكْمُ مَا بَعْدَ وَمَا لا قَبْلَ وَلا بَعْدَ، وَعِلْمُ الْبَدْءِ وَهُوَ الْعِلْمُ الْمُحِيطُ بِكُلِّ عِلْمٍ وَبِكُلِّ مَعْلُومٍ وَمَا يَعُودُ إِلَيْهِ». فَالعَلامَةُ الأُولَى أَنْ يَكُونَ مُتَخَلِّقًا

بِأَخْلاقِ الرَّحْمَةِ عَلَى قَدَمِ مَوْرُوثِهِ ﷺ، صَاحِبُ حِلْمٍ وَرَأْفَةٍ وَشَفَقَةٍ وَعَفْوٍ وَعَقْلٍ وَرَزَانَةٍ وَجُودٍ وَشَجَاعَةٍ كَمَا كَانَ مَوْرُوثُهُ ﷺ، وَالْعَلامَةُ الثَّانِيّةُ أَنْ يُمَدّ بِمَدَدِ الْعِصْمَةِ وَهِيَ الْحِفْظ الإِلَهِي وَالْعِصْمَة الرّبَانِيّة كَمَا كَانَ مَوْرُوثُه ﷺ، غَيْرَ أَنّهَا فِي الأَنْبِيّاءِ وَاجِبَةٌ وَفِي الأَوْلياءِ جَائِزَةٌ، وَيُقَالُ لَهَا الْحِفْظ فَلا يَتَجَاوَزُ حَدّاً وَلا يَنْقُضُ عَهْدًا. وَالثَّالِثَةُ الْخِلافَةُ وَهُوَ أَنْ يَكُونَ خَلِيفَةَ اللهِ فِي أَرْضِهِ، أَمِينًا عَلَى عِبَادِهِ بِالْخِلافَةِ النَّبَوِيَّةِ قَد بَايَعَتْهُ الأَرْوَاحُ وَانْقَادَتْ إِلَيْهِ الأَشْبَاحُ. وَالرّابِعَةُ النِّيَابَةُ وَهُوَ أَنْ يَكُونَ نَائِبًا عَنِ الْحَقِّ فِي تَصْرِيفِ الأَحْكَامِ حَسْبَمَا اقْتَضَتْهُ الْحِكْمَةُ الإِلَٰهِيَّةُ وَفِي الْحَقِيقَةِ مَا ثَمَّ إِلاّ الْقُدْرَةُ الأَزَلِيّةُ. وَالْخَامِسَةُ أَنْ يُمَدَّ بِمَدَدِ حَمَلَةِ الْعَرْشِ مِنَ الْقُوّةِ وَالْقُرْبِ فَهُوَ حَامِلُ عَرْشِ الأَكْوَانِ كَمَا أَنّ الْمَلائِكَةَ حَامِلَةُ عَرْشِ الرَّحْمَٰنِ. وَالسادِسَةُ أَنْ يُكْشَفَ لَهُ عَنْ حَقِيقَةِ الذّاتِ فَيَكُونُ عَارِفًا بِاللهِ مَعْرِفَةَ الْعِيَّانِ، وَأَما الْجَاهِلُ بِاللهِ، فَلا نَصِيبَ لَهُ فِي الْقُطْبَانِيّةِ. وَالسَّابِعَة أَنْ يُكْشَفَ لَهُ عَنْ إِحَاطَةِ الصِّفَاتِ بِالْكَائِنَاتِ فَلا مُكَوِّنَ إِلاّ وَهُوَ قَائِمٌ بِالصِّفَاتِ وَأَسْرَارِ الذّاتِ، وَمَعْرِفَةُ الْقُطْبِ بِإِحَاطَةِ الصِّفَاتِ أَتَمُّ مِنْ غَيْرِهِ لِأَنَّهَا فِي حَقِّهِ ذَوْقِيَّةٌ لا عِلْمِيّةٌ. الثَّامِنَةُ أَنْ يُكْرَمَ بِالْحُكْمِ وَالْفَصْلِ بَيْنَ الْوُجُودَيْنِ أَيْ بَيْنَ الْوُجُودِ الأَوّلِ قَبْلَ التَّجَلِّي وَهُوَ الْمُعَبَّرُ عَنْهُ بِالأَزَلِ وَبِالْكَنزِ الْقَدِيمِ، وَبَيْنَ الثّانِي وَهُوَ الّذي وَقَعَ بِهِ التّجَلِّي، وَالْفَصْلُ بَيْنَهُمَا أَنْ يَعْلَمَ أَنّ الأَوّلَ رُبُوبِيّة بِلا عُبُودِيَّةٍ وَمَعْنىً بِلا حِسٍّ وَقُدْرَةٌ بِلا حِكْمَةٍ بِخِلافِ الثّانِي فَإِنّهُ مُتَّصِفٌ بِالضِّدّيْنِ: رُبُوبِيَّةٌ وَعُبُودِيّةٌ وَمَعْنَى وَحِسٌّ وَقُدْرَةٌ وَحِكْمَةٌ لِيَتَحقّقَ فِيهِ اسْمُهُ الظّاهِرُ وَاسْمُهُ الْبَاطِنُ فَالضِّدّانُ مُختصان بِالْقَبْضَةِ الْمُتَجَلَّى بِهَا، وَأَمَّا الْعَظَمَةُ الْمُحِيطَةُ بِهَا الْبَاقِيَّةُ عَلَى

كَنْزِيَّتِهَا فَهِيَ بَاقِيَةٌ عَلَى أَصْلِهَا فَافْهَمْ. وَالتَّاسِعَةُ وَالْعَاشِرَةُ أَنْ يُكْرَمَ بِالْحُكْمِ بِانْفِصَالِ الأَوَّلِ عَنِ الأَوَّلِ، وَالْمُرَادُ بِانْفِصَالِ الأَوَّلِ انْفِصَالَ نُورِ الْقَبْضَةِ عَنِ النُّورِ الأَزَلِيِّ الْكَنْزِيِّ وَهُوَ بَحْرُ الْجَبَرُوتِ، وَالْمُرَادُ بِمَا انْفَصَلَ عَنْهُ مَا تَفَرَّعَ مِنَ الْقَبْضَةِ إِلَى مُنْتَهَاهُ مِن فُرُوعِ التَّجَلِّيَاتِ، أَيْ فِي الْحَالِ، وَأَمَّا فِي الْمَآلِ فَلا انْتِهَاء لَهُ لأَنَّ تَجَلِّيَات الْحَقِّ لا تَنْقَطِعُ أَبَدًا، فَإِذَا انْقَضَى هَذَا الْوُجُودُ الدُّنْيَوِي تَجَلَّى بِوُجُودٍ آخَر أُخْرَوِي وَلا نِهَايَةَ لَهُ. وَالْحَادِيَة عَشْرَةَ أَنْ يَعْلَمَ مَا ثَبَتَ فِي الْمُنْفَصِلاتِ مِنَ الْمَزَايَا وَالْكَرَامَاتِ أَوْ ضِدِّ ذَلِكَ، يَعْنِي فِي الْجُمْلَةِ وَأَمَّا التَّفْصِيلُ فَمِنْ خَصَائِصِ الرُّبُوبِيَّةِ. وَالثَّانِيَة عَشْرَةَ أَنْ يَعْلَمَ حُكْمَ مَا قَبْلَ أَيْ مَا قَبْلَ التَّجَلِّي، وَحُكْمُهُ هُوَ التَّنْزِيهُ الْمُطْلَقُ لِأَنَّهُ بَاقٍ عَلَى كَنْزِيَّتِهِ لَمْ تَدْخُلْهُ الضِّدّانِ. وَالثَّالِثَة عَشْرَةَ: أَنّ يَعْلَمَ حُكْمَ مَا بَعْدَ وَهُوَ التّكْلِيفُ فِي مَظْهَرِ التّعْرِيفِ قِيَّامًا بِرَسْمِ الْحِكْمَةِ وَسِتْرًا لِأَسْرَارِ الْقُدْرَةِ. وَالرّابِعَة عَشْرَةَ أَن يَعْلَمَ مَا لا قَبْلَ وَلا بَعْدَ، أَيْ يَعْلَمَ مَا قَبْلَ لَهَا وَلا بَعْدَ لَهَا وَهِيَ الْخَمْرَةُ الأَزَلِيَّةُ وَالذَّات الأَصْلِيَّةُ كَمَا قَالَ ابْنُ الْفَارِضِ:

فَلا قَبْلَهَا قَبْلٌ وَلا بَعْدَهَا بَعْدُ   وَقَبْلِيَّةُ الأَبْعَادِ هِيَ لَهَا خَتْمُ

الْخَامِسَة عَشْرَةَ أَن يَطَّلِعَ عَلَى عِلْمِ الْبَدْءِ وَالْمُرَادُ عِلْمُهُ تَعَالَى الأَزَلِي السَّابِقِ لِلأَشْيَاءِ قَبْلَ أَنْ تَكُونَ وَهُوَ الْعِلْمُ الْمُحِيط بِكُلِّ عِلْمٍ وَبِكُلِّ مَعْلُومٍ، إِذْ لا يَخْرُجُ عَنْ عِلْمِهِ تَعَالَى شَيْءٌ، وَكُلُّ عِلْمٍ وَكُلُّ مَعْلُومٍ يَعُودُ إِلَيْهِ وَهَذَا هُوَ سِرُّ الْقَدَرِ، فَقَدْ يُكَاشَفُ الْقُطْبُ عَلَى جُزْئِيّاتٍ مِنْهُ وَلا يُشْتَرَطُ إِحَاطَتُهُ بِكُلِّيَّة الأَشْيَاءِ وَجُزْئِيّاتِهِ، لأَنَّ ذَلِكَ مِنْ وَظَائِف

الرُّبُوبِيَّةِ، وَإِنَّمَا يُطْلِعُهُ اللهُ تَعَالَى عَلَى جُزْئِيَّاتٍ مِن نَوْعٍ مَخْصُوصٍ. وَقَدْ أَشَارَ الشَّيْخُ أَبُو العَبَّاسِ الْمُرْسِي ﵁ تَعَالَى إِلَى شَيْءٍ مِن ذَلِكَ فَقَالَ « مَا مِن وَلِيٍّ كَانَ أَوْ هُوَ كَائِنٌ إِلاَّ وَقَدْ اطْلَعَنِي اللهُ عَلَيْهِ وَعَلَى اسْمِهِ وَنَسَبِهِ وَحَظِّهِ مِنَ اللهِ تَعَالَى ». وَقَالَ آخَرُ « مَا مِنْ نُطْفَةٍ تَقَعُ فِي الأَرْحَامِ إِلاَّ وَقَدْ أَطْلَعَنِي اللهُ عَلَيْهَا وَمَا يَكُونُ مِنْهَا مِنَ ذَكَرٍ أَوْ أُنْثَى ». وَهَذَا مِنْ جُمْلَةِ الْكَرَامَاتِ الَّتِي أَتْحَفَ اللهُ تَعَالَى بِهَا أَوْلِيَاءَهُ وَقَدْ يَكُونُ قُطْبًا كَامِلاً وَهُوَ لَمْ يَطَّلِع عَلَى شَيْءٍ مِن هَذِهِ الأُمُورِ إِلاَّ أَنَّهُ عَارِفٌ بِاللهِ رَاسِخُ الْقَدَمِ فِي الْمَعْرِفَةِ، وَإِذَا أَرَادَ اللهُ تَعَالَى أَنْ يُظْهِرَ شَيْئاً فِي مَمْلَكَتِهِ أَطْلَعَهُ عَلَيْهِ وَقَدْ لَا يُطْلِعُهُ. وَقَدْ قَالَ ﷺ: « وَاللهِ لَا أَعْلَمُ إِلاَّ مَا عَلَّمَنِي رَبِّي ». قَالَ ذَلِكَ حِينَ ضَلَّتْ نَاقَتُه فَلَمْ يَدْرِ أَيْنَ ذَهَبَتْ فَتَكَلَّمَ بَعْضُ الْمُنَافِقِينَ فِي ذَلِكَ ثُمَّ أَعْلَمَهُ اللهُ تَعَالَى بِهَا. وَبِالجُمْلَةِ فَالإِطِّلَاعُ عَلَى الْمَغِيبَاتِ مِنْ جُمْلَةِ الْكَرَامَاتِ، وَهِيَ لَا تُشْتَرَطُ فِي الْوَلِيِّ قُطْبًا كَانَ أَوْ غَيْرَهُ، وَاللهُ تَعَالَى أَعْلَمُ.

وَصَلَّى اللهُ عَلَى سَيِّدِنَا وَمَوْلَانَا

مُحَمَّدٍ وَآلِهِ وَصَحْبِهِ

وَسَلَّمَ تَسْلِيماً.

المحتويات

المحتويات

المحتويات

المحتويات

Arabic Text

of

The Book of Ascension to the Essential Truths of Sufism

Miʿrāj al-tashawwuf ilā ḥaqāʾiq al-taṣawwuf